THE ABDUCTI...
BROKE AM...

THE CONFESSION OF CARY STAYNER,
HIS BROTHER,
TO THE TERRIBLE YOSEMITE MURDERS
SHOCKED THE NATION. . . .

I KNOW MY FIRST NAME IS STEVEN

Fully revised and updated with sensational new
information on one of the most incredible true
stories in the annals of American crime.

"A powerful, important book! Brilliantly written!"

—Ernest Allen, National Center
for Missing & Exploited Children

I KNOW MY FIRST NAME IS STEVEN

Mike Echols

Pinnacle Books
Kensington Publishing Corp.

http://www.pinnaclebooks.com

PINNACLE BOOKS are published by

Kensington Publishing Corp.
850 Third Avenue
New York, NY 10022

Pinnacle and the P logo Reg. U.S. Pat. & TM Off.

First Printing: October, 1991
10 9

Printed in the United States of America

This book is dedicated to my loving mother, Anne Brown Echols, and to the memory of my loving father, Walter Harlan Echols, both wonderful parents who had great faith that I could indeed write this.

. . . And to the memory of Steven Gregory Stayner, an exceptionally courageous and remarkable young man, whom I will never, ever forget.

. . . And to the memory of the thousands of children who have been kidnapped, sexually assaulted, and murdered, a few of whom were:

Frank Aguirre; Billy Baulch, Jr.; Michael Baulch; Raymond Blackburn; Michael Bonnin; Matthew Bowman; Willard Branch, Jr; William Carroll; Charles Cobble; Graeme Cunningham; Alonzo Daniels; Danny Davis; Kenneth Dawson; Johnny Delone; James Dreymala; Danny Joe Eberle; Homer Garcia; Robert Gilroy; James Glass; Gregory Godzik; Ruben Haney; Richard Hembree; David Hilligiest; Rick Johnston; Marty Jones; Richard Kepner; William Kindred; Jeff Komen; Frank Landingin; William Lawrence; Michael Marino; John Mowery; Albert Parker; Kim Petersen; Robert Piest; Randall Reffett; John Sellers; Wally Simoneaux; Richard Stetson; John Szyc; David Talsma; Jason Verdow; Christopher Walden; Donald Waldrop; Adam Walsh; Troy Ward; Robert Winch; Gregory Winkle; Danny Yates

. . . And to the thousands of children still missing today, in the hope that they may be found alive and well, some of whom are:

Ricky Barnett; Kevin Collins; Jeffrey Dupres; Curtis Fair; Amy Fandel; Scott Fandel; Keith Fleming; Tony Franko; Angelica Gandara; John Gosch; Ann Gotlib; Toya Hill; Kelly Hollan; Robert Keck; Kimberly King; Eugene Martin; Jonelle Matthews; Elizabeth Miller; Kelly Morrissey; Mitchell Owens; Etan Patz; Andy Puglisi; Kirk Quintons; Randy Sellers; Galvin Sidden; Gary Sidden; Wilfredo Torres; Reagan Uden; Richard Uden; David Warner; Jacob Wetterling

Acknowledgments

I could never have written this book without the monumental help I received from Steven himself. He trusted me completely with his innermost thoughts, fears, feelings, memories, and details of what happened to him before, during, and after his kidnapping. And my task would have been almost impossible had I not received the help that I did from Steven's devoted father and mother, Del and Kay, as well as his, brother and sisters, Cary, Cory, Jody, and Cindy. Also, I am grateful for the time and information which was freely given to me by Timmy White and his parents, Jim and Angela.

Since 1984 my eyes and ears for events related to this story, past and present, in Merced, California, have been that city's former police chief, Harold Kulbeth, and I thank him most sincerely. And my research was aided immeasurably by Parnell's appeals attorney, Daniel Horowitz of Oakland, California, who gave me complete access to his files and copies of transcripts of Parnell's trials and hearings.

Also, I am extremely indebted to my close friend and confidant, Norman O. Milford, for his extensive editorial help, to my literary agent, Natasha Kern, for her championing of my work, and my editor at Zebra Books, Paul Dinas, for his availability and professional counsel.

Last, I thank the others who provided me with substantial help and/or information, namely: Joe Allen, Bill Bailey, Gerald Butler, Tyne Cordeiro, Shona Cunningham, Daryl Dallegge, Lyle Davis, Mark Dossetti, Ruth Hailey, Pat Hallford, Dave Knutsen, Dave Johnson, Barbara Matthias, Bob Matthias, Kenny Matthias, Lloyd Matthias, George McClure, George Mitchell, Jim Moore, Ervin E. "Murph" Murphy, Mary O. Parnell, Bill Patton, John Peace, Jerry Price, M. O. Sabraw, Art and Elsa Stoughton, John Walsh, Tom Walsh, and Ruth Younger.

Author's Note

Trained and educated as a social worker and journalist, I spent thirteen years counseling emotionally, physically, and sexually abused children for several different residential programs. Indeed, my college thesis was on the subject of sexually abused boys.

When news of Steven's kidnapping broke in late 1972, I felt moved to send a card to his mother, Kay, expressing my concern about her son's kidnapping and assuring her of my prayers.

Beginning in 1973 and continuing for almost ten years, I served as an avocational therapeutic foster father at different times to five different emotionally, physically, and sexually abused boys between the ages of ten and fifteen. My experiences trying to be a surrogate father to these boys and my frequently thwarted efforts to get counseling for them reinforced my interest in and concern for sexually abused children.

On March 1, 1980, I flew from Houston to San Francisco to spend a week's vacation with a woman I knew who lived in Marin County, just across the Golden Gate Bridge. That same night, about a hundred miles north of me, Steven Stayner and Timmy White hitchhiked into Ukiah, ending Steven's seven-year-and-three-month kidnapping (the longest stranger-abduction of a child with a safe return in United States history) and Timmy's two-week kidnapping. For two days the front pages of the San Francisco Bay area newspapers were filled with little else.

On March 4, 1980, Steven and his parents, Del and Kay, appeared on ABC-TV's *Good Morning America* from ABC's affiliate in San Francisco, KGO-TV. My friend and I watched the program over breakfast before we drove into San Francisco. She had a business luncheon, and I began the day by exploring Fisherman's Wharf.

While strolling about, I spotted Del and Kay Stayner standing side by side and attempted to photograph them with the zoom lens on my camera. I waited patiently for a teenage boy with his back to me to move so that I could take the picture. When I snapped the shutter, Del and Kay noticed me and I walked over, introduced myself, and began chatting with them. I was surprised when they told me that the teenage boy I'd seen was Steven, and that he had gone off to eat lunch at McDonald's with his little sister, Cory.

We went upstairs for lunch in a local seafood restaurant. Soon, Steven and Cory returned and joined in the conversation. Before we parted, I also took pictures of Steven and Cory, and Kay and I exchanged addresses and phone numbers.

The following summer, on my way to go backpacking in Yosemite National Park, I spent several hours at Kay's invitation visiting with the entire family at their home on Bette Street in Merced, got to see Steven's scrawled signature on the garage wall for the first time and met Queenie, Steven's beloved Manchester Terrier, which Parnell had given him. Before I left that day Kay surprised me by showing me the card which I had sent to her shortly after Steven was kidnapped.

By early 1984 I had moved to Colorado and made a career change from social work to journalism. One of my first writing assignments for the small weekly newspaper for which I wrote was a series of articles about missing and sexually abused children.

The March 19, 1984, *Newsweek* carried an article about Steven and his parents which told of their displeasure with all the proposals from authors and movie and television producers to write or film Steven's story. This prompted my editor to suggest that I consider writing a book about the kidnapping, and after a great deal of prodding I phoned Del and asked him if I could do this.

Less than a week later, Del called me back with his family's unanimous approval that I be given exclusive rights to Steven's story in return for a small percentage of any monies I earned from writing it.

In June 1984 I made my first book-related trip to California and spent five weeks doing research and traveling with and interviewing Steven, his family, and scores of others. During the rest of 1984 I made three more such trips.

Even though Parnell at first granted my request to access his defense attorney's files for both trials (i.e., trials for kidnapping Timmy White and for kidnapping and conspiracy to kidnap Steven Stayner), he changed his mind when he learned about my exchange with attorney Scott LeStrange concerning the truth-serum tapes and reneged before I was able to get any information from either Attorney LeStrange or John Ellery.

However, since Parnell's accomplice, Ervin Edward Murphy, was tried with him, LeStrange and Ellery supplied copies of most of their files to Murphy's attorneys, Wayne Eisenhart and Neil Morse, who in turn—with the signed permission that Murphy gave to me—provided me with complete access to these files and Murphy's files, a veritable treasure trove of information about Parnell.

On my last research trip to California in December, 1984, I was able to interview the imprisoned kidnapper himself twice, the only interviews Kenneth Eugene Parnell has ever granted.

In its manuscript form, this book was the basis for the 1989 Lorimar/NBC Television miniseries of the same title—for which I was also the technical consultant—and is the result of nearly one hundred fifty hours of tape-recorded interviews with thirty-seven different people (including forty-four with Steven himself), widely varied information provided by a score of others, and reading and condensation of over five thousand pages of hearing and trial transcripts.

W.H. (Mike) Echols, II
New York City
July, 1991

Introduction

It was a time in which the nation faced enormous challenges: the end of a war, a crisis of confidence in government and our most cherished institutions, a period of economic uncertainty, terrorism, and the taking of American hostages around the world. We were shaken and preoccupied. We questioned our future.

For generations Americans had pointed with pride and confidence to our children as the future of the nation. We cherished them. We protected them. We nurtured them in order to ensure that the world of tomorrow would be far better than our world today. Or did we?

It was also a time in which we discovered another side of ourselves. We began to discover the victimization of our children, referred to in the title of a well-known book of the period as *hidden victims*. We saw evidence of their vulnerability to abuse and exploitation, to abduction and molestation, to injury and death.

What roused Americans to this unseen crisis in our midst? While there were many dedicated professionals and advocates who labored for years in the crusade to protect children, I submit that fundamentally it was

the children themselves who awakened the nation—
the hidden victims and the victim families who said
"enough"—who triggered a sustained period of local,
state, and national action.

The names and images of the period are burned
into the conscience of an entire country—Adam
Walsh, the six-year-old Hollywood, Florida, boy ab-
ducted from a shopping mall and murdered; Etan
Patz, the six-year-old New York City child who disappeared on his way to school and is still missing today;
Ann Gotlib, the twelve-year-old Russian-Jewish immi-
grant girl still missing from Louisville, Kentucky; Yusef
Bell and the twenty-eight other missing and murdered
children of Atlanta; the thirty-four young boys who
were victims of John Wayne Gacy in Chicago; and
countless others.

Yet there is no story of greater impact, nor one
which offers more important lessons and challenges
for families and institutions, than the story of Steven
Gregory Stayner. It should not require the story of a
victimized child to provoke action. Yet there can be
no question that Steven, Adam, Etan, the Atlanta children, and many others were catalysts for a movement,
and that their legacies are the fundamental changes
taking place in virtually every community.

What did Steven's story teach us?

It taught us the vulnerability of children. Steven
Stayner confronted us with the reality that there are
those in our society who prey on children, who seek
out legitimate access to children in order to victimize
them. We do not need to live in fear, but we need to
be cautious. We need to be sure that our children understand that they have the right to say No and that

they are empowered to tell the parent, teacher, or trusted individual if they feel uncomfortable about something happening in their lives. Steven showed us that even children in a loving, caring family can be vulnerable, and that everyone must be prepared.

It demonstrated for us the manipulative power of the pedophile and his ability to control the child. He helped us to understand why many children who are victims do not come forward and why they believe people other than their parents. Child victims feel alone, isolated, and dependent. They respond to small kindnesses, find comfort in acts that suggest normalcy, and seek to adapt to their changed, troubled new world.

It challenged our society to deal more effectively with the adult offender who preys on children. Research suggests that these offenders victimize large numbers of children, are serial offenders, are dangerous and often violent, seek legitimate access to children, are rarely apprehended, and are rarely convicted for the most serious charges. These offenders pose a major public policy challenge for the future. We must seek improved capabilities for state and national screening of child serving personnel and volunteers, as well as improved systems for monitoring and tracking habitual offenders.

It showed us the importance of communication with our children. As Steven reached out for help in his own way and in his own words, many failed to listen or at least to understand. The professional community must be willing to listen to children and try to hear the message. Similarly, parents must empower their children to talk to them. From a very early age children must be told that we love, trust, and believe them.

If there is something that they don't feel right about, we must tell them that we want them to tell us and we will help. Similarly, it is essential that busy, often preoccupied parents find the time to really listen to their children. We must listen for more than the words. We must strive to hear what they are really trying to tell us. There is nothing more important. We must find the time.

It vividly depicts the tremendous challenges for victims, even after the initial period of victimization. He taught us that the recovery of a missing child does not automatically produce "happy ever after." Victims often require years of help, counseling, and assistance. As a nation we must seek more treatment services for victims of crime, particularly children. Unfortunately, his story also helps to demonstrate the still too-frequent propensity of our society to "blame the victim."

The lessons of Steven Gregory Stayner are many and powerful, but perhaps there is none more important for our time than the lesson of hope and courage. Steven went to the police station at Ukiah to save Timmy White, and Steven told his story over and over in order to keep other children from going through what he experienced.

Steven became a symbol of hope for parents of other long-missing children, living proof that we must never stop looking, that we must never close a case until the child is found. Tirelessly, Steven told and retold his story, no matter how difficult. He helped missing children groups and cared about the fate of the many children who have not yet been recovered.

I Know My First Name is Steven is a disturbing but vital commentary on our times. But most importantly, it is a tribute to a courageous young man whose troubled life helped make a difference. Because of Steven, and Adam, and all the others, America has awakened to the victimization of its children. Progress has been made, but we have only just begun.

Ernest E. Allen, President
National Center for Missing and Exploited Children
Arlington, Virginia

Prologue

That Saturday Dennis's dad left earlier than usual for his job at The Palace Hotel in Ukiah, California. Shortly after nightfall, Dennis swiftly bundled his new "little brother" into his arms for what had become an almost nightly ritual . . . attempting to hitchhike into Ukiah. But tonight would be different. The persistent heavy rains of the past sixteen days had ended, and because little Timmy had whined every time they had set out before, Dennis, fourteen, decided that this time he would carry Timmy—far enough along Mountain View Road and away from the tiny cabin that had been their home that the five-year-old wouldn't start in again with his plaintive "Ohhhh! I want to go inside!" Once again the two boys were out on the lonely, spooky country road trying to escape from their kidnapper, the man others thought to be Dennis's real father.

Besides the rain and Timmy's whining, Dennis had had to abort their few previous attempts to hitchhike to Mendocino's county seat because of the dearth of cars traveling the desolate road between Manchester and Boonville. All their efforts had been at night, and

even the hippies down the road at the Land of Oz
commune seldom traveled this narrow, twisting road
in the dark. But after walking just a scant quarter mile
up the hill and away from the tiny Mountain View
Ranch cabin and abandoned ranch headquarters, a
Mexican national in an old dinged-up Volkswagen
square-back stopped to give Dennis and Timmy a ride.
In disbelief that someone was finally stopping for
them, Dennis froze for a moment before rushing to
the car. Once he had opened the door, he was surprised to learn that the driver was going through
Boonville and all the way into Ukiah.

The man spoke very little English, but Dennis could
understand that he was following a friend in another
car who was having some sort of car trouble. Then,
jumping into the front seat and lifting his little brother
onto his lap, Dennis quickly closed the door and they
drove off along the pitch-dark winding road and were
suddenly swallowed up by the all-enveloping, brooding forest of two-hundred-foot redwood trees and
patches of fog that wafted menacingly over their route.

An eerie, indescribable feeling gripped Dennis as
they cleared the thickly forested rolling hills and de-
scended into the clear-cut Anderson Valley. Partly because of the language barrier—but more because of
Dennis's secret and his fear that it would be exposed
before he had gotten Timmy safely home and himself
on his way south to the San Joaquin Valley 200 miles
away—Dennis told the driver as little as possible . . .
and most of that was not the truth.

In silence the trio slid past the Boonville Airport
(where Dennis had once wanted to attend Anderson
Valley High School's popular pilot training program),

turned south onto California 128, and drove into Boonville, where the Mexican abruptly pulled up near The Horn of Zeese Restaurant and went to check out his friend's car. During this stop Dennis winced as he briefly considered the likelihood of his dad discovering him with Timmy. He had brought along his Bowie knife just in case, but the thought of actually having to use it sent shivers down his spine. Then, suddenly, they were moving again.

They went south to Highway 128's intersection with 253 where, as Dennis had anticipated, the driver turned north and left the Anderson Valley behind as they chugged over the coastal range's rolling hills before dropping down into "deep valley," or *Yo-kia,* as the Pomo Indians called it before it was Anglicized to "Ukiah."

As they came down the last hill into Ukiah, it hit Dennis hard for the first time: "It's me against the world. I'm alone now. There's no one to turn to and no one to help me make the decisions."

Dennis had told the Mexican that he and his little brother were traveling from Point Arena to their new home in Ukiah, and as they drove into town, Timmy whispered to Dennis that he wanted to go to his babysitter's house and that they should get out near The Bottle Shoppe . . . and that was where Dennis had the driver drop them off.

Sixteen days earlier Timmy had left his half-day kindergarten class at Yokayo Elementary School for the daily walk to his babysitter's house. But he never made it, and his babysitter, Diane Crawford, had waited in vain for her charge, not knowing that Dennis's dad, Ken Parnell, had snatched Timmy from the sidewalk.

Now, at nine o'clock Saturday night, Dennis and Timmy walked west from State Street to Diane's house on South Avenue, but no one was home. At this point Dennis told Timmy that he would escort him to the Ukiah Police Station, but Timmy refused, saying he knew where he lived and that that was where he wanted to go. The kindergartner pointed Dennis south along South State Street, but when they reached its intersection with freeway U.S. 101 out of San Francisco, Timmy became confused. Even though they were headed in the right direction, the boys were still five miles from Timmy's house.

But Timmy insisted that Dennis take him home, and so they continued a little farther south along the freeway's shoulder until they reached the Boonville exit, where Dennis became convinced that they were lost and finally talked Timmy into allowing him to take him to the police station. The weary pair turned around and trudged nearly two miles back up South State Street until they reached The Palace Hotel, where they turned down East Standley Street.

In taking this route, at a little past eleven o'clock that night, Dennis Parnell passed the hotel where his dad was working his first night as the security guard. Dennis had his dad's latest family addition with him, but fortunately, the three of them did not meet, and it would be early the next morning before Dennis would see his dad again . . . and then under very strained circumstances.

Dennis stopped at the corner of Main and East Standley, where he instructed and encouraged Timmy to continue alone to the Ukiah Police Station just three-fourths of a block away, tell them his name, and, Den-

nis assured the frightened little boy, the police would
see that he got home. Then the fourteen-year-old
watched as his little brother slowly made his way to
the station's front door, opened it a crack, began to
cry, and then let go of the door and ran back to his
big brother.

Inside the station, Officer Bob Warner had seen the
little dark-haired boy come to the door, open it, and
run away. This was suspicious for that hour of the
night, and he went to the door and watched as the
child ran up to a much older boy across the parking
lot. Fearing that the boys would run away if he approached them on foot, Warner radioed for a patrol
unit.

Within two minutes Officer Russel VanVoorhis
pulled his cruiser up beside the two boys, stepped out,
and asked the older of the two what the younger boy's
name was. Replied Dennis, "Timmy White." Recognizing that as the name of a local five-year-old blond
boy who had been missing for over two weeks, a surprised Officer VanVoorhis squatted next to the dark-
haired little boy and asked his name again, just to be
sure. "Timmy White!" came the crisp reply.

Two hundred miles south, in Merced, California, as
they had for over seven years, Delbert and Kay Stayner
went to bed knowing the whereabouts of only four of
their five children. In another room of their home,
eleven-year-old Cory cried herself to sleep over the
long-ago disappearance of her brother, Steven, who
would be fourteen now . . . if he was still alive. And,
as she had done for most of her life, Cory prayed that
Steven was safe and that he would come home soon.

In Ukiah, Officer VanVoorhis straightened himself

up to address the older boy, but before he could speak, Dennis said, "My name is Steven Stayner, and I've been missing from Merced for seven years."

Even though he misspelled his name in his initial written report for the Ukiah Police Department that night, Dennis Gregory Parnell was on the way to becoming Steven Gregory Stayner again for the first time in more than seven years. As he said at the beginning of that statement, "I know my first name is Steven, I'm pretty sure my last name is Stainer [sic]."

Chapter One
Steven Gregory Stayner

"He was always just like a puppy dog."

Just north of the monstrous urban sprawl of greater Los Angeles, after Interstate 5 climbs over Tejon Pass, California 99—a freeway in its own right—angles off to the right and begins its descent through sparsely covered arid hills into Bakersfield, the city that pins the southern end of the vast, flat, agricultural San Joaquin Valley. The boyhood home of New York Giants' football great Frank Gifford, Bakersfield was also the boyhood home of Kenneth Parnell. Mary Parnell, Ken's octogenarian mother, still lives in Bakersfield and attends the Assembly of God Church, where as teenagers these two dissimilar boys played basketball on the same church team in the late 1940s. But as a young man Parnell had interests other than sports, and at nineteen he was arrested, tried, and convicted of kidnapping and sexually assaulting a nine-year-old boy. After court-ordered stays in two state mental hospitals—from which he made three escapes—this diagnosed sexual psychopath was sentenced to prison and effectively banished from the blue-collar community of hard-working, patriotic American families with young children.

Outside Bakersfield, semis with empty trailers rush northward to pick up their loads of carrots, cucumbers, peaches, watermelons, and other produce from the huge commercial farms that blanket the valley floor. So ubiquitous are these trucks that at harvest time they choke all four lanes north and south as they hurry to and from Delano, Earlimart, Visalia, Kingsburgh, and scores of other farming towns familiar across the United States as points-of-origin stamped on produce crates and boxes.

At 65 mph and more, the agricultural traffic rumbles up California 99 and slices through the southwest edge of Fresno, the largest city in the Valley, before rolling on north through Madera and Chowchilla— known since 1976 for its own infamous kidnapping, that of an entire schoolbus full of children. Another twenty miles north is Merced, a modest city of fifty thousand middle-class citizens, much like those in Bakersfield, 160 miles to the south. During the summer many tourists exit onto California 140, Yosemite Parkway, and head east eighty miles to the cooler Yosemite National Park, thousands of feet higher in the ruggedly beautiful Sierra Nevadas.

On Yosemite Parkway, one block past the Red Ball Gas Station at Jean Street, is Shirley Street. Down Shirley a short block, left on Dawn a block, and then right onto Bette for a long block—in a neighborhood of older, lower-middle-class homes with small, well-tended front yards and young children—is number

1655, a pea green frame house shaded by a huge elm tree, its large root running just under the sidewalk and heaving it up several inches, thus providing a ramp of sorts for the tykes who furiously pedal their Big Wheels up and down the pavement.

In 1972 it was the home of Delbert and Kay Stayner and their five children, including their middle child, then seven-year-old Steven, an active, almost buck-toothed boy with a slight mask of freckles.

In a house barely a quarter mile from the Southern Pacific Railroad tracks, the Stayners and their brood escaped the dry, blast-furnace heat of San Joaquin Valley summers in their backyard swimming pool—one of the few luxuries they allowed themselves—where they could hear the railroads' vegetable and fruit expresses thundering through town headed to markets far and near.

At five feet ten, Del is just slightly taller than his wife, Kay, and with a lean build and a deeply lined, sun-tanned face, he looks every bit like a man devoted to hard outdoor physical labor who could easily be a character from a Steinbeck novel. A folksy, entertaining spinner of tales, Del enjoys people. His favorite subjects are his family, his friends, his work, and the San Joaquin Valley. Inside or out, he is never without a stained gimmie cap, emblazoned with a farm equipment or fertilizer logo, which hides his ever-increasing baldness. Almost a decade older than his wife, Del was born during the Great Depression in dusty, remote Farmington, New Mexico. After the war, while he was still a teenager, his family moved west to California so that Del's father, Tal, could find work in the expanding agricultural industry of the San Joaquin Valley.

A robust young man, Del worked in the Valley's fruit and vegetable fields himself until his late twenties, when he struck out for northern California and found a job as a laborer at a sawmill in the isolated hamlet of Hyampom in Trinity County. He soon met pretty, black-haired, olive-complexioned Mary Katherine "Kay" Augustine, the eighteen-year-old daughter of local dairy and truck farmer Bob Augustine and his wife, Mary. After four years away from home at a Roman Catholic girls' boarding school in Redwood—four years away from boys, too—Kay had graduated and returned. Quiet but headstrong, she was immediately struck by this no-nonsense man boarding near her home. After a courtship of just a few weeks, she and Del married on July 1, 1960.

In November the couple moved south to be near Del's family in Merced. With the fruit and vegetable canning season almost over, Del was lucky to find work as a year-round machinery mechanic for the Consolidated Canners & Growers (CC&G) fruit and vegetable packing plant east of Merced on California 140. Del and Kay settled into a small rented house on Charles Street, where they were content with their simple life: nearby relatives, like-minded friends from CC&G, and, in August of 1961, their firstborn, a son they named Cary. Then, at roughly two-year intervals, while Del worked and Kay ran the household, the couple had four more children: a daughter, Cindy, in October 1963; a second son, Steven, in April 1965; a second daughter, Jody, in January 1967; and, after they moved from Merced, their last child and third daughter, Cory, in November 1968.

What the couple craved was a country setting in

which to raise their growing family, and in early March of 1967, the lure of rural life led them to buy a modest almond ranch in northern Merced County, near the small agrarian community of Snelling. Del proudly moved his growing family into one of the two older frame houses on the twenty acres of gently rolling land and began dry-farming his orchard of hundreds of almond trees, selling his small crop to the Blue Diamond Cooperative. Even though the ranch required his almost constant attention, Del continued his full-time job at the CC&G plant twenty miles away. It made for eighteen-hour days six days a week during a canning season which corresponded with Del's own harvest season.

Stevie—Del's pet name for Steven—was a dynamo of a little boy who loved being outside with his father as Del pruned, sprayed, and harvested his almond crop. Reminisced Del, "When he was small, Stevie wanted to go everywhere I went. I wouldn't let him ride on the tractor when I was goin' under the trees because the al-mond"—Del's distinctive pronunciation of the word—"branches was so low I was afraid he was goin' to get hit in the face. But he'd walk behind, and he'd just keep on walkin' . . . he'd walk miles following me. Then, when I'd come in from work and lay on the couch and watch TV, Stevie would come and curl up with me on the couch and I would bite him on the ear and he'd laugh. He was always just like a puppy dog."

Kay, as much family manager as mother, remarked that Steven liked to follow Del around, because "Papa did all the exciting things . . . and me, all I would say was, 'Go clean your room, go wash your face, go blow your nose.' "

Agreed Steve, "Yeah that was me. I was just like a puppy dog. Everywhere he went I wanted to go. That's why me and him did a lot of things together when I was little . . . a lot of things happened to us together." Years later Steve recalled his family's life at the ranch as the most idyllic period of his childhood: "I loved it. I could go just about anywhere I wanted with my dog Daisy."

"Yes," Kay recalled with a smile, "he still talks about his Daisy. She was a collie. All of the kids went with us to pick her out, but Steven considered her his. Daisy would run through the orchard with him and fetch a stick and play with him and wrestle with him on the ground. Daisy was the kind of dog that you picked up and loved. And at the ranch we never did have to worry about anything happening to Steve, because we had twenty acres of almond trees around us, and he could have been missing for three hours and we wouldn't have known it."

Having experienced a surfeit of Catholicism during her four years studying under the nuns in Redwood, Kay had deferred to her husband in the matter of the family's religion. Del's great-grandfather had marched to Mexico with the U.S. Army's Mormon battalion, which had fought under General Zachary Taylor in the Mexican-American War, and Del had been raised in a family with a Mormon faith as resolute as that of their pioneer forebears. Through the 1960s and into the early 1970s a solid, participatory Mormon faith was an integral part of the Stayners' family life. Steve's sister Cindy fondly reminisced that even when they lived at the ranch, twice a week they drove the twenty miles each way to services at the Mormon Stake in Merced, there not being one in Snelling. "Mom and Dad didn't make us go, we always liked it and wanted to go."

Kay laughed as she joyously recalled her family's rural life: "It was your average ill-run agricultural operation. But the kids did have fun there. We had cows, goats, and pigs . . . the pigs we were constantly chasing down the road. At one time we tried to raise some calves, but we didn't grow any feed, because there was no irrigation on the place, so we really didn't do it economically. And then we raised chinchillas. It was some success . . . we bought two. One died and the other ran away."

But the days of the family's bucolic existence on the almond ranch were numbered. Del's struggle to dry-farm the almonds by himself and work for CC&G finally took its physical toll on him. One morning in 1970, while he was shaving in the bathroom with Stevie at his side, he suffered a slipped disk, passed out from the pain, and fell to the floor. Kay called an ambulance to take her husband to Mercy Hospital in Merced, where he underwent back surgery. The incident so terrified Stevie that for many years afterward he thought his beloved dad had suffered a heart attack.

When he got home from the hospital a few weeks later, Del somehow found the intestinal fortitude to continue his single-handed dry-farming, but he soon thought it wise to take on a partner. He asked his good friend and cannery coworker Mac Scoggins to join him, and Mac and his wife Sandy and their three children soon moved into the other house on the ranch.

Kay and Sandy had been good friends for as long as Del and Mac had, and both women relished their new lives as farm mothers watching their children grow up and interact with each other. Even though the Scoggins' offspring were older than Steven, he played with them as much as he did with his own brother and sisters. Kay remarked that her son was so amiable that he would mix well and fit into any group of children with ease, regardless of age, adding, "He never did anything really out of line. He was just normal . . . an ordinary boy who would drive you crazy asking can he please do something."

But Del recollected an occasion when Stevie and Cindy failed to ask. "They was about three and five, and here was this cap and they got it off and here was this hole where the cap had been, and so they figured that they had to find somethin' to put in it. So they found a lot of sand and gravel in the driveway, and they just had a ball. The next mornin' I couldn't figure out what the heck was wrong with my truck. It wouldn't run . . . just sat there and idled . . . They was standin' there watchin' me cleanin' it up. Then Cindy said, 'Stevie put that stuff in there.' And he said, 'No, not me. *You* put that in there.' And they tickled me so much that I never did spank 'em, I got to laughin' so hard. I just sent them inside."

As Steven got older he continued his affectionate me-and-my-shadow relationship with his father. The two of them went on frequent hunting or fishing trips, or Stevie just rode around with his "Papa."

"Naturally," Steve fondly said, "I was around my dad a lot and, of course, I loved my dad and I admired him."

The exceptionally dry summer of 1971, coupled with the property's scant irrigation, forced the Stayners and the Scoggins to reluctantly sell their ranch and move back into Merced. It was a sad day for Stevie and his dog Daisy when his family moved to the house on Bette Street. Years later Kay told of Daisy's unhappiness after the move. The collie had had the run of the ranch and its considerable acreage on both sides, but on Bette Street she found herself confined inside the fenced backyard and she paced around its perimeter until she wore a path into the grass. Then one day Kay took her children to the local zoo and they saw a wolf pacing back and forth along the front of its cage, just as Daisy did. This so disturbed Kay that when they returned home she talked with her children and they all agreed it would be better to give Daisy to friends living in the country.

But Daisy's life wasn't the only one affected by the move. At the ranch Steven had been free to roam his family's twenty acres of almond trees and the adjoining vacant land. But in town the active six-year-old found himself getting into trouble for unconsciously cutting through neighbors' yards and flowerbeds.

And as if giving up Daisy wasn't enough, Steve had to leave behind the friends he had made in his Snelling kindergarten class. It was a very unhappy first-grader who started at Merced's Charles Wright Elementary School in September of 1971 . . . so unhappy that he cried and picked fights with his classmates. His teacher found it necessary to call in Del and Kay for a conference. His brother and sisters had adjusted well to the move, but to Steven this reordering of his life was almost the end of the world. Said Del, "Stevie didn't like the move one bit. The only thing he did the same as at the ranch was that while the other kids would play in front of the TV, Stevie would always come and get on my lap."

Kay remembers, "That first fall absolutely seemed like forever to that child. But after spring of that next year, he was a little more happy because he had some friends . . . Steve really did make friends rather quickly. But I guess he's always been a little spunky. He's never been one to sit back and let somebody walk on him."

At that time, except for his parents, grandparents, and a few aunts and uncles, Steve's contacts with adults were limited to his teacher and to the family's closest friends, like the Scogginses, with whom the Stayners frequently went camping. But as far as people he did not know, Del said, "Steve wasn't the type of guy who just walked up and started talkin' to strangers . . . he was kind of shy. But he was polite. We taught all our kids to be polite!"

On one of the family's camping trips, Steven's sister Jody recalled an incident when he was very compassionate toward her. She had been accidentally shot in the leg with a BB gun. "I started crying and I remember Steven coming up to me and trying to comfort me. He was just six, but he was tryin' to be really comforting . . . and I'll always remember that."

Many were the times that Stevie and his dad went fishing alone. But, Del and Kay laughed in unison, he never did catch anything. "The reason I never did," a chagrined Steven later recalled, "is that you had to sit there and be quiet, and I just couldn't . . . Another thing is that I was very good at snagging lines. Dad would always try to break the line, but he'd wind up breaking the pole instead. . . . And that would be all the fishing for me for a while. But I didn't mind, because then, while he kept on fishing, Dad would let me run around on the shore and play while he was in the boat trying to fish."

To Del, whether he took along just Stevie or all of his children, outings to the lake were among the joyous highlights of fatherhood. On one fishing trip, Del had all five of his active young children in the boat with him, and he thought that they were going to turn the boat over. "I was tryin' to fish while the kids were playin' around. I told them to stop, but about that time this big ol' catfish swam right under the boat and they all got to the other side of the boat to see if they could see it. And that catfish came up on top of the water and slithered onto its side and they was just a hollerin' and laughin' and it was so funny. And I can't swim a stroke and I was just sittin' there and holdin' on real tight.

"And that fish just kept on stirrin' up the water and the kids was havin' the best ol' time. I was leanin' back this way and that boat tilted, and I looked down into that water—and screamed. I think you coulda' heard me all over that lake, it scared me so bad! I just knew that boat was gonna' flip over, but it didn't."

In the early 1970s, the family went to the lake at least twice a month, camping out at least one weekend every month. Del ruminated happily, "We'd go to Exchecker, Don Pedro, or Alpine Lake . . . we'd just load up and take off and go."

But these lake outings weren't for Kay. Even though the Stayners had a backyard swimming pool, she was the only competent swimmer in the family. Disapprovingly, she recalled, "When we'd go to the lake it scared the bedeavors out of me. If I got into a boat with all that crowd of people, even though they had on life preservers, who was I going to help first?"

By September of 1972 Steven had made a good many friends at school and in his neighborhood, and it was a very happy seven-year-old who entered Mrs. Walsh's second-grade class at Charles Wright Elementary. Even though he had not forgotten the ranch and his Daisy, Steven did have family dogs Puggy and Brownie, his brother and sisters, and scores of other kids to play with . . . and the exceptionally close relationship with his father.

Each school morning Steven, Cindy, and Jody walked to school together, shepherded by unwilling big brother Cary, a sixth-grader who detested his mother's insistence on this. But each afternoon at 2 P.M. Steven enjoyed the freedom and independence of walking home alone since Cary, Cindy, and Jody didn't get out until later.

In late November of 1972 Steven started getting into trouble for going directly from school to a friend's house to play, rather than going straight home from school. Del and Kay warned him several times to ask permission first, but this apparently didn't register, and by Friday, December 1, after Del had twice threatened to punish his son for disobeying this rule, Steven went to his friend's house again without asking and Del whipped him when he got home.

"Victor was my best friend then," Steven recalled. "On Thursday, the last day of November, I walked home with him to play soccer, but I hadn't asked first.

When it started to get real dark, I headed for home. That day my dad gave me a warning. Then the next day I did it again. That's how come I got whipped. Probably, if it had been a week between each time, I wouldn't have gotten in trouble. It was just three licks with a belt across the fanny, but it made me remember!"

On December 3, 1972, Steven went to his friend Sharon Carr's eighth birthday party. Santa Claus was there, and photographs were taken while Steven and the other children gathered around the bearded old gent. After the party Steven beamed from ear to ear all the way home, as he talked nonstop to Kay about what he wanted for Christmas.

Once home, Steven bounded from the car and into the house, where he bounced onto his father's lap and told him all about the party, Santa Claus, and that among other things he wanted a G.I. Joe set for Christmas. As Stevie sat on his dad's lap, Del delighted in his son's wonder and excitement over the approaching Christmas holidays and thanked God for his family and especially his Stevie, the apple of his eye.

It was hard for Steven to fall asleep that night, what with visions of G.I. Joe sets dancing in his head. It was to be his last night in his own home and with his own family for many, many years to come.

Chapter Two

The Kidnapping: December 4, 1972

"The walk home was usual . . . at least the first part."

Outside the day was dawning cold and gray as inside Steven climbed out of his bed and padded down the hall rubbing sleep from his eyes. He peeked around the door into his parents' room and saw his dad still asleep. Canning season had finally ended, and Del was on vacation, enjoying the opportunity to sleep in. Steven turned and resumed his ambling journey down the hall, suddenly taking note of the smell of breakfast cooking in the kitchen. Quickly he ducked into the bathroom and relieved himself.

Back in his room, Steven dressed with a seven-year-old's purposefulness and then headed for the kitchen. Toast, scrambled eggs, orange juice, and milk . . . as usual, Kay's breakfast for her children was hot and nourishing. Later, as her four oldest children left for school, Kay stood at the front door and checked each one's attire to see that they were all dressed properly for the cold weather. Then Cary, Cindy, Steven, and Jody walked the twelve blocks to Charles Wright Elementary, with Cary shepherding them as far as Yosemite Parkway. Once there and out of his mother's vigilant range, Cary sprinted away from the young trio lest his friends see him.

Back at home, Kay told Cory to go to her room and play quietly while she cleared and washed the breakfast dishes, clucking to herself as she looked up from the kitchen sink and through the window, frowning at Steven's bold pencil-scrawled signature on the white wall of the garage. Kay sighed as she recalled how she had tried to get Del to punish Steven for this indiscretion . . . "He didn't even make him wash it off!" she sighed to herself.

At a knock on the side door, Kay dried her hands and opened it to find her next-door neighbor Arlene standing on the stoop with her young daughter Donna. Just now remembering her promise to watch the little girl while her friend went downtown, Kay apologized for having forgotten and ushered Donna inside to play with Cory. With two four-year-olds playing in the house, Del soon abandoned his sleep, but ever the patient father, he uncomplainingly got up, dressed, stopped by Cory's room, and cheerily greeted the girls before going to the kitchen. There he sat down and visited casually with Kay as he washed down his toast and jelly with black coffee. When the girls entered the kitchen, Del gently tousled their hair before rising to go out to the garage to work on his '56 Jeep pickup.

At 1 P.M. Arlene returned, thanked Kay, and collected her daughter. Ten minutes later Kay left for the auto parts store for Del, and to get a few groceries at Safeway. With a cold rain starting to fall, her plans included picking up Steven at school when he got out at two o'clock.

Eighty miles to the east, Yosemite National Park and the surrounding Sierra Nevadas had received an overnight blanket of light, feathery snow. In the predawn hours, kitchen cleaner Ervin Edward Murphy had gazed at the falling snow from his cozy shared employee's cabin as he planned his annual purchases of dime store Christmas gifts. Skinny, and hunch-shouldered, the simpleton worked the graveyard shift scrubbing Yosemite Lodge's huge cooking ovens, but Sunday and Monday nights he was off, and during the night just past he had fought hard to stay awake so as not to miss the daily bus to Merced. Not owning a car, and never having learned to drive, the 8 A.M. bus was Murphy's only way of getting to Merced, the primary shopping town for people in the park. But "Murph," as his friends called him, had fallen asleep. A sharp knock made him wake with a start and he scrambled to the door, a glance at the clock confirming his fear that he had missed the bus.

Opening the door, Murph discovered his peculiar bespectacled friend, Kenneth Eugene Parnell, smiling furtively as he huddled against the cold. Ken, the Curry Company's night auditor at Yosemite Lodge, a slightly stooped, introverted, self-taught bookkeeper—with no other friends among his fellow employees—and Murph, who made friends with any and all he met, were two of the oddest of the collection of social misfits, ex-felons, and alcoholics who then made up the bulk of the Curry Company's Yosemite employees.

"Let's go to Merced!" Parnell blurted, and without pause Murph smiled and happily accepted his friend's offer.

Recounted Murph, "We went down to Merced in his old white Buick. Parnell took me to Merced Mall, and I went shopping to buy my Christmas presents. Now, while I was shopping, Parnell got some gospel tracts. And after I did my shopping he give me some and he asked, 'Would you hand out some gospel tracts?' And I said I would. You see, according to Parnell, he was studying them gospel tracts and he decided to be a minister. You know, you *can* study to become a minister.

"So then he said that he was going to take me to a particular area of town that he knew to hand them gospel tracts out. And he drove me out on Yosemite Parkway and told me to give 'em to the kids walking home from school. He said that he wanted to raise an underprivileged child, and he felt he could do better than his [the child's] parents, and that he wanted me to help him pick up one of the boys walking home from school to be his son. Parnell said there were a lot of battered children out there who need a home where they can be well treated. He said he wanted to find him a boy like that and take care of him."

To Murph, though not, of course, to most people, Ken's plan made perfect sense, for during the pair's many conversations, Murph had shared with Ken that he himself had been an abused child, a fact not lost on the cunning Parnell when he'd chosen him to be his partner-in-crime.

At the auto-parts store Kay stood in line for Del's oil, filter, and nuts and bolts. It was a little past 2 P.M. and sleeting as she ran back to her car hoping that Steven would wait for her at school. Anxiously, Kay drove the freeway to Yosemite Parkway, exited, and headed east, arriving at the school's back entrance about 2:10. Fruitlessly she searched the few remaining clusters of children for her son before making a U-turn and driving straight home down Yosemite Parkway, past the Red Ball Gas Station, looking for Steven all along the way. Back home at 2:20, she got out of the car and asked Del, still working on his Jeep, if he had seen Steven. Not yet concerned, he shook his head "no." Neither had eaten lunch and Del asked Kay to fix tunafish sandwiches for them while they awaited what Del felt certain would be yet another tardy arrival by their youngest son.

A little before 3 P.M. Del, Kay, and Cory piled into the car and headed back to Charles Wright Elementary to pick up Cindy and Jody, looking for Steven along the way. Cindy and Jody were waiting at the curb, but Steven was nowhere to be seen . . . and his sisters hadn't seen him since lunch.

As they drove home, Del's emotions began to swing between anger that Stevie had apparently disobeyed him again and anxiety that something just *might* have happened to him. If Stevie had gone to his friend's without permission again, Kay said, "Del was going to get him *good* this time."

Back at home, Steven's parents phoned his friends and his friends' parents, but no one knew where Steven was. They did, however, speak with his classmate Royal Harris, apparently the last one to have seen Steven at school. Royal said he waved 'bye to Steven as he himself boarded his school bus. But the second-grader had no idea where Steven had gone after that.

At 2 P.M., less than a quarter mile from Charles Wright Elementary School, Kenneth Parnell pulled off Yosemite Parkway onto Jean Street and drifted to a stop just west of the Red Ball Gas Station. He gave Murph some final instructions and a handful of gospel tracts. A few minutes later at the school, with his mother nowhere to be seen, Steven started to walk home in the pelting sleet.

Murph remembers, "After Parnell let me out, he drives off and I didn't know where he was going, and I'm just standing there in the sleet handing out these gospel tracts. And, you know, I gave a lot of them tracts to them kids walking home from school. A lot would just say, 'Hi,' or 'I've got to get home,' and pretty soon I had only a few left.

"And, see, I'm handin' 'em out and Steven shows up and I'm talking to him and I said, 'Where are you goin'?' And he said, 'I'm going home.' And I said, 'The minister will give you a ride home.' And then Parnell drives up and calls Steven over to the car. Then I opened up the door and Steven got in and Parnell says to me, 'Let's go. I'm going to take the kid home.' And I got in the front and shut the doors and we drove off."

Reminisced Steven, "I don't remember too much about the school days—the usual, monotonous days—but that one stands out. The walk home was usual . . . at least the first part. I walked down the back way and then crossed Yosemite Parkway there by the gas station. At that age I usually walked with my head down, looking at my feet, so I really didn't notice Murphy standing there until I was right on him. And then he came up to me and gave me some religious brochures. They had a little story in them in cartoon form that says something out of the Bible.

"Murphy said he was from a church and was trying to gather donations. He asked me if maybe my mother would like to donate something to his cause. He asked me where I lived and I told him that I lived right around the corner about three blocks. Then he asked, 'Well do you think we could speak with your mother?' And I hadn't seen anybody else by then, but I said, 'Yeah, I'm sure she would love to give a donation.' Then he goes, 'Well, could you take us there?' And I agreed to. My impression was that he was a nice man, even though I later found out that he wasn't too bright; but at that age that wasn't important to me.

"Then all of a sudden I noticed a white car pull around the corner and up beside us. Murphy opened the back door for me. I got in; he got in front. Then he shut the doors and introduced Parnell to me. They both used their real names, too.

"Then they drove off and they passed my street. I mentioned it to them, and Parnell said, 'Oh, well, we're going to our place for a while and see if you can stay the night. We're gonna' call your mother from there.' I go, 'Well, why don't we just go back and ask her?' Then Parnell said, 'Well, we got some things to do down there. We'll call her from there.' Then they hit the highway for Cathy's Valley.

"They sure were sure of themselves. I mean, the way Parnell acted, as soon as he got me in the car, he acted like that was *it*. Then I just sort of sat back and enjoyed the ride. I'd never even been that way before, you know," Steven exclaimed.

Murphy said, "On the way out of Merced, I figured that there was something wrong"—with Parnell taking Steven along—"but then, I said to myself, 'The kid ain't doin' nothin'.' I *knowed* there was somethin' wrong, but after we left Merced I never heard him cry, either. Even when we got him there [a cabin in Cathy's Valley] he never cried."

The ordinarily taciturn Parnell recalled the events this way: "[At Merced Mall] we began looking for a likely prospect to be my son. During this incident Murphy talked to two other children in the shopping center. However, I thought them to be unsuitable." And referring to the kidnapping: "There was no force used on Steven by either Murphy or myself, and neither was any force necessary to keep him in our custody after leaving the area."

By 4 P.M. Kay and Del had scoured their neighborhood several times, checking with Steven's playmates as they went. Then, with increasing concern for Steven's safety, they began driving in ever-widening circles around their home and the school in the ever-colder, wetter, gloomier weather.

Finally, weary and becoming frantic, Del and Kay

returned home a little before 5 P.M. and telephoned the Merced Police. Fifteen minutes later Officer Michael Hyde arrived, was briefed by Del and Kay, and soon thereafter radioed his dispatcher: "Responded to the area of 1655 Bette Street in response to a missing juvenile from that location. The subject was approximately four feet eight inches, sixty pounds, with shaggy brown hair and brown eyes, last seen wearing a light tan coat with blue jeans and a possible zip-up type T-shirt." He then left and searched the adjacent neighborhood, the school playground, Yosemite Parkway, and everywhere in between.

By the time Hyde returned to the pea green house on Bette, Kay had phoned Steven's teacher, Mrs. Walsh, gotten a complete list of Steven's classmates and their phone numbers, and had called each one in her continuing futile efforts to locate her son.

As dark fell, Patrol Sergeant Jim Southerland arrived to help Officer Hyde in retracing Steven's possible routes home before the two began going door-to-door to the businesses along Yosemite Parkway. At the Red Ball Service Station, a female attendant told them that sometime before 3 P.M. she had seen Steven walking eastbound, his normal direction home from school, but that she had not noticed any suspicious persons in the area.

At 6 P.M. reserve police officers and local Boy Scouts were called out to help search an area which by now included construction sites along Yosemite Parkway. But the dark and soggy cold weather had driven all the children inside, and Steven was nowhere to be seen. At the same time local radio station KYOS's disc jockey Buzz Williamson began broadcasting news of

Steven's disappearance and his description, Merced's first public word about the incident. But as the dark blanketed Merced, a palpable gloom settled over the Stayners' normally boisterous home. Ignorant of Steven's disappearance, Del's close friend Mac Scoggins telephoned to invite Del and Kay to the Elks' Lodge Christmas Dance that weekend, but when he learned of Steven's disappearance, his invitation trailed off and Mac promised his friend that he and his wife Sandy would be right over.

When they arrived, Sandy's offer to take Cory, Jody, Cindy, and Cary to her home for the night was quickly accepted. Del and Mac departed for a nearby junkyard on Highway 140, where they slogged through high drenched weeds with flashlights, fearfully opened the doors on the abandoned refrigerators, and called Steven's name until they were soaked and hoarse.

At that moment, a little more than a half-hour drive up California 140, Parnell, Murph, and Steven were just sitting down to their supper. As they'd left Merced, the highway to Yosemite National Park had been almost deserted, and that had suited Parnell just fine. The trio had driven through the murky wintry weather straight to the little red cabin at Cathy's Valley that Parnell rented as his private retreat from his book-keeping duties at Yosemite Lodge, just 50 miles on up the highway.

Parnell could hardly have picked a quieter yet still accessible getaway, for Cathy's Valley is a hamlet in the truest sense of the word. During the summer tourists occasionally stop and buy old-fashioned wood and ceramic Made-in-Japan-style curios right out of the 1950s in the combination general store, gas station, and whatnot shop, but the off-season rarely saw anyone stopping, and the handful of locals felt fortunate when they went to the store and found it open.

On a bare hill a few hundred feet to the east of the store is Judy's Trailer Park, a funky, run-down mobile-home park and none-too-popular summers-only overnight stop for tourists with campers and trailers. Perched on the dry, grass-covered hillside with a few stunted scrub oaks scattered about, just east of the camper and trailer spaces are two barn-red prewar one-room wood-frame tourist cabins. In 1972 there were three, but one has since burned down. Each has a tiny porch and a single room; the toilet sits beside the metal shower stall and is screened off with a shower curtain. Minimal flea market furnishings complete the sparse interiors, and since the cabins are not winterized, off-season rent was cheap enough to attract even a penny pincher like Parnell.

No one noticed Parnell's dirty old white Buick as it lurched and bounced up the rutted, steep dirt road, earlier that evening, finally wheezing to a stop in front of the middle of the three dreary cabins, the only one occupied. The two men and the little boy got out, but Parnell made Murph wait outside while he took Steven inside the cabin and showed his captive a pile of used toys Murph had recently purchased at Parnell's behest during a flea market auction.

There were dozens of colorful little plastic Indians, cowboys, and, Steven recalls, a toy canoe. At first Steven was greedy, asking to take this one to his brother and that one to his sister; but this angered

Parnell, and he told Steven that he could pick out toys for himself only, and none for his brothers or sisters. Not realizing the sinister implication of this, Steven hushed and contentedly picked out and played with Parnell's imposed limit of four toys.

Recalled Murph, "It was kinda' chilly outside, but I stayed outside, and after a little bit Parnell comes out and says, 'Murph, if you say anything about this you'll be right in the same fix as me and you'll get the same penalty I get.' And then he says he was sorry he got me involved in this with him. 'But you agreed with me a hundred percent, and if you tell anybody, you'll lose everything you have,' he told me." Then Parnell escorted the intimidated Murph inside.

Steven played with his toys as Parnell hunkered down beside him and began quizzing him about his mother, father, brother and sisters, family life, and likes and dislikes. Recalled Steven, "I told a few lies to him, trying to make myself look good. He asked me if I had ever been whipped. If I had said yes it would have made me sound like I was a bad boy, so I said, 'No, I've never been whipped.'"

Unknown to Steven, Parnell knew differently, for the scheming exconvict had had a chance encounter with the Stayners' former mailman—then recently transferred to Yosemite National Park from Merced—and on Parnell's seemingly favorite subject of abused children the postman had mentioned to the bookkeeper the strict discipline he had observed in a certain family who lived on Bette Street down in Merced. Years later Murph remarked about this and said that Parnell had known exactly which homeward-bound schoolboy he wanted to kidnap for his "son."

That first evening Parnell asked Steven what he liked to eat and Steven replied, "I eat anything," and so Parnell sent Murph down to the general store for ground beef, canned green beans, and light bread . . . their first meal together. Steven was quite surprised when the meal was set out. "I *detest* green beans," he exclaimed years later, "but I didn't dare say anything. At first I just avoided them, but then he threatened to spank me if I didn't eat them."

With typically minimal observation Murph said, "Steven gobbled up his food like he was real hungry."

After supper Parnell had Steven take a shower, and when the boy came out wrapped in just a towel, Parnell had him remove it and crawl naked under the covers with him in the cabin's solitary bed, leaving the complacent Murph to sleep on a folding aluminum chaise lounge. It was very cold that night, the cabin's only heat coming from the tiny gas cookstove, which Murph complained he was obliged to get up and turn off and on several times during the night "so we wouldn't all be dead in the morning."

Also, Murph said that only once during the night did he hear any sound from Parnell or "the kid." This, he recalled, was in the early morning hours when he heard Steven say, "You're wrong." Apparently, Steven vaguely recalled many years later, this was when Parnell orally copulated with him for the first of many, many times.

In Merced the police department's evening shift had canvassed the south side of town, searching well past their 11 P.M. shift change, but they had not found any clues to Steven's disappearance. A little before midnight, Police Captain Dave Knutsen telephoned Del and asked him to come down to the station. Although it was a typical question, Del was not prepared for what Knutsen asked him. "Did you kill Steven?"

Del answered with a forceful, irritated, "No!"

The captain then asked Del if he would submit to a polygraph examination, and Del responded with equal conviction, "I sure will!" Knutsen explained to Del that Merced Police didn't have a polygraph examiner or the equipment, but that a state examiner would travel from Sacramento and examine him in a few days.

About 1 A.M., still not comprehending the magnitude of what had happened, Del went home to Kay and the two of them sat up all night talking and drinking coffee with friends who had gathered, and, Del said, sadly shaking his head as he recalled it, "Trying to figure out where Stevie had gone to."

The next morning, December 5, veteran Merced Police Chief Harold Kulbeth called on Kay and Del. It was the first of many meetings the tall, balding, sincere chief had with the quiet, unassuming couple, and he was immediately struck with compassion, not only because of the bewildering circumstances of Steven's disappearance, but also because his parents were so candid and straightforward in answering his questions.

A warm yet thoroughly professional man, Kulbeth advised them not to handle or open any unusual mail they received, but to be careful to pick it up only by the corners of the envelope and to call him immediately. He had an additional telephone extension installed in their home to record any possible ransom calls, and at his request Kay and Del provided him with a copy of Steven's recent school photograph to reproduce on some Missing Juvenile flyers he was having printed.

Later that day Tom Walsh, the F.B.I. agent in charge of the Merced field office, dropped by the Stayner home with Chief Kulbeth. Walsh told them that under the circumstances it couldn't be shown that Steven had been taken across a state line, and therefore the F.B.I. could not become actively involved in the case. However, he assured them, his office would cooperate fully with the local police, and, if needed, provide assistance from the F.B.I. laboratory in Washington, D.C. In short, Walsh recalled, "There was complete rapport between our office and the Merced Police, and we made ourselves readily available. The chief and I were in daily contact on the case."

That afternoon the local daily newspaper, the *Merced Sun-Star*, carried Steven's photograph with the headline "Local Youngster Missing: Search Planned Today." The article detailed the previous day's search and quoted Captain Knutsen as saying that if Steven had not been found by late afternoon that day, the police would conduct "an extraordinary on-foot canvass of the city with as many patrolmen as possible."

At home Del reviewed the previous 24 hours over and over in his mind, especially upset that the day before, he had slept in and missed seeing Stevie. "It really hurt me that I didn't get to see him before he left for school that morning," Del recalled sadly. "He was really the little guy . . . I think he was so cute. He would go in the bathroom and comb his hair in the mornings before he went to school. He would pat his hair into place . . . he was so sharp. Then Kay and me'd stand in the house and watch him leave for school. . . ." Del's voice trailed off emotionally.

Chief Kulbeth first learned of Steven's disappearance from Knutsen. "My captain came into my office and informed me that we had a missing child, which is not unusual. The thing is, most police officers fear having a missing child more than anything else. Fortunately, most of them turn up down the block, over at a friend's house, or playing in somebody's backyard. But nevertheless, it's something that I had strict orders to my department all of the years I was there, that when we had a missing child I wanted to know about it immediately.

"But in Steve's case, as time progressed, we became more and more concerned. As with most missing child cases, we did the routine things first. We put out the broadcast, had the juvenile officers check the neighborhood, the school, and with friends . . . that sort of thing. Of course, on into the first evening we suspected that we had something more than just the ordinary missing child, so we started throwing everything we had into the investigation. I told my juvenile sergeant, Jim Moore, to do everything he could to try and find the boy."

"The Stayners were pretty upset," Sergeant Jim Moore recalls. "I dealt mainly with Kay. Kay was kind of the spokesperson for the family . . . she kind of ran it. And she was very concerned about it, because she said that this hadn't really been a serious problem with Steven before. And we talked to the people along the route he took home from school over and over, and we determined that, well, the last time he was seen by anybody was at the Red Ball Service Station on Yosemite Parkway, and nobody saw anything at all after that."

The next day Moore assembled virtually all off-duty law enforcement personnel in Merced County for as complete a county-wide search as possible. Additionally, Moore and his officers interviewed virtually everybody within a ten-block radius of Steven's school and the Stayners' home, put out an all-points bulletin on Steven over California's statewide law enforcement teletype, and requested that news bulletins on Steven's disappearance be broadcast on all area radio and television stations and printed in all area newspapers.

Lieutenant Bill Bailey, the evening shift's watch commander on the night Steven disappeared, said, "Nothing like that had ever happened to a citizen of this community before, and we on the police department were so frustrated about his disappearance that we became very involved in looking for him. You know, I was thinking that the little guy can't just disappear from Yosemite Parkway while he's on his way home from school."

That afternoon Cary and his sisters were collected at school and brought home briefly, very confused by the frantic activity: people coming and going, police officers talking with their parents, friends and strangers alike bringing in covered dishes. Said Cindy, "The first thing I asked was, 'Is Steve back?' And he wasn't. And after a little while we had to go back over to the Scoggins', where we stayed for about a week. And it was real quiet and strange when we did finally come back home."

That night Mac Scoggins drove Del to see Kay's father, Bob Augustine, at his trailer in Cathy's Valley so that Del could tell him in person about his grandson's disappearance. Unknown to Steven, Bob had moved his trailer to Judy's Trailer Park in Cathy's Valley just two weeks earlier and was then living just 200 feet from and in sight of the little red cabins. Del said he loaded his shotgun and took it along. "Just in case."

At about the same time that night, Parnell and Murph, with Steven sitting up between them in the front seat, pulled away from the cabin and drove back to Yosemite in Parnell's white Buick, joining the highway and heading east at exactly the same point where Del and Mac left it. Parnell and Murph had to return to work that night and Parnell had elected to take his new "son" to his third-floor private room in employee dorm F in Yosemite Valley and secrete him there.

After dropping Murph off at his cabin, what Steven later said he had considered "an adventure" came to a frighteningly brutal, abrupt end. Parnell drove to a remote, deserted parking lot on the valley floor and forced the seven-year-old boy to fellate him. Whereas Steven may not have understood what Parnell had done in bed the night before, the lad was now scared to death. He tried to pull away from his captor's grip. Brusquely, though, the kidnapper shoved the little boy's head down over his exposed, erect penis, Steven's copious tears and entreaties to Parnell to take him home not deterring the aroused pedophile as he repeatedly ejaculated inside the trembling child's mouth.

Years later Steven bitterly recalled, "I told him I didn't like it when he ejaculated in my mouth, but Parnell didn't really care. The fellatio was uncomfortable but not painful . . . but it never, *ever* was pleasurable.

"And the next time he told me, 'This is what I want you to do from now on,' and he pulled me over and held me down and put me through the motions. I'm with him, and at that age I didn't think I should be fighting him every night or have to be forced every night, so I just did what he wanted me to do."

After that first traumatizing sexual assault, Parnell drove back to employee dorm F, parked, and in the late-night stillness spirited Steven up the stairs and into his private third-floor room. Once there he gently undressed the boy, tucked him in bed, and, telling Steven that he was going to work and would see him in the morning, gave the boy a couple of Nytol sleeping pills before leaving. As soon as his new son was asleep, Parnell slipped out the door, locked it, and strode the quarter mile through the snow to his accounting job at Yosemite Lodge.

Before dawn the next morning Murph had routinely finished cleaning the lodge kitchen's ovens. A little past 5 A.M. he showed up at the front desk, where a solitary Ken was still busy figuring the guests' bills. Parnell gave Murph his room key and told him to check on Steven. Dutifully, Murph went to Parnell's room and, finding the little boy still asleep, sat and waited for him to wake up. When Steven did wake a couple of hours later he was hungry, and Murph left him and went to the snack bar and got both of them a breakfast of junk food which, as with all of his meals in Yosemite, Steven ate in Parnell's room.

Shortly after 8 A.M. Parnell arrived and Murph left for his cabin. With Murph gone Parnell again performed fellatio on Steven. Stated Steven matter-of-factly, "Parnell wouldn't do anything to me while Murphy was around. Murphy was a sort of friendless person, and Parnell had drawn him into the whole thing because of the friendship. Murphy wasn't a kidnapper or pedophile. He didn't have any sexual interest in me. Murphy was just basically there to help Parnell with the kidnapping and that was it. He was a strange little man, but I grew to like him. I called Murphy 'Uncle Murphy' . . . and I still do." Steven smiled. Murph concurred with Steven's story, claiming that he never knew anything about Parnell sexually assaulting or molesting Steven until many years later.

About his relationship with Murphy, Steven fondly recalled, "He was always real nice to me. He got a bunch of comic books for me from a friend of his and brought them to Parnell's room. He came in with this big bundle in his arms, and when he took off the wrapping paper there were two stacks of comic books about six inches high. So we sat there together and started reading them, and I think he enjoyed them as much or more than I did."

Since the room didn't have a private bathroom, Parnell required Steven to relieve himself in a bucket in his closet, but Murph never took such precautions, and when he watched Steven he would just send the boy by himself to use the communal toilet down the hall.

Early the next Sunday, December 10, just as soon as

he got off work, Parnell hustled Murph and Steven into his car and drove to the cabin at Cathy's Valley. Parnell had seen and heard a few newspaper and broadcast reports of Steven's disappearance, yet he was smugly satisfied that his villainy was going unnoticed in Yosemite National Park and Cathy's Valley. So confident was Parnell that he felt he could casually plan his future with his new young son.

During the first week after Steven disappeared, volunteers and peace officers searched Merced County north to south and east to west but turned up no leads. Some minimal searching was done in neighboring Mariposa County, including a search of the home of a known homosexual pedophile and child pornographer just outside the county seat, but the man's treasure trove of nude photographs of young boys held no clues to Steven's disappearance.

Much of the search of Merced County was conducted by the male members of the local Mormon Stake, who carefully covered specific areas on detailed county maps in four-wheel-drive vehicles and on horseback while their wives brought a steady supply of fried chicken, macaroni and cheese, jello and fruit salads, and pies to the unofficial search headquarters at the Stayners' house. Years later Cary tearfully recounted this episode: "I don't like to be around a lot of people, so I stayed outside as much as I could. And I remember going out one night after Steve disappeared and wishing on a star that my brother would come back home. And I did that almost every clear night from then until Steve finally came back home.

I never did tell anybody about it, but I remember wishing on a star that my little brother would come back home." He finished his tale with tears in his eyes.

Sharon Carr, whose birthday party Steven had attended the day before he disappeared, was very much affected. Steven had given her a stuffed koala bear, and after his disappearance she became very protective of it. Referring to Sharon, Kay said, "If you even mentioned Steve five or six years after he had disappeared, this little gal would break into tears. We had to do a lot of whispering when she was around. I could talk about Steve when he was gone without really being upset, but Sharon just came unglued if you even mentioned Steve."

Del was by far the most upset by Stevie's disappearance. The morning after Stevie vanished, Del asked his Mormon bishop, Ben Walton, to call Stevie's name in to the prayer roll in Salt Lake City so that "if Stevie was still alive by the time his name got on the prayer roll, nothing bad would happen to him. It bothered me that Stevie had disappeared and he hadn't been baptized. He would have been baptized when he was eight years old, but he disappeared before that. And that always bothered me." Then, in awe, Del added, "And every person in this valley prayed for my Stevie . . . I just couldn't believe that."

Chief Kulbeth recalled that by the third day psychics were volunteering information. "We never did go to them. It's something that I certainly did not have any confidence in, yet at the same time, when you have a serious case like this, you're not going to ignore anything."

One of the psychics whose information Kulbeth

checked asked to be driven east on Highway 140, and as Merced Police drove her past a trio of little red cabins at Judy's Trailer Park in Cathy's Valley, she "lost the trail." The police retraced the route with her several times, but each time the trail ended for her just past the cabins, Kulbeth said. Almost unbelievably, during the seven years that Steven was missing, the cabins were never checked out.

By the end of that first week, Sergeant Moore had requested and received from Sacramento a list of all known sex offenders in Merced and the surrounding counties; however, since Parnell had never been registered as a convicted child molester as required by California law, his name was not on the list. Next, Moore asked F.B.I. Agent Walsh to contact Lee Shackleton, Chief Park Ranger in charge of law enforcement in Yosemite National Park, to obtain a list of all Curry Company employees, but this was not done until the following March, and when received, the list contained the names of only half of the employees, that half paid the week of December 4, 1972; the Curry Company then paying half of its employees on alternating weeks with Parnell's pay period ending on the alternating week. Therefore Parnell's name was not available for checking against the F.B.I.'s list of convicted sex offenders and child molesters, where his name did appear. Also, copies of the Missing Juvenile flyers were given to Shackleton, but for whatever reason, neither he nor his men developed any leads, and no one then in Yosemite National Park recalls ever having seen one of the flyers.

Outspoken F.B.I. Agent Walsh has his own feelings about these failures. "The boy was in the park for quite awhile, living with a park employee. Shackleton and his men couldn't find him . . . a seven-year-old boy. That boy should have been found by them.

"The problem was we were dealing with the rangers. *They* were supposed to get that list for us, and they didn't get us a good list. At that time we were virtually persona non grata [with the park rangers]. Shackleton was uncooperative with the Merced office of the F.B.I. At the time the Yosemite Park Company [then known as the Curry Company] had more than forty percent of their employees that had a record of felony arrests and/or convictions.*

"We and the United States Attorney were sure grim to see the number of people with sex violations working in the park. I do know that they [the Curry Company] have a propensity for hiring perverts. But the best opportunity to solve the case was in Yosemite National Park. Didn't somebody see a little seven-year-old boy nude around a dormitory?"

Chief Kulbeth agreed, though his reply was muted in comparison with his friend Walsh's. "One of the first theories concerning Steven's disappearance centered around the park. We knew from past experience that there were a lot of criminals and sex offenders up there working not for the Park Service, but in other jobs up there . . . [but] due to the mere fact that

---

*Using the payroll list provided by Shackleton, John M. Reed, Special Agent in charge of the F.B.I's Sacramento office, wrote to Shackleton on March 22, 1973, stating that fifty-six of the employees on that list had records of felony arrests and/or convictions, 14 of those for sex offenses.

Steven was last seen on the road leading up to Yosemite National Park, we asked [for] assistance from the Park Service in getting some of the flyers with his photograph on them distributed up there. We weren't up there. The F.B.I. didn't have an office up there either. Lee Shackleton was the one in charge, but somehow Parnell just slipped through their fingers."

After Steven's disappearance Kay reinstructed her four remaining children not to accept candy or rides from strangers and always to come straight home from school. But she kept a stiff upper lip as she continued to cook, clean, and care for her family. She was truly a rock for the family during this time, when Del was so deeply affected by the loss of his beloved Stevie. Said he, "I had a lot to do with my kids before Stevie's disappearance. But afterward, I was a hard guy to get along with. I just couldn't stand to see my family broken up with Stevie's bein' missing."

Chapter Three
Parnell and Murphy

"My track record is that I don't tell the truth."

Kenneth Eugene Parnell was born the son of Mary O. and Cecil Frederick Parnell in Amarillo, Texas, September 26, 1931, just at the beginning of the Texas panhandle's infamous dust-bowl days. It was his mother's second marriage, and one that proved unhappy. Kenneth was the only child of this union, but Mary had custody of her children from her first marriage to "a Mr. Costner," as she referred to him when the author interviewed her—one boy and two girls.

Ken's father became increasingly unhappy with his wife's overbearing, dictatorial, pious control of other people's lives, including his own. Among other maxims Mary Parnell insisted that everyone in her family fall toe-and-heel with her rigid fundamentalist Christian beliefs, and woe unto the child or husband who did not. Cecil Parnell did not, and in 1937 he was history.

Shortly thereafter Mary took her brood west on the Santa Fe Railroad and settled in Bakersfield, in California, the state at that time revered as the land of milk and honey by hundreds of thousands of escapees from the dust and unemployment of Texas and the Midwest. Once there she struggled mightily to start a new life.

But shortly before the family had departed for California the absence of his father so upset five-year-old Kenneth that he spent several hours pulling out four of his teeth with a pair of pliers. "My recollection of the day of separation—just as any kid would obviously be, I was upset. I wanted to go with my dad, and of course I didn't. I just simply did not want to leave where I was at. I didn't want to come to California. Children tend not to want to have their world upset," he convincingly concluded.

Once in Bakersfield, Mary began working as a nurse's aide and joined and quickly became one of the staunchest members of the Assembly of God Church. She required her children to accompany her to services every Sunday morning, Sunday night, and Wednesday evening, rain or shine. This was in addition to the compulsory weekday ritual of making her children get down on their knees with her and pray just before they left for school. Said she, "My children never did go to school without prayers. They wouldn't go to school without having their prayers any more than they would go without their books or clothes. They all expected that." And daily she taught the Bible to Kenneth and his half-brother and half-sisters.

After a few years in Bakersfield, Mary felt she could better provide for her family back in Texas and so packed her brood up and returned, this time to Waxahatchie, just south of Fort Worth. For three years she worked hard and saved her money, but in early 1944 she returned with her children to Bakersfield, this time for good. She immediately invested her savings in a boardinghouse—housing and feeding the oil field roughnecks—so as to take advantage of the war-related oil boom then in progress in Bakersfield and nearby Oildale. This was not, however, a happy time for Kenneth.

In the spring of 1945 one of his mother's boarders befriended the slender, troubled thirteen-year-old and, after establishing a degree of trust in the fatherless boy, coerced the lad to engage in fellatio. This—young Kenneth's first-known homosexual encounter—was the apparent catalyst for his setting fire to a pasture very soon thereafter. He was found out, taken into custody, and locked up in Bakersfield Juvenile Hall. A psychiatrist who examined him at the time, Dr. Richard D. Lowenberg, recommended temporary placement for Parnell in the Juvenile Hall "in the hope that his marked emotional immaturity mixed with his sophisticated disposition toward perversion might be overcome."

After several months in Juvenile Hall, Kenneth was released in the early summer of 1945. But that fall, shortly after his fourteenth birthday—and still chafing under his mother's strict rules—Kenneth stole an automobile, was arrested, and, after a court hearing, was sent to the California Youth Authority's Fred Nelles School in Whittier, a residential facility for juvenile male offenders. Parnell remained there from October 1945 to February 1947, during which time, he later reported, he engaged in homosexual behavior both passively and actively.*

Upon his release from Whittier in 1947 Kenneth returned to live with his mother in Bakersfield. He entered the ninth grade but was already so far behind in his studies that his promotion to the tenth grade the following September was really a disservice to him. In December 1947, sixteen-year-old Kenneth was "arrested as a homosexual"—as the legal record of the time so quaintly put it—for public sex acts. Released to his mother's custody, just two months later Parnell stole another car and landed in the California Youth Authority's Lancaster facility.

Parnell, virtually out of control by this time, escaped from Lancaster within weeks and returned to Bakersfield, where he became sexually attracted to a young boy, his freely stated reason for returning. Parnell was at liberty only a few days before he was again arrested and placed in the Kern County Jail in Bakersfield, where he attempted suicide by drinking disinfectant. After emergency treatment at Kern General Hospital, Parnell was sent to the state mental hospital at Napa, northeast of San Francisco, for ninety days. But before the ninety days were up Parnell escaped again, went to San Francisco, where he stole another car, returned

*Psychiatrist Joseph E. Brackley's 1951 report stated, "After [Parnell's] admission to Whittier School and his later admission to Lancaster"—another C.Y.A. facility—"he started to have irregular homosexual experiences. He speaks rather lightly of these procedures such as placing his penis in some other boy's rectum or taking some boy's penis into his own mouth or having some other boy take his (the patient's) penis into the mouth—as being practically normal procedures in these schools."

to Bakersfield to see the young boy with whom he was so infatuated, and was re-arrested and returned to the Lancaster facility, where he remained until his release as a seventeen-year-old in May 1949.

Ken returned to Bakersfield and moved back in with his mother, and a few months later he began a series of short-term jobs, first as a kitchen worker at Kern General Hospital, then as a stock boy for Smith's Market, and later as a stock boy for the local Sears, Roebuck store. During this time he married Patsy Jo Dorton and she, too, moved in with Ken's mother.

But Parnell's sexual attraction to young boys caught up with him on March 20, 1951. Driving Mary's pre-war black Chevrolet coupe, Parnell approached three young grade-school boys playing near Kern General Hospital. Flashing a fake deputy sheriff's badge he had bought at a Bakersfield Army-Navy surplus store that morning, he talked one of the trio—nine-year-old Bobby Green—into accompanying him.

He drove the frightened youngster east out of Bakersfield and into a remote area in the Kern River Canyon where he sexually assaulted him. For an instant he thought about killing the child to prevent him from telling what had happened, but nineteen-year-old Parnell decided against it and instead casually drove the terrified lad back to the hospital and let him out. Immediately young Bobby ran home and tearfully told his parents what had happened.

On the morning of March 26, 1951, Bobby Green's father signed a complaint against Kenneth Eugene Parnell before Justice of the Peace Stewart Magee alleging that Parnell had committed three felonies on his son: "First count, child stealing; second count, the infamous crime against nature;"—Parnell had anally sodomized the boy—"third count, the act of copulating the sexual organ, to wit: the penis of him, the said Kenneth Eugene Parnell, with the mouth of Bobby Green." The Kern County sheriff's office wasted no time in arresting Parnell at the Sears, Roebuck store late that morning, and neither did Justice Magee: he held Parnell's preliminary hearing at two o'clock the same afternoon.

Justice of the Peace Magee offered Parnell the opportunity to retain an attorney, but Parnell declined the offer. Magee then began the preliminary hearing questioning him. For what was quite possibly the first and last time in his life Parnell answered each question honestly and straightforwardly.

Magee: Now, it is alleged here in this
           complaint, the first count in this
           complaint, that on or about the
           twentieth day of March, this year, in
           Kern County, you did take and entice
           one Bobby Green from his natural
           parent. Is that true?

Parnell: Yes, sir.

Magee: In the second count in this complaint
           it alleges that you did commit the
           infamous crime against nature. Is that
           right?

Parnell: Yes, sir.

Magee: In the third count in this complaint
           there is a violation of Section 288a,
           which you heard me read to you in

specific language. And did that occur
too, here in Kern County?

Parnell: Yes, sir.

Deputy D.A. Clayton Cochran began his cross-examination of Parnell by establishing that Parnell
drove to an area near Kern General Hospital, flashed
the fake badge at the three young boys, and coerced
one of them to get into the car with him. Next he led
Parnell through the drive out of Bakersfield into the
rugged Kern River Canyon, up a remote road, and to
the point where he had stopped the car. Then Parnell
matter-of-factly told about his sexual assault on scared
nine-year-old Bobby Green.

Cochran: What did you do then?
Parnell: Well, I told the boy to get out,
            that I wanted to stretch my legs. And
            so then we walked up on one of the
            hills there and set down and talked
            awhile. And that is when I told him
            what I was going to do, and committed
            the act.
Cochran: What did you say to the boy at that
            time?
Parnell: Well, at first I asked him what he had
            in his pockets, and he showed me.
Cochran: In his pockets?
Parnell: Yes. And then I asked him if he had
            any scars on him, and he said no at
            first. Then he showed me two or three.
            Where they were at the time I don't
            remember. And then I asked him if he

had done anything similar to the counts that are held against me. And he said no. And so then I told him that I was going to do those things. And so then is when I done those things.

Cochran: Did you ask him to take his clothes off?

Parnell: Yes.

Cochran: Did you have him take all of his clothes off?

Parnell: Yes.

Cochran: And did you take any part of your clothing off?

Parnell: No.

Cochran: The little boy resisted, did he not?

Parnell: Yes.

Cochran: He did not want to do that, did he?

Parnell: No.

Cochran: Did he cry at any time?

Parnell: Yes.

Cochran: Did you have to use force with him?

Parnell: No.

Cochran: Did you not, at some time, hold his hands?

Parnell: No.

Cochran: Then after his clothes were removed what was the first thing you did? Did you open your trousers and take from your trousers your sexual organ?

Parnell: Yes.

Cochran: And what was the first thing you did to the little boy?

Parnell: Well, I put my penis in his rectum.

Cochran: You got the penis between his buttocks, the little cheeks of his buttocks, I presume, did you not?

Parnell: Yes.

Cochran: How long were you in attempting this act by the rectum?

Parnell: As to the exact time, I don't know. Maybe two or three minutes.

Cochran: Then what did you do after that?

Parnell: Well, I placed the penis in his mouth.

Cochran: You placed your penis in his mouth?

Parnell: Yes.

Cochran: And then you forced him to suck on the penis. Is that right?

Parnell: That is correct.

Cochran: How long did that act continue?

Parnell: Oh, a minute, maybe; maybe not that long.

Cochran: Did you reach a climax so there was any . . .

Parnell: Yes, I did.

Cochran: An emission?

Parnell: Yes.

Cochran: Then after this, what did you do then? Did you tell him to put his clothes on again, or what?

Parnell: Yes, I did.

Cochran: And you got back in the automobile, did you?

Parnell: Yes.

Cochran: Did you attempt to harm him in any way?

Parnell: No.

Cochran: Did you have in mind at one stage harming him?

Parnell: A flash like . . .

Cochran: You did? But you controlled yourself and you did not?

Parnell: Yes. As soon as it come to me, well, I dropped it just as quick.

Cochran: What was it that you thought of doing to him in that momentary thought there?

Parnell: Well, I was going to strangle him.

Cochran: You were thinking that you should strangle him so that you might conceal from anybody that this took place. Is that correct?

Parnell: That is correct.

Cochran: It was your thought to strangle him and then some way to dispose of the body when he was dead?

Parnell: I didn't think that far.

Cochran: But you thought of strangling him in order to kill him, did you not?

Parnell: Yes.

Next, Parnell told how he walked Bobby back to Mary's black Chevrolet, got in, and drove the trembling boy back to Bakersfield in a manner so casual that he stopped along the way for a drink of water before dropping off the terrified boy at the hospital.

Then Mr. Cochran asked a few final questions.

Cochran: When you picked up the little boy in the first place, you had in mind doing

	exactly what you did. Is that correct?
Parnell:	Yes, sir.
Cochran:	Did the arresting officers at all times treat you with consideration, or did they at any time make any threats towards you?
Parnell:	No. They treated me very nice.
Cochran:	They never used any force or made any threats?
Parnell:	No force and no threats.
Cochran:	Let you freely and voluntarily say whatever you cared to relating to the matter?
Parnell:	Yes.

Through his questioning of Parnell, Justice Magee then confirmed that Parnell did indeed know that Bobby Green was only nine years old and thus under the legal age for consensual sex in California. Bobby's mother then took the stand and confirmed that Bobby was her son and only nine years old. Parnell was then given a chance to question her, but he declined. Justice Magee then closed with his announcement that probable cause had been shown that Parnell was guilty of all three counts, and that he therefore ordered Parnell delivered to the Kern County Jail and held in lieu of $5,000 bail.

Mary Parnell had hired private attorney Wiley C. Dorris to represent her son. Mr. Dorris felt that since Parnell had already testified extensively as to his guilt, the only course was for his client to agree to be bound over to Kern County Superior Court and once there plead guilty. Parnell was bound over, but nine days later Mary bonded her son out of jail by paying $50 to the National Automobile and Casualty Insurance Company to write his $5,000 bond.

On April 20, 1951, Parnell appeared before Kern County Superior Court Judge William L. Bradshaw and formally pled guilty to a lesser charge, "the crime of felony, to wit: lewd and lascivious conduct on and with the body, members and private parts of a male child under the age of fourteen years." Judge Bradshaw then canceled Parnell's bond and ordered him held in the Kern County Jail for examination by three psychiatrists: Dr. Louis R. Nash of Camarillo State Hospital, Dr. Richard D. Lowenberg of Bakersfield, and Dr. Joseph E. Brackley, also of Bakersfield. (Dr. Lowenberg had examined Parnell on six previous occasions, beginning with Parnell's stay in the Bakersfield Juvenile Hall as a thirteen-year-old in 1945.)

Dr. Nash drove the six-hour round trip from Camarillo on May 1, spending almost two hours interviewing Parnell. On May 4, Dr. Brackley devoted a similar amount of time to evaluating the slightly built teenager. On May 5, Dr. Lowenberg devoted the better part of his afternoon to talking with his long-time patient, drawing extensively on his files for his probing questions.

The three physicians wasted no time in completing and filing their reports with the Court, and on May 11 Judge Bradshaw held a hearing on their findings.

According to Dr. Brackley, Kenneth Parnell "apparently had very little parental control or disciplinary supervision from the family unit." Parnell also told the doctor that he ejaculated into the nine-year-old boy's mouth, but said that he got no sexual satisfaction from the act. However, the doctor observed that Parnell appeared "somewhat nervous" during the examination and that he was not "over-willing in communication of his troubles [but] rather matter-of-factly volunteers the details of his erotic acts."

In his summation Dr. Brackley wrote, ". . . this patient is a sexual psychopath and it is our [sic] opinion that he should be committed to an institution for such unfortunate patients."

Camarillo State Hospital psychiatrist Dr. Nash dryly reported: "Prisoner states that on March 20 of this year, while driving around the vicinity of the county hospital in Bakersfield, he enticed an 8-year-old [sic] boy into his car and took the youngster out of the city toward Kern Canyon, where he committed sodomy upon the boy and then had the youngster accomplish the act of fellatio on him." The doctor went on to report that Ken had told him about his marriage and "normal heterosexual relations with his wife."

His conclusion: "It is the examiner's opinion that this prisoner is a definite psychopathic personality with well-defined homosexual drives, and as such has a tendency and predisposition to commit sexual offenses to a degree constituting him a menace to the health and safety of others, and it is recommended that he be committed to a suitable institution for the care and treatment of this disorder, namely psychopathic personality and sex psychopath."

The most detailed and informative report, however, was Dr. Lowenberg's. He drew on his considerable earlier records on Parnell and detailed the story of five-year-old Kenneth pulling out his teeth, eight-year-old Kenneth shining a bright light into his eyes in an effort to blind himself, and a slightly older Kenneth jumping off a shed into a pile of old lumber with protruding nails to try and injure himself—" 'One step off; it's all over: one step off; it's all over,' " Dr. Lowenberg quoted a thirteen-year-old Ken as having said about the incident.

More recently, Lowenberg's report continued, "While driving a stolen car one night he was conscious of a desire to drive it directly into oncoming lights of other cars. . . . He has repeatedly thought of suicide ('oftener than once a year, not so often as once a month') and usually thought of plans involving gunshot or knife wounds in the abdomen, rather than less unpleasant ways of committing suicide." Then the doctor recounted an incident which had occurred in Mary Parnell's presence: Kenneth had taken the safety catch off a loaded .22 pistol and held it against his abdomen and threatened suicide.

During this jail examination Parnell also told Lowenberg that he was sick after having committed the acts on nine-year-old Bobby Green: " 'I confessed to my wife and I wanted to see you. I did not get any thrill out of it. . . .' "

Dr. Lowenberg continued, "The defendant is cooperative and sincere in his statements. His sex activities may be described as polymorphous perverse; they are not fixed in any one undesirable pattern. . . . His intellectual capacities, his memory, his knowledge, and general grasp are probably slightly above the average. It is necessary to review this defendant's peculiar life history and emotional development, at least in its highlights, to understand and evaluate his present condition."

Dr. Lowenberg's professional, detailed summary conclusion said in part, "Upon reviewing the lengthy history and my various observations and examinations over the last six years, it cannot be overlooked that we are dealing with an extremely unstable emotional personality whose instinctual anxieties and insecurities work themselves out periodically in both car thefts and sex offenses. Gifted with good intelligence, his deeply rooted disturbances are grounded in an impulsive character. . . . They seem to imply a search for trouble and punishment. His present predicament is especially tragic because of his young, apparently congenial marriage, which resulted in the birth of a daughter a few days ago. When the undersigned brought him a letter from his wife, who had just delivered their first baby, he showed genuine excitement and asked most anxiously about ambulatory treatment possibilities after his release.

"As used in Chapter IV of the Welfare and Institutions Code, paragraph 5500, he must be considered a sexual psychopath who is affected in a form predisposing him to the commission of sexual offenses and in a degree constituting him a menace to the health or safety of others, due to a character neurosis legally called a psychopathic personality, with marked departures of his sexual activities. In view of his youth, it is hoped that he might benefit from a systematic treatment and rehabilitation program in a state hospital."

Parnell and his recently hired attorney, Mr. Dorris, were in Kern County Superior Court for the brief hearing on May 11, 1951. Judge Bradshaw agreed with the doctors' evaluations and found "the said Kenneth Eugene Parnell to be a sexual psychopath" and ordered him sent to Norwalk State Hospital in Los Angeles "for observation and diagnosis for a period not to exceed ninety days."

In a 1984 prison interview, Parnell said, "[My] attorney says, 'Well, you will go into prison, okay, but what we can do is that if you will plead guilty and be good through this, we can get you to the hospital.' Which was worse than the prison. But he kept telling me, 'It doesn't matter what you do. You are going to prison.' Now at my age [then nineteen] the fear of prison was greater than confessing to anything, and I could have confessed to murder. I just should have done more in the legal process."

The staff at Norwalk State Hospital did not need the full ninety days Judge Bradshaw had allowed for them to evaluate Parnell. On June 14, 1951, Acting Superintendent and Medical Director Dr. Hyman Tucker wrote to Judge Bradshaw, "His case was reviewed by the medical staff on May 29, 1951, and he was diagnosed as a sexual psychopath without psychosis. He is considered legally sane. The staff has recommended that he be returned to the court and committed as a sexual psychopath for an indeterminate period."

The authorities returned Parnell to Bakersfield for another hearing on June 22, at which Judge Bradshaw committed Parnell to "Norwalk State Hospital for an indeterminate period."

Back at the hospital, Parnell wrote an intelligent, literate letter to Judge Bradshaw on July 15, complaining about what he felt to be a lack of treatment opportunities there and asking the judge to consider returning him to Bakersfield for outpatient therapy and supervision. It was the first of hundreds of similar letters, briefs, and the like that Parnell would compose and send to judges, penal authorities, attorneys, and public officials during his adult life.

Parnell did not receive a reply from Judge Bradshaw and on September 11, 1951, he took matters into his own hands, and sawed a lock from a clothes room window at Norwalk State Hospital and escaped. On September 24 authorities arrested him and returned him to the hospital, where he was placed in a maximum security ward. But three weeks later, on October 14, Parnell went AWOL again and this time made his escape good for three months, hitchhiking to Albuquerque, New Mexico, taking a job as a short-order cook in a downtown cafe where he was happily at work on February 22, 1952, when Albuquerque police walked in and arrested him. Kern County deputy sheriffs "called for him" at the Bernalillo County Jail on February 25, and he was driven to Bakersfield and again lodged in the Kern County Jail. Then, while Parnell was in custody, Judge Bradshaw made efforts to have him readmitted to Norwalk State Hospital; however, the judge was rebuffed in a March 17 letter from Hospital Superintendent and Medical Director Dr. Robert E. Wyers, and this in turn was underscored by an April 16 letter from State Director of the Department of Mental Hygiene Dr. Richard Tallman.

On April 22 Parnell, accompanied by a new attorney, John M. Narin, was present in Judge Bradshaw's courtroom. Even though the Assistant District Attorney, Robert A. Farrell, joined Mr. Narin in arguing quite strongly for a court order to place Parnell in another state mental hospital, Judge Bradshaw resisted and in the end stated:

"It is the order of this Court that the defendant, Kenneth Eugene Parnell, be committed to the California Institution for Men at Chino for the period prescribed by law [five years-to-life]. There is no alternative in a case like this. I don't think it was the intent of the Legislature that our hands be tied, and we just couldn't do nothing because some recalcitrant defendant didn't want to behave himself, so that is the order.

"This defendant has been a consistent violator ever since he was very young. He is obviously a homosexual of the more or less dangerous type, and it is the recommendation of this Court that his sentence be for a long period of time."

Assistant District Attorney Farrell was so upset by Judge Bradshaw's seemingly callous handling of young Parnell that he refused to sign the sentencing document as required, leaving it for Deputy District Attorney J. F. Meeks to sign several weeks later.

Three days later, on April 25, Kern County sheriff's deputies transported Parnell to the California Institution for Men at Chino, a minimum-security prison thirty miles east of downtown Los Angeles. Since Parnell was a convicted child molester, prison officials felt he would be in danger if placed in the general prison population, and so on May 1, the Department of Corrections exercised its authority and transferred Parnell to the medium-security Soledad Correctional Training Facility near Salinas, the only prison in the system with a protective-housing unit. However, after prison officials received and reviewed Parnell's files from the state mental hospitals and duly noted his record for escapes, they transferred him to California's maximum security prison at San Quentin on August 30, 1952.

Parnell remained behind bars at San Quentin for three and one-half years while the parole board denied his requests for release at hearings in April 1953 and April 1954. Finally, April 1955, the board paroled Parnell on the condition that he "receive psychiatric treatment while on parole" (a condition which Parnell adamantly refused to meet); inexplicably, Parnell's official release on parole was not recorded until late October that year.

Parnell requested parole to San Francisco, bitterly recalling, "You know, in San Francisco, it was not like I was raised there or some shit. It was pretty difficult and, of course, that was a large city, and for a person who has to tell his employer he is on parole and everything, that narrows the employment situation quite a bit. After a couple of months of unemployment, I wanted to go down to Bakersfield."

But the Department of Corrections refused his request to move to Bakersfield, so Parnell pressed and received permission from his parole officer to visit his mother there. Once there he got a job and applied for transfer of his parole, but as this was a violation of his parole conditions, authorities arrested and locked him up yet again in the Kern County Jail. At his parole violation hearing in September 1956 Parnell was sent to Folsom State Prison, where he spent the next three months before the board again paroled him—on December 17—this time officially to Bakersfield.

In early 1957 Ken's first wife, Patsy Jo, divorced him.

He had not lived with her since March 1951, and he had never even seen his daughter, the divorce effectively having closed this chapter of his life. On August 8, 1957, Ken married Emma Naoma Schafter, ten years his senior. During this marriage she gave birth to Ken's second daughter.

Little is known about Parnell's personal life, especially the periods from August 1957 to September 1960 and from September 1967 to March 1972. He has said repeatedly that there were people he wished to protect.

Even the California Department of Corrections records contain nothing more than the notation that Parnell successfully completed his parole in December 1957 . . . and that on May 23, 1959, the Department formally noted his discharge. However, one can assume that Parnell went back to drifting from job to job, taking positions as a short-order cook, a bookkeeper, and a door-to-door salesman of shoes, brushes, and other consumer goods.

In the summer of 1960 Ken moved to Ogden, Utah, where he continued his unsuccessful job search at the time. Desperate for money, he armed himself with a snub-nosed revolver and went to Salt Lake City, where he randomly held up service station owner Scott Neilson as the man was closing for the night, a crime that netted the ex-convict just $150. At first Salt Lake City police showed Nielson several hundred mugshots, but none were of Parnell. However, the break in the case came when the police brought in Ken's roommate for questioning about another crime and on a hunch brought Ken in, too, and took a mug shot of him. When the police showed both men's pictures to Nielson he immediately identified Kenneth Parnell as the holdup man.

Salt Lake City police charged Parnell with armed robbery and grand larceny and jailed him. Unable to post the $2,500 bail, he remained in the Salt Lake County Jail until his jury trial in February 1961. He was convicted on March 6. District Judge Stewart M. Hanson sentenced Parnell to five years-to-life for robbery and one-to-ten years for grand larceny, and the next day Kenneth Eugene Parnell was taken to the Utah State Prison at Draper, south of Salt Lake City.

While he was serving this sentence, Ken's second wife, Emma Naoma, divorced him. He represented himself in the divorce proceedings and tried to argue for his legal right to be present in court in Salt Lake City. Short of his desire to irritate prison officials and to get a trip into Salt Lake City, his actions gained him nothing. The divorce was summarily granted and authorities returned him to prison. But Ken did improve himself educationally while in prison by earning his G.E.D.—equivalent to a high school diploma— and by taking some college-level accounting courses.

In September 1967 Utah released Parnell from prison with the proviso that he never again enter the state of Utah. At that time this was a common practice which states used to reduce their prison populations; however, when neighboring states began reciprocating, the Utah State Legislature had the wisdom to repeal its law.

According to an employment application Ken completed in 1972, he then headed to Phoenix, Arizona, where he worked as a short-order cook at the greyhound racetrack. During an interview Ken stated that following this two-month position he worked as a cook for the ABC Vending Company in the Adams Hotel in Phoenix before becoming the acting chef at the Phoenix Playboy Club. However, Ken gave the lie to that on the aforementioned employment application wherein he wrote that he was only a "broiler cook" at the "bunny club." Then, for a short time, Ken claims, he owned and operated the Haynes Café on West Van Buren Avenue in Phoenix. This venture lasted six months and, Ken admitted, ended in financial failure.

In 1968 Ken married for the third time. He would not say to whom but admitted only that the marriage lasted less than a year. However, no records could be found to substantiate this third marriage or the subsequent divorce.

At this point Ken left Arizona and went to several states before returning to his mother's home in Bakersfield in early 1972.

On March 7, 1972, Ken drove from Bakersfield to Yosemite National Park and applied for a job with the Curry Company, the park concessionaire. On the application he fudged a good deal about his past educational and employment history and mentioned absolutely nothing about his felony convictions and his years spent in mental hospitals and prisons. For a time the application languished in the personnel office, but in April the Curry Company notified him that they wished to hire him, and on May 1, 1972, ex-felon Kenneth Eugene Parnell began working as a night auditor for the Yosemite Lodge.

Born in Alcester, South Dakota, on July 11, 1941,

Ervin Edward Murphy remembers his mother as having been abusive to her ten children. "She would always fly off the handle too quick," he recalled. "I remember one time the kids were playing noisy outside, and she came out and stood there and started screaming and yelling at us to go in. And we said, 'Oh. Do we have to go in now?' And she went back in and got the strap—and she could really hit with a strap—and she came back out and started beating the hell out of me, and then she found out that I wasn't even the one who did it!"

The incident Murph recounted occurred when he was about three, and shortly thereafter his mother deserted the family and Murph's father had to assume the task of raising his ten children single-handedly. In order to support them, Mr. Murphy moved his brood to Sioux City, Iowa, thirty miles south of Alcester, where he went to work at Chilly's Ice Cream Factory. Murph went to public school there until the age of sixteen, when he dropped out and struck out for California on his own.

Shortly before his departure from Iowa, Murph's older brother, Arnold, was convicted of an attempted sexual assault on an eight-year-old girl in the Sioux City Public Library. Observed Murph, "He was way past the adult age, but they put him in the Glenwood State School for Boys."

In 1957 Murph arrived in the San Joaquin Valley, having hitchhiked and ridden freight trains from Sioux City to Fresno. From there, he said, "I walked all the way to Tulare, where I got a job in those fields chopping cotton." There followed half-a-dozen years of drifting from job to job, some as a field hand, some washing dishes, and doing other menial work. At one point Murph lived with his sister and her husband, who themselves had moved to California, but for reasons which Murph still puzzles over, his brother-in-law threw Murph out and his life of wandering resumed.

In the mid sixties Murph joined the Job Corps and started learning "kitchen work," but one day he got into an argument with a black trainee and a shouting match ensued, complete with racial slurs from Murph. The Job Corps terminated the slow-witted South Dakotan. Murph headed back to Sioux City and tried to find "my poor parents," as he calls them, "but they were gone and I didn't know where they were." He hung around Sioux City for a week and then hitchhiked back west, settling in California.

Once back in Fresno, Murph took a position performing odd jobs at the Salvation Army, where he stayed for nine months. Next he pitched in with a group of farm laborers—most of them winos—headed by a crew boss whose wife treated Murph like her son. Then, in the summer of 1969, Murph heard that good jobs were to be had with the Curry Company in Yosemite National Park. "I went up to see about it," Murph said. He was hired on the spot and went to work immediately at the venerable Ahwahnee Hotel, transferring to the modern Yosemite Lodge in 1972.

It wasn't long after Ken and Murph met in the summer of 1972 that Parnell started telling the gullible Midwesterner about his desire to have a son. But instead of adopting one, Parnell told Murph, he wanted Murph to help him pick one up off the street. *"Kidnap one!"* Murph shockingly ruminated. Later that summer, when Parnell drove himself and Murph to Sacramento to visit a fellow employee's mother, Murph recalled that Parnell tried to talk him into helping "find some young kid for him." But Murph declined to help, and when they got to the woman's house, Murph stayed there while Parnell went off on his own for twenty-four hours.

During the drive back to Yosemite, Murph recalled, Parnell kept talking about being lonesome and "telling me that he would like to have a boy to be able to raise him up in a religious-type deal." Murph said he then steered the conversation to the subject of getting married to have kids, but Parnell ignored him and kept talking about kids and how he wanted a "son" to raise by himself. Murph also remembers a lot of other times that Parnell wanted his help in picking up a boy to be his son, but Murph said that he made up excuses not to help him. "I thought maybe he'd just get off the subject," recalls Murph.

Murph said that his and Ken's relationship "was a friendly type, 'cause he never did anything to me in the way that I could look at him twice. It was just a casual friendship. But I was warned about him, and this was way before the kidnapping. Buzz Colisimo, a friend of mine [in Yosemite] who shared my cabin with me, said, 'Murph, I don't trust that guy.' He was thinking maybe I would get the message, but I didn't."

Perhaps Murph's personality can be best understood through the impressions and remarks of his friends and fellow Yosemite Lodge employees which were gleaned by a private investigator, retired F.B.I. Agent Mel Shannon, in March 1980.

During the 1970s Charles Hudspeth was a second cook at Yosemite Lodge. He described Murph as a person who liked people and wanted other people to like him in return. He said Murph was a lonesome type who was easily influenced by others and that there was practically nothing that Murph wouldn't do for his friends.

An employee of the Yosemite Lodge Bar and Restaurant, Ralph Lerkin, described Murph "as the kind of person that if you needed twenty-five dollars, and he only had twenty, he would give you the twenty that he had and then go out and borrow another five dollars to give to you."

Station cook Peter Gillespie noted that Murph was a good, willing worker who did much more than was required or expected of him, and that Murph was generous, always buying small gifts for his friends.

A very interesting story about Murph was told by Ahwahnee Hotel storeroom clerk Russell White. He related that several years earlier a fellow employee had stolen a brand new pair of shoes from Murph. When Murph found out that the man who had stolen the shoes was badly in need of a pair, Murph let the thief keep the shoes. White added that Murph had originally planned to stay in Yosemite only a short time, but he had stayed as long as he had because it was one of the few times in his life that he'd had any real friends.

Finally, Murph's roommate of many years, Myron "Buzz" Colisimo, described Murph as "a fantastic person who cannot do enough for other people." He also stated that a person with a strong personality could convince Murph to do something just on the basis of friendship, that he was easily misled, and that he had a tendency to believe everything he was told.

On several occasions Buzz had encouraged Murph to visit his mother in Arizona when he was on vacation, and, he said, Murph was a perfect gentleman . . . "I wouldn't send a nut to visit Mother!"

In Murph the image of a lonely, pathetic, naive man emerges. He believed his friend Kenneth Parnell—whom he did not know was an ex-con—when he told him that he was a minister and that he wanted to take in some poor, abused boy to help by raising as his son "in a religious-type deal."

Though Murph thought it odd, he did not question his friend when on December 4, 1972, Parnell asked him to pass out gospel tracts to the young boys walking home from Charles Wright Elementary School in Merced, and then to help him get Steven into his car, or even when Parnell then drove off with the little boy in the car. Murph believed in and trusted his good, loyal, generous, kind friend Kenneth Parnell. And he felt that Ken would never do anything to hurt him . . . and certainly nothing to hurt an abused little boy.

Chapter Four
Dennis Gregory Parnell

"Parnell just ignored me and kept on doing it."

At daybreak on Monday, December 11, 1972, Kenneth Parnell, his balding head bowed and lost in concentration, figured the Yosemite Lodge's guests' bills. A little before 8 A.M. Murph quietly shuffled into the lodge's lobby and peering over his thick horn-rimmed glasses, silently fixed a gaze on his friend. Moments later, Ken realized with a sudden start that he was being watched and sharply yet softly rebuked Murph before turning back to his work. A few minutes later Parnell finished his shift and the pair made their usual after-work trek to check on the little boy living in Parnell's third-floor room in dorm F . . . usual since Steven's kidnapping the previous week. As the twosome trudged under snow-laden redwoods, Parnell unctuously approached Murph to babysit Steven at his little red rented cabin in Cathy's Valley while he made a day trip out of town and Murph agreed, as always, happy to be needed.

When the pair reached his room, Parnell gently

shook Steven awake and then turned and quickly packed his and Steven's clothes and meager possessions, almost forgetting the comic books Murph had given the boy until he was reminded. While Murph stood watch in the hall, Parnell hustled Steven down the stairs, outside, and into his old white Buick, Murph quickly following. With their captive sitting between them in the front seat the kidnappers drove off and after a quick stop at Murph's cabin for him to dash inside to get some clothes, they headed out of the park to Cathy's Valley.

Remarked Steven's father, Del: "We could have met Parnell and them on the highway. We had so many people going up and down that road looking for Stevie . . . so *many* people looking. And that character just driving up and down the highway with Stevie sitting up front next to him . . . Stevie said they never made him get down . . . had him sit right up there between them!"

The trio arrived at the cabin in Judy's Trailer Park at 9:15. It was bewildering to Steven to be left in the charge of "Uncle" Murphy as Parnell hurriedly drove off for Bakersfield to pay a rare visit to his mother, Mary; but Steven and Murph got up on the cabin's sole bed and together read their beloved comic books. As Parnell smugly drove southwest, through Planada and straight into Merced, the little boy in Cathy's Valley occasionally played with his collection of worn flea market toys on the lonely cabin's bare floor.

In Merced the search for Steven continued as Parnell boldly stopped at a self-service gas station on Yosemite Parkway, barely a quarter mile from the Stayner home. After tanking up, Parnell self-assuredly strolled inside and just happened to spot one of Steven's "Missing Juvenile" flyers. While another customer paid the clerk, Parnell astutely made a quick mental note of Steven's middle name, date of birth, and physical description, all the better to make plans for his captive's new identity. Later Parnell particularly recalled that Steven *Gregory* Stayner had been born on April 18, 1965, and was described as having "light brown, shaggy collar-length hair." Smiling conceitedly at his craftiness, Parnell got back into his car and drove off at a respectable speed, passing the Red Ball Service Station before entering the freeway, California 99, where he settled back for the 160-mile-drive to Bakersfield.

Mary Parnell was retired, in her seventies, and had silvery-gray hair. Even though she no longer worked, she still greeted each day well-groomed and wearing a fashionable though modest dress. Late that morning her son paid her a surprise visit. She welcomed her son Ken's visit, although as usual he needed money . . . but as usual she readily gave it to him. Ken visited her more often than her other children, sporadic though his visits were. Their conversation revolved around family news and Ken's work in Yosemite, but her son said nothing about the recent disappearance of a little boy from the streets of Merced.

As their visit drew to a close Mary surprised her son by presenting him with a gift to remember her by: a six-week-old female puppy from her Manchester Terrier bitch's litter. Ken mumbled his gratitude for his mother's generosity, gently wrapped the trembling black and tan puppy in his doubleknit plaid sport coat, and tenderly cradled the tiny form in his arms as he carried her out to his car for his return trip to Cathy's Valley.

Ken completed the 370 mile round trip early that evening and proudly entered the cramped little red cabin with the tiny puppy hidden inside his gaudy coat. Murph was sleeping on the lawn couch, and Steven sat forlornly in a corner playing with his toy canoe and plastic Indians. Parnell's entrance startled the boy, but Murph continued to doze when Ken called Steven to him and grandly presented the puppy to the boy as his own. Overjoyed, Steven immediately named his new pet "Queenie" and profusely thanked his captor. Ken smiled cheekily to himself, for this was *exactly* what he had expected and it set the stage for the plan he had cannily concocted during his return drive from Bakersfield.

Parnell sat down in the cabin's single, ratty, overstuffed chair and gently lifted the seven-year-old onto his lap. Tenderly he stroked the boy's hair as he began a skillful lie about having gone to court that morning where a judge had given him custody of Steven. Parnell also lied to Steven saying that his parents didn't want him anymore because they couldn't afford to take care of him. The kidnapper then completed his story by telling the numbed Steven that he was now his son, his name was now Dennis Gregory Parnell, and from now he was to call Parnell "Dad."

Tears of protest welled up in the thoroughly confused little boy's eyes as he indignantly contradicted

Parnell's story and demurred about staying with his captor because, he insisted, his mom and dad needed him at home. What was more, the hurt, shocked little boy blurted that he had three sisters and a brother and his mom and dad wanted him to help with them. Coldly Parnell corrected, "Well, I don't think that they really need you right now."

By then he was bereft of his own family, and years later Steven recalled with visible emotion how he at that point began the slow, painful resignation to his new life as Dennis Gregory Parnell . . . but, he made it infinitely clear, he never, ever forgot his family back in Merced.

The next afternoon long shadows stretched across the brown, grass-covered hills at Cathy's Valley as Parnell, Dennis, and Murph piled into the Buick to return to Yosemite. Murph had to clean the Lodge ovens that night; however, Parnell had decided to fold his tent, as it were, quit his job, and depart for points as yet unknown, even to himself. When they arrived at Yosemite Lodge, Parnell asked Murph to wait in the car with Dennis while he went inside and told his boss that his mother had suffered a heart attack—an out-and-out lie—and therefore, he continued his fabrication, he was quitting his job and returning to Bakersfield. When he returned to the car Parnell told Murph what he had done and that he was going to move but that he would spend the rest of the week at the cabin with Dennis. Then he dropped Murph off at his employees' cabin before driving himself and Steven back to Cathy's Valley.

Night fell during the pair's return trip, and with it the darker side of Parnell's twisted relationship with the boy he now called his son resumed, for as soon as they had entered the musty tourist cabin Parnell made Dennis remove all of his clothes. With the child naked, the now-aroused Parnell experienced a frisson as he feverishly began fondling the shivering second-grader's genitals as a prelude to yet another session of forced fellatio with Dennis. With Murph at work, Parnell again felt free to molest his frightened young captive.

The next morning after breakfast Parnell called Dennis to him and, without explanation, sat the frightened boy on a camp stool, wrapped him from neck to toe in an old bed sheet, and trimmed his new son's hair with a pair of sheers until it had lost its shaggy look. That finished, Parnell walked Dennis to the chipped old sink and dyed his son's hair a dark brown. After rinsing and drying the boy's hair Dennis's new dad perfected the charade by restyling his son's hair into a parted fashion quite unlike the soup bowl look evident on the "Missing Juvenile" flyers. Years later Dennis visibly tensed as he recalled his having been too terrified to ask his captor a single question. Parnell then walked Dennis and Queenie outside to play in front of the cabin, less than three hundred feet from the highway to Merced and within sight of Dennis's maternal grandfather's trailer. With Dennis dressed in flea market clothes and the tonsorial transformation complete, Parnell cockily went back inside and took a nap.

Parnell spent the balance of the week reading his get-rich-quick books and figuring ways—some illegal but appealing greatly to his cupidity—to make money, plotting his next tactical move with Dennis, and having oral sex repeatedly with his resident child-sex partner-cum-son. But even for Parnell this routine quickly became tedious.

The wickedest side of Parnell's perversion with his young son surfaced the night of December 17, 1972, Dennis bitterly recalled. Parnell again made his son remove all his clothes and, Dennis recalled, "explained what he was going to do to me and that there was going to be some pain involved." Immediately Parnell made the naked, scared, sixty-pound second-grader lie face down on the bed while he himself undressed, then mounted and spread the boy's small buttocks apart and roughly smeared Vaseline deep inside the immature anus and onto his own by-now-erect penis. Without pause Parnell roughly thrust his engorged member deep inside and painfully sodomized his crying, confused young sex partner. After his organ had completed its orgasm inside the seven-year-old, Parnell withdrew, wiped himself off, and gave his sobbing young son a couple of Nytol sleeping pills. Then the pederast turned out the light and pulled the sheet and blanket up over his own naked body and that of his young son. Throughout the night Parnell snuggled his own naked body against that of his son as he excitedly fondled the boy's small buttocks and genitals and masturbated himself again and again.

Of that first time Parnell raped him, Dennis acerbically recalls: "There was a lot of fear and confusion. I was *very* confused. I didn't know what was happening. I'd never seen anything like that before. I mean, that's the age when you still think that Mr. Stork brings the little babies. It was *real* confusing. *Real* scary!

"I knew it wasn't right mainly because it was never done to me [before]. My father didn't do it! I just basically thought that it was something sorta' normal that I never had known about before. And it *hurt*. It hurt a lot, and I kept crying . . . but Parnell just ignored me and kept on doing it."

The next morning Parnell awoke early and left his son to finish his drug-induced sleep. When he returned a few hours later he found Dennis engrossed in play with Queenie. While gone, Parnell had traded in his old possibly recognizable white Buick and, using some money given him by his mother, bought an equally old but unknown and better-running white Rambler American.

Parnell told his son that they were going on a trip. Unknown to Dennis, while exchanging automobiles the previously complacent Parnell was startled to learn of Bob Augustine's—Dennis's maternal grandfather's—recent relocation: he had moved his house trailer to Judy's Trailer Park, just a few hundred feet from the little red cabin. Said Murph succinctly, "Parnell decided to split." Although Bob's grandson had never visited him there, and neither one knew of the other's proximity, Parnell was taking no chances. He was anxious to leave the San Joaquin Valley where Dennis had been born and had spent all of his young life with his own family and head for northern California.

In response to a phone call from Parnell, Murph hitchhiked to Cathy's Valley that afternoon and brought with him—as the ex-con had instructed—

Parnell's last paycheck and some blank signature cards to open a new savings account at the Wells Fargo Branch Bank in the Yosemite Valley. Parnell had hatched a scheme to blackmail the simple-minded kitchen cleaner by threatening to identify him as *the* kidnapper unless Murph agreed to deposit a portion of each of his own paychecks into this new account; and since he no longer had a job, Parnell could certainly use the money, for he further dictated to Murph that only he would make withdrawals.

Then, shortly before dusk on Monday, December 18, 1972, Dennis Gregory Parnell climbed into the Rambler's front seat with his puppy, Queenie; his new dad and rapist, Kenneth Parnell, climbed into the driver's seat; and they both waved good-bye to Murph and drove off.

From Soledad Penitentiary in 1984 Parnell boasted that he drove Dennis "right through Merced" that night. However, Dennis is certain that they traveled north through Mariposa and then northwest toward Mt. Bullion. But then the seven-year-old fell asleep for the balance of the trip, apparently through Oakland, across the Richmond-San Rafael Bridge, past San Quentin Penitentiary, and another fifty-five miles on north to Santa Rosa.

It was long after ten P.M. when "Kenneth E. Parnell and son" registered at the Tropics Motel on Santa Rosa's south side and were assigned to room 18. Parnell parked at the door and tenderly carried his sleeping son inside. Gently, he laid Dennis on the bed, undressed the boy down to his briefs, and covered him up. Santa Rosa was the Sonoma County seat, the heart of the fabled California wine country, a small yet bustling city of 50,000 . . . and an innocuous middle-class "hometown" that Parnell had carefully and shrewdly chosen.

When they awoke the next morning, Parnell took Dennis to a nearby café for breakfast. As they walked back from breakfast Dennis saw the cracking stucco walls and weathered, tilted signs that typified the Tropics and its equally dilapidated neighbors along Santa Rosa Avenue, former tourist courts that dotted this backwater that had once been U.S. 101. Now bypassed by the freeway from San Francisco, they languished as low-income transient accommodations by the week or by the month, cramped accommodations which would serve as Dennis's home for most of the next eighteen months.

Four days later, fearing that someone might discover them, Ken moved himself and Dennis to another aging motel, the Pelissier, across town on quiet Mendocino Avenue. It was a family-type place, clean and run by an accommodating yet reserved Pakistani family . . . just right for the anonymity Parnell sought. It was amid the sparse furnishings of room 16 at the Pelissier that Dennis spent his first of eight Christmases away from his own family, quietly opening the three presents from his new dad, a toy rifle, a toy bow and arrow, and a Hot Wheels Race Track set, playing idly with them as Ken smugly sat back, lit a cigarette, and watched the holiday fare on TV.

Christmas was bleak at the Stayner home in Merced. Everyone in the family bought and wrapped a special present for Steven, partly because they still considered him a very real part of their family, partly because they felt that doing so would somehow help to bring him home. But it didn't, and Christmas was very sad.

Del couldn't bear to see his other children opening their presents without his Stevie there and so he slipped quietly into his room and cried as he talked to Stevie's picture, asking his son where he was and when he would be coming home.

Being a single parent was difficult for Ken. When he wasn't in prison, he lived a bachelor's life, going and coming as he pleased. But in Santa Rosa he always hired someone to stay with Dennis while he went job-hunting and, later, when he worked. Usually he got sitters through a local babysitting service, but before the first one arrived, Ken indoctrinated Dennis with some Parnell family background, though not the complete truth, and Parnell cautioned Dennis to *never, ever* say anything to anyone about his being taken from Merced or the by-then almost daily sexual abuse, threatening Dennis with a severe spanking and being locked up in a children's home should he ever say anything about their secrets.

After Christmas, Ken began work as a day front desk clerk at the Santa Rosa Holiday Inn. On January 2, 1973, he registered his son in the second grade at Steele Lane Elementary School in the Bellevue Union School District, stating on the enrollment form: Name, "Dennis G. Parnell"; Date of Birth, "April 18, 1965"; Place of Birth, "Merced, California"; Former School, "Yosemite Elementary,

Yosemite National Park" . . . a real school, but one
never attended by Dennis Parnell or Steven Stayner.
That same month the Bellevue Union School District Office in Santa Rosa received the following letter:

Mr. and Mrs. Delbert Stayner
1655 Bette Street
Merced, California 95340

County Superintendent of Schools:

Would you please distribute the enclosed bulletins to all primary schools in your district? Hopefully we are sending enough; if not, please let
us know.

George Hogan, Special Consultant, Office of the
Chief Deputy, in Sacramento, suggested this as
a means of getting the bulletins to all schools.

Steven may not be in school, but a child may
have seen or heard of Steven in his or her neighborhood. We must cover any and all possibilities.

We appreciate your cooperation and thank you
for any help.

Sincerely,
[signed] Delbert & Kay Stayner

A copy of this letter and bulletin (i.e., the "Missing
Juvenile" flyer) never reached Steele Lane, and it was

years later that Del and Kay learned that the letters
and bulletins they had so hopefully sent were thrown
in the trash at the Bellevue Union School District Office, as well as at many other California school district
offices. But an anonymous Steele Lane Elementary
School office employee wrote on the back of a form
forwarded to Dennis's next school: "Steele Lane did
not receive any records from former school." However, like Steele Lane, the next school also failed to
insist on receiving his records, and this brief note was
the extent of concern for Dennis G. Parnell's lack of
records and a birth certificate shown by any of the
half-dozen public schools he attended as Kenneth
Eugene Parnell's son.

From prison in 1984 Parnell smugly said of his use
of Dennis's real middle name, date, and place of birth,
and the name of a real elementary school: "You have
a lot of qualms about a lot of things in that situation.
And I had various reasons for listing Yosemite Elementary. First of all, I had come out of the Park. And I had
worked down there." He paused and then ventured,
"It just followed the pattern." Still failing to discern
acceptance in the author's expression, Parnell lamely
added, "It fell right in."

So, on the day that school Christmas holiday
ended, Dennis was back in school, albeit with a different name and a new dad, and 170 miles from
home . . . and, too, with a new family history to remember, one taught rather than remembered. But
although he was not happy at this new school—once
again he was a new kid without friends—Dennis was
beginning to settle into his forced identity as Kenneth Parnell's son. After all, he was just seven years

old, and he had to look to Parnell as his primary
caretaker—as social workers like to phrase it—and
he wasn't even sure where he was. Dennis had always
been extraordinarily close to his real father, continu-
ally following him around. Thus acclimated to having a strong father figure to whom he could relate,
what with the nurturing, affectionate, dependent
closeness Ken showed his youngest son the vast majority of the time, Dennis quickly adapted to being
Kenneth Parnell's son. Therefore the two readily
gave the appearance of "father and son" oft recalled
by their acquaintances years later when the truth
finally became known.

In late January, even though he was employed full-
time, Ken went to the local office of the California
Department of Human Resources, claimed that he was
underemployed, and filed for financial aid. The request was denied.*

On February 24, 1973, Ken and Dennis moved from
the Pelissier Motel into an old, forty-foot long, dilapidated rental house trailer with peeling grayish-pink
paint at the scruffy Mt. Taylor Trailer Park out on
Santa Rosa Avenue. But Dennis relished their new

---

*Curiously, Ken was—for him—quite honest about his back-
ground with Human Resources caseworker V. Holmes . . .
even to the point of stating that he had a son, Dennis G.
Parnell, living with him, and that he and his son had previously lived in Yosemite National Park, where he had worked
for the Curry Company. Holmes wrote to Curry, and their
employment manager, Derrick Vocelka, wrote back confirming
Parnell's employment and stating that he had quit the job
"because of illness in his family."

home, for there were trees for him to climb and for Queenie to sniff, and other children to play with, and, as Dennis later recalled, Ken liked to do whatever made him happy . . . except, that is, for ending his repetitive sexual assaults on his young son. However, on the whole, Dennis saw his lot as improving. He was quickly becoming assimilated into his second-grade class at his new school, Kawana Elementary. He really liked his teacher, Ms. Englehart, and she him, for on April 6—just five weeks after Dennis had entered her class—she wrote in a report, "Dennis has adjusted quite well to the work and routine of our classroom. He is well liked by the other children, and I am glad to have him."

But Eleanor Lindvall, the school secretary, thought Mr. Parnell's behavior strange, for almost every day Ken would call her to give specific, ever-changing instructions about whether he would pick up Dennis after school, or whether Dennis should go to a babysitter's, or whether Dennis should ride the school bus home. She thought this odd, for he was the only parent who did this on a daily basis, but she never did or said anything to question Parnell's behavior.

Early 1973 was a very difficult, emotional time for Del and Kay. During that first winter a little boy's cowboy boot, somewhat like those Steve had been wearing when he disappeared, was found washed up on the bank of Bear Creek in north Merced. Steve's sister Cindy said, "They started dragging the creek, looking for his remains. Dad got real upset, but then he and my mom looked at it and realized that it wasn't Steve's boot after all."

Steven's parents next wrote to Walter Cronkite at CBS-TV and Frank McGee at NBC-TV, asking that they help try to locate their son through their news programs, but both wrote back saying that Steven's disappearance was old news and that therefore they couldn't help. Next Del and Kay sent copies of the "Missing Juvenile" flyer to TV stations all over the United States asking for the same kind of help, but the responses were nil there, too.

On into spring Del's friends and fellow employees searched until it seemed that they had covered every square foot of Merced County. Recounted Del, "About half of them were organized, but some, like friend Otto Doffee, searched on their own. And he was searching along this little irrigation ditch bank and he ran into a gunny sack. And he said his heart kind of jumped into his throat, because he knew there was something dead inside of it. So, he takes his pocket knife and goes to cutting it open. And when he got it partly cut open he could see hairs, but when he got it all the way cut open . . . well, it was a baby calf. Otto said he sat on that ditch bank after he got through doing that for about fifteen minutes, shaking like a leaf."

Also, Steven's disappearance was a factor in the messy business breakup of two Chinese brothers who had operated a supermarket on Yosemite Parkway and lived in the Stayners' neighborhood. When their business failed, they had a falling out which each blamed on the other, one starting a rumor which accused the other of killing Steven, cutting up his body, and dumping it into the sewer at the store. Del heard about this from co-workers at the CC&G Cannery and went to the police. They tried to get the accused brother to voluntarily take a polygraph examination, but he refused. Just to make sure, though, the police dug up the sewers up and down Yosemite Parkway, but no body or body parts were found.

Late that spring, when Cary helped Del repaint the garage, Del cautioned his oldest son not to paint over the pencil-scrawled signature, "Steven Stayner," one of the last reminders to his family of six that once they had been seven.

At the Mt. Taylor Trailer Park Dennis's new father continued his secretive sex assaults on his young son. One night after a particularly odious, painful session of anal intercourse, Parnell fell asleep; seeing this, Dennis got dressed and, making doubly sure that his dad was asleep, the eight-year-old stole out the trailer's front door, intent on running away and returning to his family in Merced. Hurriedly he walked south several blocks along busy Santa Rosa Avenue before he became lost, panicked, and gave up. Sobbing and shaking with fear, he finally found his way back to the trailer before his dad awoke. This was to be Dennis's last attempt to return to his own family for many, many years to come.

Finally summer arrived and with it the opportunity for Dennis to meet and play with more of the neighbor children, his popularity with the boys increasing considerably when he had finally saved enough of his allowance to buy a G.I. Joe set. Also during that summer Ken began letting Dennis drive the car when they went places around Santa Rosa. Remembered Dennis, "When he first let me drive we were on our way to a flea market in the park. I sat on his lap and he worked the pedals and I just worked the steering wheel. But I only got to drive for about five minutes because I spent most of the time off on the sides of the road."

Summer vacation didn't last long enough for Dennis, and on September 6 he entered the third grade at Kawana Elementary. He soon discovered a neighbor boy he hadn't known before in his class, but they had yet to become friends. According to Dennis, at first he and Kenny Matthias were enemies: "We rode the same bus, and when the bus stopped on the way home I would run through the bus door. Kenny would be right on my butt, but I was faster and so I'd get on down the road, and he'd give up chasing me. Then I'd turn around and yell, 'Fuck you, you stupid jerk,' and stuff like that. I used to get him pissed!"

In 1973 Kenny Matthias was a jug-eared kid with a pixyish smile. He looked much the same in 1984 as he recounted the initial animosity between him and Dennis: "He started saying smart things to me on the bus. I let it slide for a couple of days, and then finally it built up inside of me and I had to get him back. So I started chasing him down the road when he got off the bus, and one day I did catch him and we got in a fight. I beat him up, too! And that made his dad mad, so Ken came over to see my parents.

"I didn't get in trouble about it because my dad always told me to stick up for my rights and fight. I guess Ken didn't have that same philosophy, because he said he would rather see Dennis walk away from a fight. And it was then that we shook hands and we were friends ever since then. We got pretty close, too. In Santa Rosa we had an acre lot, and we would always go out in the back and play army on the mounds with his G.I. Joe sets."

Soon Dennis headed for the Matthias' home every day after school. Ken quickly realized that his son had stumbled onto the ideal babysitting arrangement, so he asked Barbara, Kenny's mother, if she would keep his son after school and feed him supper. Recalled Dennis, "She said, 'All right.' He paid her for it. And so I got *real* acquainted with the Matthias family."

In the late fall of 1973, third-graders Dennis and Kenny decided to experiment with an adult vice . . . smoking. Ken chain-smoked unfiltered Camels and Dennis stole and hid a pack from his father's carton. Then, when Kenny came over, Dennis pulled them out and they lit up. "We sat there and acted big and tough, and did little things like Parnell would do, like blowing smoke rings," Dennis recalled.

As Kenny tells it, "I came over and Ken was in the back bedroom sleeping. I had been trying to get Dennis to smoke, so naturally I smoked some cigarettes, too. But then Ken woke up and came in and caught us hiding behind the couch smoking. He started yelling and grabbed Dennis by the arm and slapped him open-handed and then he told me to go home."

That fall Dennis was ill a good deal of the time, first with the mumps and then with impetigo, ailments which caused him to miss twenty-seven out of thirty-nine school days and resulted in Ken's taking him to a doctor for the first time since the kidnapping. Ken stayed with Dennis during the entire appointment and made a point of answering all the doctor's probing background questions—even those directed to Dennis—himself.

With his relative job security (he'd worked at the Holiday Inn for ten months), in early November Ken felt flush enough to rent a large wood-frame house at 1107 Sonoma Avenue in central Santa Rosa. It was a wonderful place for Dennis and Queenie to romp and play together, what with a tall spruce tree for Dennis to climb in front and a fenced yard in back for Queenie, and seven rooms which afforded Dennis more space and privacy than he had ever before experienced.

In some ways, though, Dennis looked on the move as a setback, for he had to leave the comfortable environment of his third-grade class at Kawana Elementary to attend a new school, Doyle Park Elementary, and he felt that the move also meant leaving behind his new best friend, Kenny Matthias. But Dennis's father surprised him when, right after the move, he allowed Dennis to have his first-ever overnight guest, Kenny. At the time there was more to Ken's relationship with the Matthias family than his son's friendship with Kenny. Not only was there a not-so-platonic relationship developing between Barbara and the occasionally heterosexual Ken, but the crafty pedophile-kidnapper had also begun to eye young Kenny as yet another sexually attractive boy. But Parnell didn't move in on Kenny . . . yet.

By this time Parnell had happily realized that living in Santa Rosa fulfilled his expectations perfectly: he had neither seen nor heard any newspaper, radio, or TV accounts of the kidnapping since his arrival and therefore felt the danger of his son's identity being discovered was almost nonexistent; he had a good job, earning him good money; his life with Dennis had settled into what was for him a happy routine; and he had a live-in sex partner who compliantly satisfied his perverted sexual needs and provided him an entrée to other young boys. Indeed, so confident was Parnell about his life in Santa Rosa that he occasionally treated his son and himself to a meal at the Denny's Restaurant on the freeway from San Francisco . . . an odd choice in that it enjoyed a considerable traveling clientele from all over California.

While living on Sonoma Avenue, Ken sold his Rambler American and in its place purchased an even older beige station wagon of unknown make. Dennis remarked that the wagon was a klunker. In late fall 1973 Ken tricked some Mexicans into buying it at the K-Mart parking lot, the local informal Saturday morning car mart. Said Dennis, "Then the Mexicans decided that they didn't want it and they tried to get their money back, [but] they were stuck with it. Then he bought an old blue-and-white two-door Ford which he kept for about a year and a half. He changed cars pretty often."

As Christmas 1973 approached, reporter Janice Cruickshank of the *Mercury* in San Jose (California) traveled to Merced to interview Kay. Wrote Cruickshank: "The only unique thing about Steve, she [Kay] said, was that he got along well with everyone. 'His friends included older children as well as younger ones. He loved babies, and dogs, and kitty cats and anything that was alive,' she recalled." Cruickshank continued: "There are reminders of Steven everywhere in the Stayner home. He liked to write his name, his mother laughingly recalls. Then with a slight crack in her voice, she said, 'He had his name written on fences, outside walls, in his bedroom. So we don't scrub too many walls—we don't paint, either.' "

As to hope for Steven's return, Kay concluded: " 'Sure, I know that there is a fifty-fifty chance that Steven is dead and that at any time they could come and say, "Well, we found him—it's not good, but we found him—at least you know." I pray that if he is dead, please let us know, because this not knowing is enough to drive you insane.' "

Chapter Five

The Parnell Family

"You know your dad's a faggot?"

In 1973 Barbara Matthias's husband, Bob, was a blue-collar worker with the City of Santa Rosa Street Department, a man of average height with a muscular build . . . and a man who frequently drank to excess. An amateur watchmaker who haunted local flea markets, Bob invited Ken to join him that fall in what soon became a mutual interest, spending their weekends going from one peoples' market to another in Sonoma and Marin Counties while back at home Barbara took care of her four children still at home—Lloyd, 4; Kenny, 8; Vallerie, 11; Christy, 12—and Dennis. Two older boys whom Dennis never knew—Robert, Jr., and Gary—were in jail: one for dealing drugs, the other for manslaughter.

Rather quickly the two men became close friends, though Ken wasn't a heavy drinker like Bob. Dennis said that Ken was a light social drinker who never touched anything stronger than wine, and that rarely; when he did drink, a couple of beers in the literal sense were his preference and self-imposed limit. An entertaining, candid fellow with a folksy manner of speech, Bob was gaunt and balding when the author interviewed him in late 1984. He admitted that back in the 1970s he had been a heavy drinker, but was quick to add that those days were long gone. However, remembering those days, Bob particularly recalled Ken's omnipresent craving to get rich quick and the several soured business deals Ken convinced him to go halves on: "Ken had a saying, 'One of these days I'm gonna make it rich!' And I would kind of look at him and say, 'Well, Ken, more power to you. If I can make a damn good living, I'll be satisfied.' "

One of the various money-making schemes in which Ken involved Bob was a cattle feed lot on Bob's single acre in Santa Rosa. This happened the winter of '73-'74 when, against his better judgment, Bob went in with Ken and bought two calves to fatten for sale. It was very cold, and the would-be feed lot operators didn't provide any kind of shelter for the animals. But Ken wasn't concerned, said Bob. Then one morning Bob went out to check on their investment and both calves had died of exposure.

Like a raconteur on a roll, Bob chuckled with the author before launching into his tale about the feckless Ken buying scores of old, broken TV sets with plans to repair them and then sell them at a profit, pointedly remarking that it didn't concern Ken that neither of them knew a thing about electronics, let alone TV repair. They took the sets to a TV repair shop for an estimate and the owner told them the sets were all beyond repair. Bob said, "But then Ken wanted me to go in with him and buy the parts anyway, and I says, 'I don't want no part of that!' "

The next spring, undaunted but now a solo act, Ken decided to start a lawn-mowing service. He got started by purchasing an old rope-start mower of Bob's. "I sold it to him and showed him how to crank it," Bob recalled, ". . . told him to pull the rope away from him. But, no, Ken had to do it *his* way. He pulled the rope straight up and busted himself in the lip and split it from there to there wide open! I had to run around the side of the house 'cause I just couldn't help laughing. Then he comes around and says, 'Goddamn, Bob! How bad is it?' And I says, 'You better go see a doctor. You're gonna need some stitches.' Then I went in the house and thought, 'How stupid can a guy get?' "

But even that wasn't the end of it, for several days later, after having his lip sewn up, Ken went to Bob and told him that he had broken the mower's starter rope and needed his friend's help to install a new one. Said Bob, "I told him it is simple . . . just like that [he snapped his fingers]. But when he tried to do it himself, he got the rope all wound around it and we had to use a knife to cut it off and start all over again."

Dennis recounted that in 1974 Bob often came home drunk: "Bob liked to go out to the bars with his buddies and get toasted and come home and beat up on Barbara. But he was nice to his kids when he was drunk. Boy! He was the nicest guy in the world!

"One time he came home drunk while Barbara was babysitting me and he got to ranting and raving while he was taking off his boots. They [the boots] were just sitting there on the floor, and he went and kicked them like he was going to kick up a storm . . . like all the way across the room and through the wall! But the boots just went, 'bloop . . . bloop,' and fell over on their sides. They didn't go nowhere. Then he just fell down on the floor with them.

"His kids and me started busting up laughing, and he says, 'What are you laughing at?' And he called me over and says, 'Dennis, you know I love you like my own son. You know that radio and tape recorder I gave Kenny? Well, I'm gonna give you one, too.' And then he stumbled down the hall into the back room where he kept all his flea market stuff, and pretty soon he came out with the biggest reel-to-reel tape recorder and radio that I'd ever seen and gave it to me. And I thought that that was pretty neat!"

Ken's relationship with the Matthiases developed to where Ken occasionally acted as a surrogate parent and babysat and disciplined the children when Bob and Barbara went out. But Bob's drinking and his beatings of Barbara got so bad that one night Ken intervened. When he did, Bob responded, " 'Ken, you just stay out of this!' "—Dennis recalled—" 'This is a family matter. I know you like the family, but this is between me and my wife!' Then Bob turned back to Barbara and slapped her a couple of times and started yelling at her."

For a while Ken's frequent presence had a somewhat calming effect on Bob, but after yet another late-night beating, Barbara left. Ken learned of it by phone minutes later and got in his car and went looking for her, stopping her as she walked along Santa Rosa Avenue. He took her to El Tropicana Motel and rented a room for her, but a few days later Barbara went back to Bob. But the Matthiases' marital problems were rapidly coming to a head. Bob had entered into business deals with Ken and lately Bob had allowed Ken to park his rickety old cargo trailer in the Matthias' drive and work on it there. But there was a point at which Bob drew the line, recalling: "One day I came home and there he was, sitting down next to Barbara with his arm around her, and I got mad. I had tried to help him, let him use my tools and everything, but I wasn't gonna let him use my wife, too.

"So I put my hands on my hips and I says, 'Ken, get that trailer out of here. I don't want to see it in here anymore.' So he backed up his car and got it out. And as he was doing that, I says, 'I don't want my wife babysitting for you anymore, either.' " But Barbara did continue to keep Dennis.

In February 1974 Ken lost his job at the Holiday Inn because, a lifelong chain smoker, he refused to abide by the new no-smoking rule at the front desk. Pressed for money, he soon took an early morning motor delivery route for the Santa Rosa *Press-Democrat*. Dennis recalled that at first Ken made him get up well before dawn every morning and accompany him on his rounds, but the eight-year-old grew weary of this and asked his dad to let him sleep in. Reluctantly Ken agreed. "But," Dennis ruefully recalled, "I made the mistake of saying something about it one day when I was over at Kenny's and Parnell was picking me up. I just said, 'I get to stay at home by myself at night.' And with that, Parnell very politely rapped my head with his knuckle, and then later after we had left he explained why. He said that I shouldn't be telling them stuff like that because they might tell welfare or a social worker and they might come and take me away from him."

Earnings from the paper route weren't enough, and after barely four months in the spacious rental house, on the last day of February 1974, Ken, Dennis, and Queenie had to move out. As usual, Ken was behind in his rent, and all he could manage was yet another aging motel room with one double bed which, as before, father and son shared. This time they were at the Holiday Motel, again south of town on Santa Rosa Avenue, low-rent lodgings frequented by welfare families and poverty-level transients. But there was one positive thing about the move in that it put Dennis back in his favorite school, Kawana Elementary, and back in the classroom with his best friend, Kenny Matthias.

Finally finances got so bad that one night Ken walked Dennis to the pay phone in front of the motel and used some of his scarce cash to place a long distance call to Murph in Yosemite. By then Murph had quit depositing money into the blackmail account, but until he lost his Holiday Inn job this had not concerned Parnell. Now broke and unemployed, he decided to again try and extort money from Murph.

Remembered Murph: "Parnell called me up, and as we was talking he put Dennis on the line, and he said, 'Hi, Uncle Murphy!' And then Parnell got back on and asked me to start putting money in again. I told him, 'What are you trying to do? Do you want me to give you money the rest of my life?' Then I said to him, 'I ain't sending you nothing else, Parnell. I can't afford it!' And I hung up." It was their last contact for six years.

During Easter break in 1974, eight-year-old Dennis was visiting the Matthias home when a twelve-year-old friend of Christy Matthias's tried to get Dennis to have sex with her, the first time that he had been so propositioned. "She called me into the girl's bedroom," Dennis recalled, "and asked me if I had ever done *it* before, and I didn't answer her. Then she asked me if I would go out to the barn with her and 'get it on.' I gasped and said, 'No!' and that was it. And then Kenny started making fun of me about it when he found out."

Late that spring Ken landed a desk clerking job at El Tropicana Motel and soon thereafter moved him and his son back to the Pelissier Motel on Mendocino Avenue, a slight step up from the Holiday Motel. Then late one night Bob came home drunk and beat up Barbara again, and for a few days Ken again rented a room for her at El Tropicana. But Ken and Dennis had their lives reordered after Bob's next beating of Barbara. Once again Ken put her up at El Tropicana before asking her to move in with him and Dennis . . . into a room with one double bed at the Pelissier Motel. And she did.

Dennis said that at first the three of them just slept together, but then one night Ken and Barbara went out and left Dennis in the room by himself. Remembered Dennis: "They came back a little tipsy and they were obviously feeling horny. I was in the same room watching TV, but without paying any attention to me they got undressed and got into bed and started having sex with each other. Then Parnell told me to come over to the bed and he made me undress and get into bed with them. He rubbed my dick until it got stiff and then he rolled me over on top of her and she reached under me and put my dick in her. Then Parnell told me what to do—to go up and down—and I did. I stayed on top of her for a couple of minutes and then I said I was through and got off. Then I got dressed and just sat and watched TV while they went at it some more."

Years later Dennis told of his embarrassment about having had sex with Barbara: "I was their [Barbara's children's] best friend and we were like brothers and sisters, and she was their mother, and it wasn't right! I felt guilty when I was around them."

In late June the Holiday Inn rehired Ken as a day desk clerk with the strong stipulation that he not smoke while on duty. The position paid much better than did the El Tropicana, and with his increased wages Ken bought a sixteen-foot travel trailer for his little family's new home and moved it to the North Star Trailer Park, still another of the seemingly endless locations he chose on Santa Rosa Avenue. So, after just three weeks back at the Pelissier, Ken, Dennis, and now Barbara moved into their very own tiny new home, and from that point forward Ken and Barbara represented themselves and Dennis as a family . . . man and wife, and son. This arrangement could possibly have added some degree of normalcy to Dennis's life, especially had Barbara's children come with her, but they remained with Bob. This was just as well, though, for the small trailer had only one bed, a double in which the three of them slept together . . . and on eight additional occasions, Dennis said, these two amoral adults participated in a menage à trois with the nine-year-old boy they represented to others as their son . . . himself.

During the eighteen months the trio lived together, Dennis says that Barbara met almost all of Ken's sexual needs and that Ken never had sex with him while she was present: "That was the only reason I put up with her. I did not like her. She was the sort of person that was real stupid but thought she knew everything. But I thought that as long as she was around, Parnell wouldn't be fucking me. In fact, I thought that if she stayed around forever, he wouldn't have sex with me *ever again.*" Unfortunately, Dennis's assumption was only partially correct, for while Ken and Barbara lived together, Ken did engage in sex with his son four times when Barbara was gone or when he and Dennis went somewhere alone. Also, Parnell continued to egg on Barbara to have sex with Dennis while he played the voyeur.

Bob, however, did not consider his marriage with Barbara over. One hot July night a loud, truculent Bob unexpectedly showed up at Ken's trailer drunk as a skunk and looking for trouble. He tried to pull Barbara outside, but Ken got between them, swiftly pinned Bob to the ground, and hollered to Barbara to call the cops from a neighbor's home. The Santa Rosa Police responded and hauled Bob to the drunk tank.

It was also about this time that Ken took Dennis out of California for the first of three times, just the two of them driving to Reno, Nevada, where Ken tried his book-learned techniques at the blackjack and craps tables while Dennis stayed in their hotel room under the watchful eye of a sitter Parnell hired from a Reno service. A few days later Ken and his son returned to Santa Rosa flat broke.

That fall, as the three of them slept together in the tiny trailer's sole bed, Barbara grew weary of having to share it with Dennis—at least when asleep—and so she asked Ken to build a small single bed into the trailer wall for their son. He obliged and, crude though it was, the new bed relieved Dennis's anxiety somewhat, though it did not dramatically improve the family's cramped living conditions.

Dennis was always adequately clothed by Parnell, but he wasn't happy with Parnell's eclectic tastes. Most of Dennis's wardrobe consisted of worn boys' clothes from Ken's extensive collection of used apparel which he bought compulsively at flea markets: outerwear of doubleknits and imitation satins in bright colors, the racetrack tout's wardrobe which Ken himself preferred. Said Dennis in 1984, "Today, I wouldn't be caught dead in about ninety percent of what he got for me to wear!"

Finally Ken got so deep into the flea market scene that, when he lost his job at the Holiday Inn for a second time—he still refused to stop smoking at the front desk—he opened his own flea market. Called The Ad Market and located in downtown Santa Rosa, next door to the Greyhound Bus Station, Ken tried his damndest to make it provide a living for himself and his little family by wheeling and dealing in, as Dennis exasperatedly put it, "used junk." But it didn't work, and after two months Ken closed up and found a minimum-wage job as a greasy-spoon fry cook at a diner near the run-down Holiday Motel.

That fall Dennis entered the fourth grade at Kawana Elementary in the same room as his best friend, Kenny Matthias, now his stepbrother . . . sort of. But one day after school Parnell walked up behind Dennis as he sat in a field beside the trailer park, idly lighting one match after another. He marched his son inside to punish him, but when Ken went to get a belt Dennis quickly stuffed paper down his pants. He didn't do a good job of it, though, for Parnell saw the paper and made him remove it before he gave his son seven or eight licks across his bottom. This dampened Dennis's interest in playing with fire for a while, even though it fascinated him; however, it is quite likely that Dennis's fascination had a darker catalyst . . . Ken's frequent sex assaults on the by-then nine-year-old.

With his son back at Kawana Elementary, Ken resumed his daily telephone calls to the school secretary, Eleanor Lindvall, to advise her of that day's particular after-school arrangements for Dennis. "It was unusual for anyone to call daily to make such arrangements for their child," Ms. Lindvall remarked, "but I recall Mr. Parnell calling about these arrangements more in the fourth grade than when Dennis was a smaller child." As Parnell explained these calls to one Kawana teacher, "Dennis might be picked up by some weirdo on the street. You never can be too careful, you know!"

In Merced, Del still had deep suspicions that a lot of people knew something about his Stevie's disappearance but weren't talking. One day he had his family out for a drive when he spotted a man idly—ominously, to Del—standing beside a mound of dirt at the roadside. This so upset Del that he turned around and drove back and, much to the embarrassment of his family, parked across the road and stared at the stranger. Startled, the man got into his car and drove off. Del then went to the police and tried to get them to dig up the mound to see if Stevie was buried there, but they would not do it and for years afterward Del felt that just maybe that man knew something about his Stevie's whereabouts.

Kay's parents divorced, and her mother, Mary, moved in with them on Bette Street. As another Christmas approached, this kind lady did her best to keep the family's, and especially her son-in-law's, spirits up by playing excitedly with her grandchildren, but it just didn't work. Finally, on Christmas Day, Del internalized all he could before again retiring to his bedroom to talk to Stevie's picture, cry, and sniff his lost son's clothes.

Del reminisced morosely years later, "I kept all of his clothes. I wouldn't let none of his clothes be thrown away. And I would take them out and smell them. I just wanted them close to me. I had his little shoes and socks—and maybe someone would think it was silly—but I would smell them just to see what his little body smelled like."

That Christmas in Santa Rosa Dennis thought a lot about what Parnell had told him, that his family had not been able to afford to take care of him and that that was why the judge had sent him to live with Parnell. "Maybe he is right," Dennis recalled having thought to himself at that time. "Still, it was a compromise. I never did give up hope of returning home to my family someday."

At school just before Christmas Dennis and his classmates made cards for their parents, his own green-and-red construction paper card to Ken reading, "Merry Christmas to Dad from Dennis." Just before school was out for the holidays Ken and Barbara accompanied Dennis to school to see him in the Christmas play. Dennis doesn't remember the part he played, but he does recall Ken and Barbara introducing themselves to his teacher as "man and wife."

During the Christmas holidays Dennis recalled that Parnell attempted—with his help—to kidnap another boy, driving him to Santa Rosa's Codding Town Shopping Mall and instructing Dennis to go up to a particular boy near his age. Said Dennis, "Parnell watched a particular kid for fifteen or twenty minutes, and after he made sure that the kid wasn't with anyone, he said, 'Go over to that kid.' And I went over to the kid and said, 'Hey, have you seen a kid around here about so high with blond hair?' And he said, 'No.' And I said, 'Thank you.' And then I went to Parnell and told him, 'He doesn't want to go with me.'

"Parnell didn't get mad. We just stayed there and tried for another one! And we did this for two whole hours! He wanted me to try and approach the kids because he thought that he would stand out as a man going up to a boy and asking him questions and stuff, so he never took the chance. He always put me or somebody else up to it."

With Barbara present, Christmas 1974 slightly resembled Dennis's Christmases past in Merced in that he got several gifts and there was someone besides Ken with whom he could share the joys and pleasures of the holiday. But Dennis longed for his own large family 160 miles to the south, even though by the time the holidays had ended, Dennis's life with Barbara and Ken had smoothed out . . . except, that is, for the rare, totally abnormal, coerced heterosexual intercourse with his "mother." But Dennis kept quiet, saying nothing to anyone about that side of his relationship with Barbara.

In the spring of 1975, at Ken's urging, Dennis joined the Santa Rosa Boys' Club where he often swam, played ping-pong, and enjoyed the company of other boys. But one day when Ken and Barbara picked him up at the club, Parnell asked Barbara to lure a certain young boy into the car with them. Barbara did exactly as Parnell had instructed her and didn't ask any questions, but when she approached the car with the boy, the lad hesitated. Sensing trouble, Parnell shouted at Barbara to hurry and get into the car. She obeyed and the trio quickly drove home in silence without the boy, as if nothing had happened and, even though Dennis and Barbara do not recall Ken ever saying anything more about the episode, soon thereafter Parnell pulled up stakes in Santa Rosa.

On the last Sunday of October 1984, the author tracked Barbara to a remote mountaintop in rural northern Mendocino County, where she then lived on twenty rugged, wooded acres with her common-law husband, John Allen, and youngest son, Lloyd. A Mendocino County Sheriff's Deputy provided detailed directions to the place but refused to escort the author "cause John raises 'funny stuff' up there and you never can tell what he'll do."

The road to the property is seven desolate miles of unsigned, rutted track, and that Sunday afternoon thick fog hid the mountaintops while fat fingers of the brume wafted down through the many small valleys crisscrossing the road and enveloping the road's sole traveler. The property itself was crudely fenced and posted with homemade signs reading "No Tresspassing [sic]" and "Tresspassers [sic] will be shot." Once across the cattleguard, a drive wound around a quarter-mile maze of derelict wrecked trucks, autos, and abandoned farm and road machinery with a backdrop of dark, forbidding pines, ending at an old, twenty-foot-long decrepit house trailer that looked as if a final lurch had left it in that position.

At some point in the dim, distant past the now-peeling trailer had been painted a bilious light green. One end of the trailer poked from the fog-shrouded pine forest and was surrounded by several dark forms low to the ground, forms which quickly found their voice as the author braked to a halt . . . they were large, mangy, vicious guard dogs. Another equally decrepit house trailer sat a short distance away, and beyond it were a couple of small metal sheds, one of which had still more loudly barking guard dogs chained to it. All in all, the scene was one of an ethereal Tobacco Road West.

Except for the dogs, the place appeared totally deserted. Soon, though, a gangling, gaunt teenaged boy emerged from the bilious green trailer and shouted above the din to ask what the visitor wanted. The author shouted back an introduction and explanation and thus met Barbara's then-sixteen-year-old son, Lloyd. The boy shushed the dogs and said that Barbara and John—"my parents"—had gone to San Francisco, but that the author was welcome to talk with him inside the trailer which, it turned out, was the small family's home.

The inside was dirty and trashy, a thin layer of dust-covered frying grease coating doorknobs, light switches, walls, cupboards, the floor, the ceiling . . . everything one touched or saw. The kitchen counter, chairs, and a small, rickety old dining table were all piled high with refuse, unwashed dishes, and food-encrusted pots and pans. There was no running water, telephone, or electricity, although a cluttered shelf held a small battery-powered black and white TV flicking a pro football game. The forlorn-looking teenager invited the author to sit with him on his narrow wood bunk slung along the trailer's wall and watch the game.

The author began his interview and over the next two hours this kindly, soft-spoken young man with milk-white skin and finely chiseled features enunciated his answers slowly and with some hesitation. (Later Lloyd's mother confirmed the author's suspicion of the child's slight mental retardation.)

A good deal of the interview involved Lloyd's telling with moving honesty about Parnell's sexually assaulting him as a nine-year-old and his still-evident emotional grief over this. Once again the author found himself both touched and angered by the long-lasting emotional damage Parnell's insatiable lust for young boys had caused.

On Halloween the author returned and met Barbara and her common-law husband, John Allen. But before John would allow his wife to be interviewed, he sharply interrogated the author while he himself sat on the toilet. Finally emerging from the trailer's tiny bathroom, John—a rough-and-tumble, self-described former federal drug agent with broken front teeth and matted hair—pointed to several bulletholes in the ceiling and told the author that he had put them there with his AK-47 (a grimy finger pointed to its location under Lloyd's bunk) "when I got pissed with a fellow who asked too many questions.

"Now," he commanded the author, "you go get your tape recorder and interview Barbara." Warily, the author did so.

With a hard face wrinkled well beyond her forty-odd years and strands of black hair hanging over an almost toothless smile, Barbara looked every bit the backwoods woman she now is. Illiterate—a fact which she unsuccessfully attempts to hide—and lacking most of the social graces, she is a talkative person who, during the author's two hours with her, offered some arresting observations about Parnell's interest in Dennis's agemates. "Ken used to tell Dennis to make friends with other boys, but Dennis would say, 'No, I don't want to make friends with those kids.' And one time a bunch of boys were walking up the street and Ken asked Dennis, 'Do you know those boys?' And Dennis said, 'No, not really.' Ken was always looking at boys, but everybody looks at kids, I guess."

Probably because of the botched kidnapping attempt at the Boys' Club, Dennis didn't get to finish the fourth grade at Santa Rosa. Just a few days after that incident, Ken, Barbara, and Dennis pulled up stakes and moved very suddenly to Willits, eighty miles north in remote, peculiar Mendocino County. "Never-Never Land," one lifelong county resident calls it. For months Ken had been unemployed in Santa Rosa and no job awaited him in Willits, but for whatever reason, he had hitched up his sixteen-foot travel trailer and moved his family to the Quail Meadows Trailer Park on U.S. 101, just north of Willits.

Located in the northeastern quarter of the Redwood Empire—famed for its gigantic redwood trees and the scenic California & Western tourist railroad from Ft. Bragg on the coast—Willits is a quiet little town of three thousand in bucolic Little Lake Valley, and it gave Dennis his first taste of life in a small town. But there was no vacation from school for Dennis: Parnell checked him out of Santa Rosa's Kawana Elementary on May 12 and the next day enrolled him in Brookside Elementary in the Willits Unified School District . . . again a school district to which Dennis's real parents had sent their plaintive form letter and a supply of "Missing Juvenile" flyers. But once again, it was a school where their mailing had been thrown away.

Dennis said that it was while he was in Ms. Tuppman's class at Willits that he first learned what the word "homosexual" meant: "You always know pretty much what your vocabulary is at a certain age, and [it] was around the end of my fourth grade year in Willits when I started knowing what 'faggot' and 'dyke' meant, and I started calling people that. That was when I started knowing that the sexual aspect of what Parnell was doing to me was wrong. I had figured out that it was probably wrong, but I knew that Parnell always did what was wrong. Therefore, if he knew it was wrong, and he was still doing it, he didn't care.

"If I came up to him and confronted him with it, there might be trouble, and I wasn't looking for trouble at that age. In fact, I've never been the type who would say, 'Hey! Hold it here! You're doing something wrong here!' I've always been the quiet type. I'd say in kind of a small whisper, 'Did you know you're doing something wrong?' First of all, I don't like arguing with people, and I avoided discussing anything sexual with Parnell. I was afraid that if I did say anything about sex he'd just want to do *'it'* again.

"Anything to do with sex was always *hush* with me. If Parnell was around and any of my friends came to our place and mentioned anything about sex, or used the term 'faggot,' I just gave them a dirty look and said, 'Hey, let's go . . . let's get out of here.' "

In Merced, Police Sgt. Jim Moore was still working Steven's case and had now turned to checking reports of unidentified children's bodies that had been discovered from California to New England. "Luckily," he recalled, "none of them were Steven. But you know, you continue to look for the child, but from past experience you also know the possibility that he might be dead."

Lt. Bill Bailey, Sgt. Moore's supervisor, added, "In fact, we got calls from the Midwest, and even a police sergeant working a murder case of a little boy up in Maine called us up, but it wasn't Steve."*

*During 1983 and 1984, near Omaha, Nebraska, Airman John J. Joubert—then stationed at Offutt Air Force Base—was arrested, charged, convicted, and given a death sentence each for his brutal kidnapping-murders of thirteen-year-old Danny Joe Eberle and twelve-year-old Christopher Walden. During the late 1970s—when police in Maine phoned Lt. Bailey—Joubert was a teenager in Portland, Maine, suspected of having sexually assaulted several young boys. Such crimes against children occur all over the nation . . . a problem detailed in this book's Epilogue.

Shortly thereafter Merced Police Sgt. Leon Martinez replaced Moore as the Juvenile Department Sergeant and he remembers his own investigation leading to many cases of physical and sexual abuse of children that the department would not have known about otherwise: "When I was put in charge of the investigation the case was getting a bit old and therefore we were following up all kinds of leads. It led us to a lot of other situations involving juveniles being sexually abused by adults. I thought, 'It just doesn't happen here.' But, my God, the weirdos that surfaced here!"

Try as he might, Ken couldn't land a job in Willits, and it was only thanks to his mother's beneficence that his little family remained financially afloat. Less than a month after arriving in Willits, Ken again hooked his travel trailer to his old Ford and he, Barbara, Dennis, and Queenie chugged west, toward the coast. It took nearly half a day for the overburdened, frequently overheating car to crawl over twisting California Highway 20, up and down hills blanketed with towering redwoods, into and out of occasional fog banks, the spooky, desolate, uninhabited forests making a profound, lasting, sinister impression on Parnell.

In Fort Bragg, Ken quickly found a home for his family at the Harbor Trailer Park, high on a cliff overlooking the mouth of the Noyo River and the Pacific Ocean. To Dennis it was a beautiful, idyllic location, and with the exception of Yosemite National Park, by far the best in terms of natural beauty in all the time he had lived with Ken.

With a population of 4,500, Fort Bragg is the second largest town in Mendocino County, a pleasant, mostly

blue-collar town with a large Georgia Pacific Mill turning out lumber, plywood, and other wood products
from redwood and Douglas fir logs trucked in from
throughout the region. Tourism is a major local industry, and there are scores of motels and restaurants
catering to sightseers and rail buffs who come to enjoy
the dramatic northern California coast and ride the
renowned California & Western "Skunk" tourist
trains round trip to Willits.

In the 1850s Fort Bragg drew its first immigrants
from the Portuguese Azores, immigrants who first
worked at the area's pioneer lumber mill and later
used some of the large trees themselves to build family
fishing boats. Today one of the largest concentrations
of Portuguese on the Pacific Coast continue this fishing industry in both Fort Bragg and the nearby pic-
turesque fishing village of Noyo.

Ken spent weeks trying unsuccessfully to find a job
and then made one of his infrequent trips to Bakersfield to visit his mother. As usual, he left Dennis and
Barbara behind. Once at Mary's, Ken convinced her
to underwrite his plan to open the Fort Bragg Bible
Book Store and to buy her son a brand new Chevrolet
Impala. Even though Dennis never met Mary Parnell,
he said that from what Ken told him she is a very frugal
yet financially well-off woman, having managed to save
money from her World War II boardinghouse operation, invest it, and then add to it money from Ken's
half brother, at one time the president of an oil company. But when the author asked Ken about this in
1984, he would neither confirm nor deny this information, but rather showed consternation that it was
known. Said he angrily, "I won't verify or deny any-

thing in those regards! One way or the other! Just let it stand at that!"

To a certain extent, starting the Bible Book Store was not all that foreign to Ken, who explained, "I usually don't discuss it, but I've had a lot of study in the Bible. I have taken extensive courses—and I'm not going to get into detail—but I have held a minister's license and a Doctorate in Bible degree. I've had times when I wanted to get into the religious field, and it weighed out in the bookstore. Financially, of course, it was a disaster." Ken's boasting notwithstanding, the author found no evidence of his ever having received a minister's license or a college or seminary degree.

About Ken's Bible knowledge, Barbara said, "On Sundays he used to sit down and read the Bible to us. And one day he was saying something about a certain part of the Bible and Dennis says, 'Well, why don't you get the Bible down and read it to us?' And Ken says, 'I know it all by heart.' So I says to Dennis, 'Well, there's the Bible right there. Get it and see if he does know it by heart.' And so Ken told us the page and the paragraph and such, and then Dennis follows along and then he says, 'He *does* know it by heart!'"

So, with neither of them attending church, Barbara illiterate, and Ken a convicted kidnapper and pederast, and *both* of them practicing perverted sex acts on their nine-year-old son, albeit at different times, this very odd, amoral couple opened the Fort Bragg Bible Book Store in a rented A-frame just across Highway 1 from the mobile home park where they lived in a sixteen-foot travel trailer.

Dennis recalls that Ken often left Barbara to handle the store alone and that she was unable to make out receipts and give change for the sales she handled while he was gone. During these times Ken was usually drinking with his buddies at the local Eagles' Lodge, where he was soon a well-liked, well-known member and where for several years he led the membership in sales of tickets to their annual pitch-till-you-win dungeness crab feeds, their annual fundraiser. At the election of officers in 1976, Ken was chosen treasurer. He held this post for nearly three years, until the membership decided that they should bond their treasurer; fearing his criminal past would be exposed, Ken resigned the post.

A good friend of Dennis's back in the late 1970s, Joe Gomes described the scene at the Fort Bragg Bible Book Store. "They had a full stock: Bibles, pencils with scriptures on them, and different types of religious pictures . . . but not many customers." Also, Joe recalled that Ken and Dennis ". . . always seemed like they were trying to hide something. I knew Barbara and Ken weren't really married. Dennis told us that, and he called Barbara his 'Mother-friend.' But—you know the way kids get together and just talk about everything?—well, we'd go down to the river a lot and just sit and talk, but Dennis never opened up to anybody and let them know about the past."

The owners of the Harbor Trailer Park, husband and wife Leroy and Dorothy Neilson—no relation to the Nielson whom Parnell robbed in Salt Lake City—also found Barbara and Ken somewhat strange. Said Dorothy, "Barbara was a rather queer bird. She complained constantly of men peeking in the shower in order to see her take a shower in the public facility.

She wouldn't use the bathroom, but rather urinated right at the rear of their trailer."

Remarked Leroy, "Parnell was very slipshod in the hours he kept at his shop. He was very erratic, opening and closing at his convenience rather than the public's." It was this attitude about business which cost Ken the position of manager for Mr. Neilson's flea market when the job opened up and Ken applied.

That first summer Parnell caught Dennis playing with matches, this time trying to set fire to a field atop a cliff overlooking the Pacific surf. Dennis recalls, "I was out in this field where the grass was real dry. Plus, it was a non-burn day. I had a clump of grass in my hand and I was trying to set it on fire.

"So Parnell comes out there and says, *Dennis!* What are you doing?' I jumped up and dropped the matches. He came out to where I was and saw the pile of grass and the matches and says, 'What have I told you about playing with matches? Go back to the trailer and wait for me.' And I went back to the trailer and he came in and he gave me this big lecture about what happens when little kids catch places on fire and the trouble they get into with the fire department.

"Then he says, 'Now, I'm going to blister your ass!' And he took off his belt and said, 'Bend over!' And this time he made sure that I didn't have nothin' in my pockets. And he went at it . . . hit me eight or nine times . . . hard, too!"*

*Years later, when Dennis told the author about this incident and the previous one in Santa Rosa, with his background in social work the author suggested to him that there might have been a connection between his fire-setting and Parnell's sexual abuse, but Dennis refused to even consider such a thing, dismissing his actions as simply "a kid playing with matches."

That fall Dennis enrolled in Miss Friend's fifth-grade class at Dana Grey Elementary School on Chestnut Street. On the enrollment form dated September 2, 1975, Ken listed himself as Dennis's father and "Barbara Parnell" as Dennis's mother, and Ken admitted as much to the author in 1984: "I may have represented her as my wife in the [school] registry over on the coast." Also for the first time, Dennis's real middle name, "Gregory," was spelled out on a school form, and as before, his actual date and place of birth were listed.

As a ten-year-old in Fort Bragg, Dennis was rather independent, often spending Saturdays wandering around this just-right-sized town for a boy his age, buying and chewing fist-sized wads of grape-flavored bubble gum, gazing in shop windows, watching the "Skunk" trains (so named for the noxious fumes their gas-electric engines emit) arrive and depart from the local depot, and nosing around the commercial and sport fishing docks in Noyo Harbor.

It was on such a Saturday, with Barbara busy minding the Bible Book Store while Ken made his social mark at the Eagles' Lodge, that the police picked up Dennis and Joe Gomes for shoplifting. While they were in the Ben Franklin five-and-dime, Joe dared Dennis to slip some Silly Putty into his pocket. The two then casually strolled out the front door and a clerk and the store manager nabbed them.

The police arrived, put Dennis in the back of their cruiser, and delivered him to Barbara—who identified herself as his mother—at the Bible Book Store, where they told her what he had done. "It was the first time I had come into contact with the police since I had been kidnapped," Dennis recalled, "but I wasn't thinking about saying anything to them about that. I was *extremely* scared of having been caught shoplifting. My mind wasn't into, 'Oh, boy! There's a cop! All right! I want to tell him that I was kidnapped and I'm going to go home!' Well, *shit*, I was worried about, '*Oh, no!* My ass is going to get whipped!'

"But when Parnell got there he gave me this big bullshit line about good people and bad people. What he did is, he took a piece of paper and drew a black line and he says, 'You see this line? This line represents all the people who have committed a crime. The empty space on either side is the people who have not. You have now been added to that black line. Now, how do you feel about that?' And I told him, 'Well, everybody does that! It was just a little thing . . . just a little toy!' But I didn't say anything about him being a part of that black line. I wasn't out to be killed! *No thank you!*"

There was insufficient demand for a religious bookstore in rustic Fort Bragg, let alone one run by business and church neophytes like Ken and Barbara, and when Mary finally cut off her son's supply of money, the business's days were numbered. Struggle as he might, Ken knew this was a losing proposition. Finances were so tight there was not even money for much-needed school clothes for Dennis and, said Barbara, "[Ken] called up his mother on the phone and begged her for money. I was standing right there when he made the call. He just said, 'I need money for clothes for the kid.' And I assumed that she knew about it, because she didn't question him. She just said, 'I'll send you two hundred bucks . . . would that help you out?' And he says, 'Yeah.' And she did send it, because I was there when the check came in the mail.'' Although Mary maintains that she knew nothing about Dennis living with Ken—and Dennis concurred—did she, perhaps, think that "the kid" was one of Barbara's children?

In the spring of 1976 Barbara's divorce from Bob—who had remained with their children in Santa Rosa—came through, and with it she gained custody of her four youngest children: Lloyd, Kenny, Vallerie, and Christy, and suddenly an ill-prepared Ken found himself the head of a family of seven. It was a rowdy brood and far more than he had bargained for, especially in terms of the attendant financial responsibility. To begin with, there was absolutely no way the seven could live in a sixteen-foot travel trailer, so Ken bought an old, motorless, converted school bus which in the past was painted a dusky, noxious shade of blue, a remnant of the hippie exodus to Mendocino County in the 1960s. It could sleep eight on crude wood berths slung under the windows, and there were, after a fashion, cooking and dining facilities, plus a primitive bathroom with a shower that at best sprinkled one with a few drops of cold or warm water, depending on whether it was winter or summer. But the Neilsons were not about to allow such an eyesore to mar the decorum of their establishment, and when Ken and an Eagles' Lodge brother unexpectedly showed up towing the bus—prepared to exchange it for the travel trailer—Mr. and Mrs. Neilson rushed from their office protesting the monstrosity and Ken had to find another place for his enlarged family's new home.

Fortunately, there was such a place nearby. Below

the spectacularly high Noyo River Bridge, in the mal-
odorous fishing village of Noyo, the Anchor Trailer
Park had a collection of pickup campers, old house
trailers, motor homes, and a couple of similarly converted school buses—though none as ghastly a hue as
Ken's.

Located on a tidal flat between two cliffs, Noyo had
air heavy with the unmistakable smell of the predominant local business, yet it was a fascinating place for
the kids and it wasn't long before Dennis and Kenny
and a couple of their friends went for a day's fishing
on a raft—and failed to return by dark. Upset, Barbara
wanted to call the sheriff, but at first Ken wasn't at all
keen to do so. He was worried, she said, but had her
wait a while before allowing her to call the Mendocino
County Sheriff's Office. After she did call and a deputy
arrived, Barbara said, "Ken was kind of worried because he was walking back and forth and smoking
more and more cigarettes. Then, while the deputy was
talking to Ken, here came Dennis and them. They was
cold and wet and everything else, and I just let Ken
talk to the deputy and I took them inside to get some
dry clothes on."

In prison, when the author recounted Barbara's version to Ken, the prevaricator bristled, "I *wanted* Barbara to call the sheriff! There was no question there!
For me, believe it or not, there was a difference in me
facing whatever penalties I might have [for kidnap-
ping] and Dennis's life! He was out fooling around in
the ocean . . . Okay? . . . so I had to face that situation . . . *right?* . . . to tough it out and hope that I
could explain anything that came up!"

It was while living in Noyo that Barbara's eleven-year-old son, Kenny, was first propositioned by Parnell. One day Dennis and Kenny were sitting on a dock shooting the breeze when out of the blue Kenny said, "You know your dad's a faggot?" Unnerved that someone knew, an embarrassed, shocked Dennis lied and denied any knowledge of such a thing. But Kenny persisted and went on to tell Dennis that Parnell had grabbed his balls and tried to get Kenny to fellate him. Dennis ignored Kenny's accusations; for the time being, the subject was dropped and nothing was said to Barbara.*

When the Bible Book Store went out of business, it put additional strain on an already strained relationship between Ken and Barbara. But Ken explained the rift to Dennis by saying, "Well, sexually I can't relate to her [anymore]."

Soon thereafter Barbara took a job washing dishes at The Captain's Cove, a fried-fish restaurant on a cliff overlooking Noyo Harbor, and it was there that she met John Allen, the self-described former drug agent, and fell for him. Compounding family matters, Dennis and Christy had a knock-down-drag-out fight: Christy accused Dennis of stealing things from her, and Dennis countered by screaming insults at her. But when the hitting and kicking started, Barbara drew the line: for her this was the last in a series of problems, and she and her children moved out, leaving Ken and Dennis.

*In the author's several interviews with Kenny in October and December of 1984, Kenny claimed that Parnell had only "tried" to molest him. However, in October of 1984, John Allen recalled that in 1978 Kenny had told him that Parnell had had sex with him on several occasions . . . and in 1980 Barbara reported the same—including Parnell's sexual abuse of Lloyd—to several law enforcement officers.

The split occurred when school ended in early June of 1976. Barbara and her brood immediately moved into John Allen's own small trailer in the tiny coastal hamlet of Caspar, a few miles south of Fort Bragg, while Ken and Dennis remained in the old blue bus at Noyo. Dennis said that the bus was not very clean, that it smelled and was cramped. But almost unbelievably, it had served as home to that odd family of seven for nearly six months. Then, in celebration of Barbara and her kids' departure, Ken took Dennis with him on another trip to Reno. Again he unsuccessfully tried his luck at the gaming tables while Dennis—wishing he was old enough to go out onto the casino floor—roamed their hotel alone.

After a few days in Reno the father and son drove back to Noyo and the old blue bus. On their arrival Parnell undressed and had Dennis do the same before he fondled the boy's genitals "as foreplay to his having sex with me," Dennis sighed. Then, as Parnell caressed the eleven-year-old's naked privates, he forced his son to reprise the humiliating act of fellatio and put his open mouth over Parnell's naked, erect penis. With Barbara gone, Parnell's frequent sexual abuse began again, and Dennis faced a dilemma: even with his dislike for Barbara, he would have preferred putting up with her ignorance and the occasional sex acts with her just to have had her around to satisfy Parnell sexually rather than his having to submit to his father's almost daily requests for oral and anal intercourse.

As Dennis said years later, "From the start I recognized my situation"—being kidnapped and sexually abused by Parnell—"as life-threatening, and I knew that I had to do what he wanted me to do. When he first forced me to suck him off, I knew that he might kill me if I didn't do it. There's some times that you just have to go along with things. You have to learn to *never say never*, because you never know when you're gonna have to do something just to survive."

Two hundred miles away, Del and Kay were going through yet another version of their own private hell. Kay's father had picked up and fed a starving, mentally deficient young man whom he then took to meet Steven's parents. Said Del, "I told the kid the story about Stevie and how much easier it would have been if Stevie had just gotten sick and died . . . that we could accept death because that is a part of life. You know, if we had had his funeral and his little body had been dedicated and we would know where he was at, we could go visit his grave.

"So after a while this kid goes off down to Bakersfield and goes into the Salvation Army down there and tells them this story, that he killed Stevie and buried him off somewhere in the hills. And, of course, they called the Merced Police and they brought him back up here. Then he tells them where he's buried Stevie, and it's out toward Cathy's Valley, out beyond the cannery.

"And so the police took him out there with a backhoe and they start digging up the place he said he buried him. And the police was keeping it all real hush-hush, but somebody from the *Sun-Star* found out about it and came out to the cannery where I was working and asked me about it. I got so damned upset that I was bawling and I tried to stick my hands through the wall. But then they didn't find nothing; he confessed that he had just made up the story because he'd felt sorry for us."

In late June Ken was hired as the bookkeeper at Wells Manufacturing, a small, family-run dental equipment factory near the tiny Mendocino County community of Comptche, thirty miles southeast of Fort Bragg. Ritchie Wells, the owner, was pleased to find as competent and detail-oriented a bookkeeper as Kenneth Parnell. But he was a devout Baptist and would have been aghast had he known about his new employee's criminal convictions, not to mention Parnell's continuing sexual assaults on the quiet, well-mannered boy Wells thought was Ken's son.

For a month Ken commuted along the marvelously scenic coast highway, California 1, south along the Pacific headlands from the Noyo River to the nineteenth-century New England-style village of Mendocino City where, just after crossing the Big River, he turned east into the 200-foot-tall redwood forests that smother the rolling hills between the sea cliffs and the relatively open Comptche area.

Dennis said that he felt it was primarily Mendocino County's beautiful scenery that attracted Ken to the area in the first place and that it was only later that Parnell realized that he had happened onto an area peopled by some of the most liberal, free-thinking individuals in a state known for an excess of such folk. However, Ken discovered early on that most coastal Mendocino County inhabitants observed few social constraints, on the whole allowing their neighbors to do just about what they wanted so long as they didn't infringe on or dictate their lifestyle to anyone else.

Chapter Six
Comptche, California

*"I never wanted to leave there because
I was happy."*

In late July 1975 Ken rented a spacious double-wide mobile home from fellow Wells employee Tyne Cordeiro, a move which placed him just a mile from his work. Ken was well aware of Dennis's love of country living, and since he seemed to do things to please his "son," it was no surprise that he moved himself, Dennis, and Queenie to this strange, remote, rustic little hamlet. Ken had learned during his first few weeks at his new job that the two hundred folks in Comptche might gossip about their neighbors, but on the whole they let others live their lives as they pleased. Whereas Fort Bragg is the most conservative town one will find in the coastal half of Mendocino County, Comptche's population is as independently minded and diverse in personal philosophies as one could find anywhere in California.

The hamlet has a country store with a couple of gas

pumps out front, a tiny post office, a Grange Hall, a
volunteer fire station, a primary school, and The
Chapel of the Redwoods, the Baptist church which
Ken's employer, Ritchie Wells, built with locally cut
redwoods as a gift to his community. Situated in a small
logged-over valley 200 feet above sea level, Comptche
is a world apart from the damp, foggy, breezy coastal
weather in Fort Bragg and along the Mendocino coast
where summer rarely sees thermometer readings
above the mid 80's. In Comptche—just 15 air miles
inland but protected by coastal hills—temperatures
of over one hundred degrees are common in the summer.

After picking up his mail at the post office, Ken
drove south along Flynn Creek Road for less than a
quarter mile before he turned left onto a dusty,
bumpy private road which took him over a hill, past
a rustic, unpainted wood residence with a few marijuana plants growing among the tomatoes, and past
Tyne Cordeiro's mobile home, and then pulled up
in front of the rambling trailer which he and Dennis
would come to call home for the next three years.
Once Dennis went in he was thrilled to see that he
had a bedroom of his own, furnished with a dresser,
double bed, desk, and chair. It was Dennis's first
room of his own since the short stay in the house
in Santa Rosa. In addition, Comptche offered a
growing boy countless trees to climb . . . so many
that "at Comptche there was too many trees for
[Parnell] to keep me out of," Dennis laughed in
joyful recollection.

Dennis remembers his years in Comptche as filled
with almost constant outdoor activities. "I spent a nor-

mal life at Comptche. I went through school, I played on the football team, I went through the routine of marijuana that kids experience, and I experienced my first date as every kid has experienced. I had a lot of friends. I loved the place! I didn't think too much about my own family back then. I was afraid I might end up at a boys' home, so, really, I thought, 'Why don't I leave well enough alone?' "

While living in Comptche, Ken and Dennis raised their own meat—rabbits, pigs, and chickens—and grew their own vegetables in the community plot provided by the Wells family. Ken put up much of what they raised in a huge chest-type freezer he'd bargained for at a flea market. In that way they didn't have to spend much for store-bought groceries, and therefore, Dennis said, ground beef for his favorite food, hamburgers, became a rare store-bought treat.

Farther out Flynn Creek Road lived lumberjack Ronnie Mitchell, his wife Joann, and their eight children, five sons and three daughters. It wasn't long before Dennis and the three youngest boys—"Babe Ronnie," 13, George, 11, and Michael, 8—became constant companions. Just across a valley pasture from the Mitchell clan lived Larry and Judy Macdonald, their two daughters, and their toddler son. Larry was a carpenter, a community leader, an officer in the local Grange, and Chief of the Comptche Volunteer Fire Department; and their oldest daughter, Lori, an olive-skinned tomboy, soon became Dennis's first girlfriend.

On Dennis's first date ever, Lori's parents chaperoned them, taking them to a movie in Fort Bragg.

"I can't remember what we saw because I was too nervous," he chuckled. "Her parents sat right behind us." Dennis and the Mitchell boys spent the long, hot summer days frolicking naked in the cool water of the "pothole" in Flynn Creek. One day, unknown to the boys, Lori saw them from her house a couple of hundred feet away. As soon as they were in the water, her brunette hair flying in the wind, Dennis laughed, "She came up on us and we just stayed in the water. She said, 'I can see your bare butts shining when you run around on the bank. You better be careful or someone's gonna see you from the road.' Then she asked me to go swimming with her, too, but I wouldn't go skinny-dipping with her."

That first fall Dennis started smoking marijuana as a sixth grader at Mendocino Middle School. A friend, Ronald Harris, had asked him "to stay the weekend" in the tiny coastal village of Elk, and after breakfast Saturday morning the two boys set out to explore the nearby abandoned beach houses. While wandering about they encountered a fellow classmate who had just got his weekly allowance of weed from his parents.

The three boys stopped at the largest of the abandoned houses, a ghostly two-story vine-covered structure with a crumbling garden wall. Inside the house they took cover from the onshore wind and smoked up the lad's pot. A neophyte at "blowing dope," Dennis said the other boys had to show him how. After that, Dennis admitted that he smoked it during school hours, all the time. "Whenever we didn't have any, we'd just make a pot raid to one of our neighbors'. There was always someone who had it growing."*

At home Dennis stuffed his marijuana into 35-mm film containers and then hid them inside the mobile home's heating vents. Parnell never did discover this, but Dennis said that he was always afraid that he would. "Parnell told me that if I was ever caught smoking pot he'd tear my ass up. That's how strongly he was against it at that time . . . until he found out that he could make some money selling it."

A retired nurse, Ruth Hailey, nearly got Dennis in trouble with Parnell over pot. A short, stocky, elderly lady, Ruth was always tending to the business of others. "She has a good eye for a pot smoker," said Dennis. "She thought that my experience with pot was known to Parnell, and she mentioned it to Parnell by accident. I wasn't around at the time, but Parnell brought it up to me. I denied it, of course. He was satisfied with that. I always told him what he wanted to hear. He was slightly gullible and a pretty easy individual to fool. I got very good at telling a lie, but not really lying . . . just sort of bending the truth. That's what made it easy for him to believe me."

During Dennis's first year in Comptche the John Peace family lived directly across Flynn Creek Road from the Macdonalds and Mitchells and Dennis

---

*Over the past twenty years the commercial and private growing and use of marijuana has become rather acceptable in the coastal half of Mendocino County. In the 1980s the California Commissioner of Agriculture was quoted in *Time* as estimating the street value of the Mendocino and adjacent Humboldt Counties' pot crop at over $3 billion, making it the largest cash crop in the state.

quickly developed a close platonic relationship with their thirteen-year-old daughter Kim—she later married his friend Joe Gomes—which lasted until well after she had moved to Caspar on the coast and he had left Mendocino County. Kim's mother Sherry quickly took on the role of surrogate mother to this "motherless" boy. But from the start her husband sensed something very odd about Dennis and his "father." "Dennis was strange," John said. "There was always something different about him. He never could confide in me. I knew something was wrong sexually. I knew that, but I didn't know what it was. In other words, he [Dennis] felt *it*—whatever *it* was—was wrong. But Dennis was really close to my ex-wife. He would spend time talking to the wife.

"And Parnell, he was always fairly strange. I never could understand why, when he would take off to see his mother—which I thought was Dennis's grandmother—he never would take Dennis with him. But Comptche, I mean, just living out in the middle of no place with a lot of squirrelly people, we thought that Parnell was just one of 'em."

"Because of the sexual abuse, I was always scared of Parnell," Dennis recounted, "and a lot of time I felt violence toward him. The sex was just whenever he felt like it. It was really quite fast, actually. When he was in the mood, we did it . . . just took a couple of minutes and it was over. Boom! I was dressed and out the door! The anal intercourse was painful. Parnell screwed me about a hundred times, and about half the time he split my butt. It hurt, but he just ignored me. It was like in the case of a man raping a woman. The man is not thinking about the woman's feelings.

Parnell had a split personality. When the urge hit him he was somebody different. And after he'd done it with me, he always just went on like nothing had happened. We'd sit down and have a meal or something . . . just do what we'd normally do. But due to the sex abuse, I really didn't look to Parnell for any attention. I did look to friends and my friends' parents for the attention I needed . . . at least to some extent to Mrs. Peace. Really, I tried to stay away from Parnell as much as possible. However, there were times when I really made my presence known to him because no one else was around."

Occasionally Parnell would take Dennis into Fort Bragg for pizza and pinball at the Pizza Place, and periodically Tyne Cordeiro invited them to a meal at her home. Usually these were holiday feasts when the widow entertained other older single women friends who, interestingly, were Parnell's choice for adult companionship. Tyne and her friends would dote on Dennis. One Thanksgiving, at her home, she said, "We fixed a big turkey and I tried to get everybody to carve it, and Ken said he didn't know how. Then Dennis said, 'I can carve that turkey! I've watched them do it on TV.' And Dennis got up there and, by golly, he carved that turkey! He did a beautiful job on it, too."

At work Tyne said Ken was a quiet, proficient bookkeeper, totally unobtrusive in his habits. "He wasn't a very outgoing person," she remarked. "We always used to set around and talk—you know how you set around and talk about people's backgrounds? Well, he'd only go so far and then he'd clam up. And he never did invite any of us into his home, although he stopped here [at her house] many times."

But Ken's dearth of hospitality did not extend to his ersatz son's young male friends. He often invited them to the trailer home without telling Dennis. On one occasion, he'd invited twelve-year-old Kenny Matthias who, though he lived in Caspar, attended the same school as Dennis. At Parnell's suggestion, Dennis asked Kenny to spend the weekend, Dennis telling Kenny that he and Parnell would pick him up at his house after school. Then, when Dennis got home from school, Parnell arranged for him to go to another friend's for the weekend, telling Dennis that he would call Kenny and cancel the weekend. But Parnell didn't call Kenny. Instead, he went and picked up the boy, not telling him that he was to be *his* guest for the weekend.

"When we got to Comptche," Kenny said, "I saw Dennis wasn't there, and I asked Ken where he was, and he said, 'Dennis is over staying the night at a friend's house.' Then I ~ id, 'Well, why am I here?' And he didn't answer me." The two went into the mobile home and just sat around and talked for a while. "Finally," Kenny recounts, "it was getting late and I said I was getting kind of tired, and he said, 'Well, hit the hay.' So I went in and took a shower and when I come out of the shower I had just my underwear on. And Ken picked me up and threw me over his shoulder and said, 'I want to fuck you!' And I said, *'No you're not!* I won't let you! You just let me down!' And I was frightened. He put me down and I went in the other room and shut the door and sat down and thought about the situation while I smoked a couple of cigarettes, and finally went to sleep. The next day I told him to take me home and he did.

"The next time I went over, I made sure that Dennis was there, and that night when we went to bed I told him what had happened. Then he said, 'We've already had sex with each other.' Him and Ken. And he spilled his guts to me and told me that Ken was sexually molesting him. He told me that he didn't want to do it, but Ken would force him to . . . that Ken had done blow jobs on him and had anal sex with him, too.

"Dennis seemed upset about it, like he didn't want it to happen, and I said, 'Why don't you turn him in?' And he said, 'I can't. He's my dad.' "

In the spring of 1978, after a heated argument with John Allen, Barbara loaded up Kenny, his sisters, and brother Lloyd—then nine—and went to Ken's in Comptche for a few days. One day, however, everyone except Lloyd, Kenny, and Ken went shopping in Fort Bragg. Alone with the boys, Parnell took full advantage of the situation, tricked Kenny into removing his shirt, started rubbing the boy's shoulders, and then quickly slid his hand over Kenny's stomach and down inside the boy's briefs, where he grabbed Kenny's privates. Immediately Kenny jumped up and ran outside, leaving his little brother Lloyd alone with the now-aroused Parnell.

Parnell wasted no time in forcing the frightened boy into the master bedroom, locking the door behind him, and forcibly stripping off the crying child's clothes, removing his own clothes, and ordering the naked boy to "Get on the bed!" Scared out of his wits, Lloyd did as told, "Face down!" he tearfully recalled.

When Barbara and her children returned to Caspar, Lloyd and Kenny told their mother and stepfather that Parnell had sexually assaulted them. Barbara telephoned the Mendocino County Sheriff's Office and reported both incidents but, she said incredulously, "The sheriff didn't believe it!" However, Barbara had no further contact with Parnell and Dennis.

William "Bill" Patton was Dennis's sixth-grade teacher. A balding, courtly, well-educated conservative man who is somewhat out of his element in Mendocino County (having settled there years before the 1960s influx of hippies and liberal freethinkers), the retired teacher recalls a great deal about Dennis's years at Mendocino's grammar and middle schools. "I remember it was rather unusual because he didn't have any records, but during that time the whole society was breaking down . . . [Dennis] was just a little kid that said very little out of line."

In 1977, during the spring of his sixth-grade year, Dennis went on Patton's four-day class trip to San Francisco, where they stayed at the Presidio Boys' Club, saw the Giants play the San Diego Padres in Candlestick Park, went to the Exploratorium and Golden Gate Park, and ate dinner at a restaurant in Chinatown. Never once, Dennis emphasized, did he even think about trying to get from San Francisco to Merced; "I was having too good a time."*

---

*The author showed Dennis his sixth-grade class group portrait in July of 1984, and as he looked over the twenty-four young faces one by one, he pointed to four boys (all with dark blond, brown, or black hair) who, he said, were sexually assaulted, propositioned, or requested as weekend guests by Parnell. Dennis went on to say, however, that Parnell was not interested in any of the light-blond-headed boys, including one with whom he was close friends.

While living in Comptche, Parnell continued to make trips to Bakersfield to visit his mother; and whether because Mary really didn't know about Dennis, or because of some newfound fear of risking discovery of the boy's true identity, Ken always left Dennis behind with the Macdonalds, the Mitchells, or the Peaces. When Lori Macdonald asked him why he didn't go to see his grandmother, Dennis responded, "She would get mad if I went down there."

During Dennis's stays with Judy Macdonald, she was put out with Ken for allowing his son to smoke—something that she did not permit her children to do—and it especially irked her that Ken would even hand her money for Dennis's cigarettes. Also, she couldn't understand why Ken allowed Dennis the freedom to come and go as he pleased, again very much unlike the way she ran her own family.

In the summer of 1977 the Peace family moved out of the rambling red house across from the Macdonalds and Mitchells and relocated in Caspar. Kathryn Vinciguerra and her playwright husband, Louis, moved into the house with her twelve-year-old son from a previous marriage, Damon Carroll. Damon and Dennis had known each other casually at school, but Damon's move to Comptche marked the beginning of a "best friend" relationship between the two. Kathryn said that one day Damon brought Dennis home with him, introduced him, and pointed out that he lived down the road. "I felt all right about the relationship," she said. "However, I did feel that Dennis was odd . . . you know, there was something in his eyes." Also, she revealed the rather startling knowledge that "from Dennis's information, his parents were separated and his mother and a brother and sisters lived in Merced." But she never questioned Dennis or Ken about this.

From the fall of 1977 and on through 1978 and into 1979, Dennis and Damon—a handsome boy with brown hair—spent the night with each other nearly every other weekend. Also, Ken frequently took the two boys to the movies in Fort Bragg, beachcombing along the Pacific Coast, and out for pizza. And when Damon stayed at Dennis's, they would stay inside but a short while before Dennis would suggest that they go somewhere together. Years later, when told of Parnell's sexual assaults on Dennis's young friends, Damon paused and professed shakily, "Perhaps it was because he knew my parents real well. But he never did anything at all to me. He never tried to take any nude pictures of me . . . nothing." Indeed, both boys asserted Parnell never did "try anything funny" with Damon. But Damon hesitated again as he recalled with awe, "Dennis *never* left me alone there with Ken."

But another of Dennis's seventh-grade classmates was not so lucky. Jeff Norton was a good-looking brunette without a father. True to form, Parnell arranged for Jeff to spend the weekend with Dennis and then picked Jeff up after school while Dennis rode home on the school bus. Driving along the winding road to Comptche, Parnell asked Jeff, "Can I put my dick in your hole?"

A shocked Jeff responded, "I don't have a hole."

Countered Parnell, "You know what I mean," and offered the twelve-year-old some money for the upcoming county fair. But, according to the 1980 police report about the incident, Jeff successfully rebuffed Parnell's proposition.

After supper that night Parnell threw a little beer party for Dennis and Jeff and then took advantage of their drunken state to take nude photographs of them with his Polaroid camera. Said Dennis, "Toward bedtime I took a shower and Jeff took a shower. That's when we had the pictures shot . . . in the shower. We both posed for them in the nude. There were no sex acts."

However, these weren't the first nude pictures of Dennis that Parnell had taken, for when he'd originally bought his Polaroid, he'd had Dennis pose for several nude photographs and then kept them, Dennis recalled, on the coffee table in their living room, often pointing them out to the boy. "He didn't care what I thought about them . . . it wasn't important to him," Dennis spat angrily.

Beginning with their residence in Comptche, Ken got in the habit of giving his ersatz son the most expensive Christmas and birthday gifts he could afford. One Christmas he gave Dennis a motorbike. Another Christmas he gave him a brand-new $300 ten-speed bicycle. By this time Ken had also begun to buy more fashionable adolescent clothes for his son: "Levi jeans, cords, new-style shoes, and a lot of T-shirts with logos on the front," Dennis happily recalled.

During Dennis's last two years in Comptche his friendship with Damon blossomed into a Tom Sawyer-Huck Finn alliance. Reflected Damon with obvious joy, "We'd go skinny-dipping at the pothole. We'd try fishing sometimes, but we never really caught anything 'cause we'd get rowdy. We'd have rock fights, apple fights . . . we just did whatever thirteen-year-olds did in Comptche in the summertime!"

As chief of the local fire department, Larry Macdonald could testify to that, since one day he found the two "playing with matches and lighting these little bundles of grass . . . lighting them and then putting them in these little wheels and letting them roll down the hill and laughing." Macdonald phoned Dennis's dad about this and Ken's response, "Boy, I'll check into it right now and see what's going on," sounded weak to Larry. A similar call to the Vinciguerras resulted in Damon's getting grounded for weeks.

A few days later Macdonald drove by the trailer home of Ruth Hailey. Ruth was a talkative elderly woman who wore heavy, bright red rouge and hats that would rival those of Bella Abzug. He saw Dennis smoking a cigarette on a roof that he was helping reshingle. "I mentioned to Dennis he should be real precautious [sic] about putting it out, and I said something about him getting scolded for playing with fire the other night, and he says, 'Oh, no! I didn't get scolded. Ken just told me that there was some concerned people.' And I often wondered what the extent of Ken's scolding was."

During the whole of Ken's residency in Comptche he tried first one and then another part-time, door-to-door sales job. For one he sold scented artificial flowers—announcing to several of his acquaintances that he was going to be "the area sales manager" for them. Later he sold Mason Shoes. He'd even had stacks of business cards imprinted with the name of his planned bookkeeping service—"A Aardvark Bookkeeping—

Parnell's Bookkeeping—Over 25 Years' Experience."
Nothing seemed to work.

During the 1970s the Comptche Store—a country
store lacking only the cracker barrel—was operated
by Art and Elsa Stoughton, and there wasn't much
that went on in and around Comptche that got past
them. When Ken's door-to-door sales efforts failed he
used his purple and white '68 Ford Maverick—having
sold his previous car, a Chevrolet Impala, during hard
times in Fort Bragg—as collateral to borrow $2,000
from the couple to set up the bookkeeping service.
Said Elsa, "And we thought, 'Well, you know, he was
a nice guy and [we] might give him a boost and help
him along.' "

Interjected Art, "We loved him!"

The couple found Ken to be eccentric, but that
didn't bother them one bit, since he fit in perfectly
with their other acquaintances in Comptche. But, Elsa
remarked, "I noticed that Ken never did have any men
friends. It was always ladies. Ken went out of town a
lot, and whenever he did, he left Dennis here with
someone. And the main thing I can say through seeing
him was that he loved that boy. He loved him and was
so thoughtful of him that if the youngster wanted
something, he got it. And I never doubted for a moment that Dennis was his son."

Not only were the Stoughtons convinced that Ken
and Dennis had a wholesome father-son relationship,
but Louis Vinciguerra, Damon's stepfather, remembers this: "There was a part of their relationship that
I saw that was supportive . . . there was a giving and a
concern. And I don't think that is something that you
just put on because you are with people. That's what

makes this thing so paradoxical [sic]. I mean, this is going to be a challenge for people to accept it. They don't want to see that side of it."

Concurred Damon, "Ken demonstrated a lot of affection toward Dennis, and the affection seemed to be reciprocal. To my knowledge, Dennis had nothing but admiration for Ken, and he acknowledged him to be his father."

But Damon's and Dennis's seventh-grade teacher at Mendocino Middle School, Gerald Butler, a stocky, jovial, rural renaissance man, tells a chillingly bizarre tale which hinted that Damon knew the truth about Dennis and Ken. "There was quite an extensive article in *Junior Scholastic* about lost children, missing children. We read it together and discussed it . . . had quite a discussion about it, and the bell rang for recess and most everybody went outside. But Damon and Dennis stayed by the door and Damon said, 'You know, Dennis claims that he was taken away when he was real young, and his parents said that they didn't want him anymore.'

"Damon and I were standing right near the door and Dennis was standing back a little ways," Butler continued. "Damon is a real exuberant kind of person, he just kind of comes up . . . kind of overpowering. And Dennis acted a little frightened. He kind of moved back from me, very shy, and he had kind of a funny little smile on his face. I asked him. 'Do you ever have the opportunity to visit with your parents?' He kind of shrugged his shoulders and said, 'No.' And at that time I thought it was rather strange, but so many other strange things happen in Mendocino County relative to children and parents, the relationship that they have. I should have followed through on that, because I really thought an awful lot about it. But somebody interrupted, and there were other kids waiting around for them to go out and play, and they just took off.

"But I remember going into the teachers' lounge and talking about it with some of the other teachers. And I heard from some other person on the staff—I'm not really sure who it was—that the story had been repeated at least one other time," Butler concluded.

Both Damon and Dennis later insisted that this incident never happened. However, among his peers Gerald Butler has a reputation as an honest, straightforward teacher with a sharp memory . . . and at least one other teacher, Bill Patton, recalled hearing Gerald tell of the incident in the teachers' lounge on that day years ago.

In the large Mitchell family Dennis was closest to his agemate George. On occasion George's mother kept Dennis during Ken's out-of-town trips, and when Ken dropped by to pick up Dennis he always paused a few minutes to give this handsome boy with brown hair some extra attention. One day Parnell gave the twelve-year-old a ride home from school . . . alone. As usual, Ken had told his son to take the bus. On the drive to Comptche, George asked Ken if he would buy a pack of cigarettes for him and Ken responded, "Sure, if we could have a little fun tonight."

Said George, "I didn't know what he meant by that, and so I said, 'Sure!' "

Dennis was home when they arrived, and within minutes Parnell was serving the boys beer. George recalled that after three apiece, Parnell told the boys,

"Take off your clothes. We're going to dance around, just fart around."

Recalling his naive, bewildered feelings, George said, "I thought we were just farting around, some kind of game, you know. And then Ken went into the bedroom and told me to come in there and I did. And he was just standing there naked . . . aroused. And he had this open jar of Vaseline in his hand and he wanted me to get up on the bed." But, George insisted, Parnell did not have sex with him, although when he went home George told his mother that Parnell had raped him.

According to a police report Joann Mitchell later made about the incident, George obeyed Parnell, got up on the bed, and was mounted and sodomized by Parnell. The report concluded, "She was positive that the incident had occurred. He [Dennis] and George had become somewhat intoxicated, and that at this time Parnell engaged in sodomy with George."

Dennis, however, knew full well what was going to happen to his friend from the time Parnell opened the first beer, but when his father called George to the bedroom, Dennis admitted years later he just sat naked in a living room chair, his head buried in a book. He said that he had "always" kept quiet when Parnell invited his friends over. "I just kind of figured that if he was fucking them he wouldn't be fucking me."

Parnell's sodomizing George became common knowledge around Comptche, but as usual the taciturn residents kept it to themselves, once again adhering to the local "live and let live" code lest, perhaps, their own idiosyncratic behavior be scrutinized.

In the eighth grade Dennis was regarded as a quiet, slightly below average student. Teacher Bob Krebs coached him in several sports and described Dennis as "a very fierce competitor, but a very quiet type of fierce . . . very intent, and very good, but he was not the take-charge, quarterback-type kid. He was somewhat withdrawn but was not reluctant to participate."

Krebs also related that among the parents of students in Dennis's school Parnell wasn't the only father who sexually abused his child. He recounted a number of cases—far too many, considering the small population base—including one involving a girl in Dennis's class who was known to have been involved sexually with her father from the age of six until she was well into her teens.

That case and the others were confirmed by Mendocino County Sheriff's Deputy Sergeant Daryl Dallegge, who in the early to mid 1980s was his department's professionally trained expert in the investigation of sexual abuse of children. At the time Ken and Dennis were living in western Mendocino County, Dallegge said that he knew them but had heard nothing about Parnell's sexual assaults.

Kim Peace said that soon after Ken and Dennis moved to Comptche, Parnell invited her to his home, but that she hadn't felt welcome. "I didn't like the way that Ken was looking at me. He has this strange look he gives people, and that scared me. He was doing that to people that were there, like Donnie Mitchell and Alan Stenback"—then handsome, dark-headed thirteen-year-olds—"and so I left and never went back." Also, Kim described the interior of Parnell's home as being dirty and not well kept. About Dennis's personal cleanliness she remarked, "He wore his clothes for days and days and days. But I don't think anyone ever said anything to him about it . . . Comptche people are kind of like that."

But when asked, Dennis blamed his lack of clean clothes on Ken's slatternliness, saying, "Parnell had to have to do laundry. He'd rather wear clothes over and over than to have to wash them."

As the years passed, the subject of Steven's kidnapping didn't arise very often between Parnell and Dennis. As for Parnell, he had always been very insistent that his son forget about it because, Dennis said, "He wanted me to get it off my mind. He didn't want me to think that I had been kidnapped. He wanted me to think that I had been given to him by the judge. But I got to wondering about that."

In the late spring of 1978, when he was thirteen, Dennis went to a party with a group of older Comptche teenagers where he drank beer and Jack Daniels, smoked marijuana, and then began to prattle on about his true past. One of the teenagers present, Kurt Poehlman, recalled, "This party was over at Beak's land. Dennis was next to the fire and he just started crying. He said, 'I want to go home.' And nobody really understood him—he never explained himself— but he didn't mean back to Ken's." Alan Stenback was present, too, and he recalls events as did Kurt . . . as did Donnie Mitchell, George Mitchell, Lori Macdonald, and many others who were also there.

When the author confronted Dennis with these recollections in June 1984, he denied ever having told *anyone anything* about the kidnapping, the sexual assaults, or his own family back in Merced.

Throughout 1978 Ken remained in his unassuming bookkeeping position at Wells Manufacturing where he was, said Angela Peterson—an older, now-deceased Comptche lady friend—"the original Mr. Milquetoast." But in early 1979 Ken got so upset over his low pay and lack of benefits that he quit and took a similar job at Eastman Trucking Company in Fort Bragg, a change which again required his making a daily round-trip commute over the crooked Comptche-Mendocino City Road and up the Coast Highway.

As Dennis got older, Parnell's sexual interest in him waned and he began actively seeking younger boys to satisfy him. One such lad was Ricky Frietas of Fort Bragg, the handsome ten-year-old son of first-generation Portuguese immigrants and a cousin of Dennis's friend Joe Gomes. Ricky had known Dennis and Ken casually when they lived in Fort Bragg, but when Ken saw Ricky in Fort Bragg one day he lusted for the youngster and had Dennis invite him for the weekend. Dennis complied and telephoned the lad, telling Ricky that Ken would pick him up on his way home from work the next Friday. Recalled Joe Gomes, "Ricky said that Ken had tried to offer him money for sex with him. He said that it happened at the trailer, and Ken offered him five dollars for some kind of sexual favor, but Ricky wouldn't do it. And after that he never went there again."

In the late spring of 1979 Ken happened to spot a classified ad in the *Wall Street Journal* for a rural cabin and acreage in northern Arkansas, and, sight unseen, he scraped together the $1,000 down payment and mailed it to the owner. Then, early that summer, on impulse he loaded Dennis into his Maverick and the two drove cross-country to see the place.

Pointedly avoiding Utah, Ken went through Las

Vegas—where he stopped to gamble—then into Arizona and onto Interstate 40 through New Mexico, Texas, and Oklahoma before entering Arkansas at Fort Smith and heading to the cabin just outside the small Izzard County town of Mount Pleasant. Once they had arrived, Dennis irately recalled, Ken insisted on having sex with him: "He had both oral and anal sex with me there.* But at that time we were just beginning to drift apart, sort of like a man and wife after they've been married for a while. And the sex was slow in tapering off. At first it was maybe once a night. Then once a week. And then it would, maybe, stop for a week. Then it would go maybe three times a week. It was just sort of whenever he felt like it."

In early July of 1979 the *Ukiah Daily Journal* carried a story about the discovery of the bodies of a young teenage boy and girl in shallow graves in the dense redwood forest along Highway 20 about ten air miles from Comptche. A few days later, without telling anyone, Ken suddenly and inexplicably moved out of the mobile home, hooking up and loading his trailer before quickly driving off with Dennis and Queenie to an isolated caretaker's cabin on the unoccupied Mountain View Ranch in extremely remote southern

---

*Steven had never before said anything to anyone about these sex assaults until he told the author about them in June of 1984, when he said that he wanted Parnell prosecuted for them. With Steven's concurrence the author phoned J. C. Skinner, Assistant Prosecutor for Izzard County, who stated that—since Arkansas' statute of limitations would not expire until July 1986—his office might be interested in prosecuting Parnell for these previously unknown crimes. However, Kay felt that her son had been through enough already and dissuaded Steven from pursuing the matter.

Mendocino County, fifty road miles from Comptche.*

Dennis was very upset by the move. "Living in Comptche, I thought, 'Why not leave well enough alone?' I never wanted to leave there because I was happy. But then we moved. I was very upset. I cried all the way to the cabin when we moved."

*The identities of these young victims have never been established and the cases are still open.

Chapter Seven

Mountain View Ranch

"The man seemed to be really interested in the boy."

The caretaker's cabin on the desolate, unoccupied Mountain View Ranch is twelve miles from the nearest community . . . twelve narrow, twisting, frequently wet, fog-shrouded miles of blacktop leading to California 1, the famed, scenic Coast Highway, and the small unincorporated coastal settlement of Manchester, home to a few hundred widely scattered residents, many of whose homes are surrounded by slanting cedar-tree windbreaks as they cling to windswept cliffs above the pounding Pacific surf. Four miles south and directly on Highway 1 is Point Arena, the commercial center for southwestern Mendocino County. With five hundred people and a slightly Bohemian character it boasts a handful of restaurants, two gas stations, a grocery store, a weekly newspaper, a picture show operating weekends only, a motel-lodge, and an eclectic assortment of small businesses besides the area's public schools. Thus it became the town most often visited

by Ken and Dennis after their move to the remote
Mountain View Ranch.

The ranch is owned by the Stornetta brothers, Charlie, Leslie ("Duke"), and Bill, all over sixty and de-
scendants of nineteenth-century Italian immigrants.
The ranch's modest headquarters house sits vacant
next to the caretaker's cabin on the infrequently traveled Boonville-to-Manchester roadway. However, in
summer the brothers occasionally rotate stays there
to escape the seasonal fog that smothers their main
ranch house at the mouth of the Garcia River north
of Point Arena.

As Ken drove down the coast from Comptche, Dennis asked about their new neighbors and was shocked
to learn that there were none. They would be the only
people living on the ranch's 4,400 acres of hilltop pasture, woodlands, and valleys. Turning off the Coast
Highway they passed the homes of a dozen residents,
the only people living along the road to the ranch save
the hippies secreted back in the woods at the Land of
Oz commune on the north fork of the Garcia River.
For Dennis this desolation was confirmed as they approached the ranch through a bleak, uninhabited
landscape of grass-covered hills, scattered cedars,
scrub oaks, and occasional redwoods.

As Ken's tired, overburdened old Maverick wheezed
pulling the trailer cargo of possessions and pets over
the last hill, the teenager sadly drank in the forlorn
expanse of gamma grass dotted occasionally by grazing
sheep. When he saw the cabin he could hardly believe
his eyes: they were going to live in a small, old, weath-
erbeaten wood cabin with faded streaks of white paint.

There was no drive, so Ken parked on the road's

shoulder. Dejectedly Dennis got out and waded through waist-high grass around the cabin with Parnell to carry their clothing and personal possessions into their "new" one-room home.

Immediately across the road Dennis spied the gray, heavily weathered old barn, adjacent sheep-shearing shed, and holding pens. But on the trip up from the coast Dennis had seen only one other car and the silence was almost deafening. As Dennis soon found out, he could count the day's total of cars and trucks passing the cabin on his fingers and toes.

Recalled Duke Stornetta, "I was looking for a caretaker because we had some thieves rob some stuff out of the barn. And I run into Louis Vinciguerra on Mountain View Road, up at the ranch, and he says, 'I would like to live there in that cabin.' So then he decides that he wasn't interested, but he said this fellow he knew in Comptche was looking for a place. So Parnell, he called me and made an appointment and met me at the ranch. He looked at me and says, 'Yes, this is just what we want. We have chickens, and we have rabbits, and I have a young boy. I'll start moving in.'

"When he came back with his belongings, he had Dennis with him, whom he introduced to me as his son, and they set up living there. I thought it was father and son all the time. The boy had a lot in common with his so-called father . . . both were quiet. They kept to themselves and they had few friends. They were just like drifters living there."

The cabin had a potbellied wood stove for heat, a propane gas water heater and cookstove, and indoor water, though the shower was out back and the toilet an old-fashioned outhouse 25 yards behind the cabin at the edge of the thick, dark wood . . . and there was no electricity for miles around, the nearest being nine miles away toward the coast, so at night they used kerosene lanterns for light. However, there was a telephone for what seemed to Dennis their only link to the outside world. But there was no television to watch while they lived at the cabin since Parnell procrastinated about putting up an antenna and using a car battery for power as did the Pipers, their neighbors a mile down and a quarter mile off the road to the coast.

Ken's impetuous trip to Arkansas the previous month had lost him his job at Eastman Trucking in Fort Bragg, and he was still unemployed when he made this latest move. Soon, though, he found a job as the graveyard desk clerk for The Palace Hotel, a restored nineteenth-century inn in downtown Ukiah, the distant Mendocino county seat. It was a job that Ken grew to like even though it required an hour-long commute inland through Boonville along forty twisting miles, over two coastal mountain ranges, with only four miles of straight pavement on the whole route.

As usual, Ken was a quiet, unobtrusive employee. One of the few fellow employees he met during the seven months he worked at The Palace Hotel was Robert Sandkila, the hotel barber, who remarked of Ken, "Suddenly he was here and he had come in to get a haircut. He never had much to say at all. I only cut his hair, maybe, once a month. He was very low-keyed, very unusual . . . never had anything to say. Just came in and did his job and then left."

After three years in the Mendocino City Schools—the longest he had ever attended a single school system—Dennis was very upset about leaving that comfortable environment with his friends, and in short order he convinced Parnell to allow him to attend Mendocino High School's ninth grade. At first Ken accommodated Dennis by making a point of dashing home early each morning to take him part way to school in Mendocino City. "I told Parnell that he could drop me off at Boonville and I'd hitchhike to school. He said, 'Fine.' And so that's what I did. I usually did whatever I wanted." Also, Dennis was dead set against transferring to Point Arena High School because, he said, "They had a lousy football team. Mendocino had a good football team." And that fall Dennis tried out for and won a starting position on the Mendocino High freshman football team.

Dennis was very proud of this, his first and last involvement in organized school sports, and Ken even attended some of the games, remarking, "I don't recall he was as aggressive as some of the other players."

But when football season ended Ken refused to continue his five-times-a-week mad dash from Ukiah through Boonville to the cabin and then, with Dennis, back to Boonville again, and so Dennis had to transfer to Point Arena High School in mid November. However, this arrangement presented its own transportation problems, since the Point Arena school bus ended its route where the power lines did, nine miles down the road to the coast. Because of this, during the fewer than sixty school days that Dennis was registered at Point Arena High he was absent more than twenty.

Even though he was there for less than forty days, Dennis's teachers at Point Arena gathered an accurate yet sketchy assessment of their laconic new student. World history teacher Rose Gartner remarked, "Dennis was very quiet. He had good manners and seemed to be fairly interested in things. [In class discussions] he was interested in what we were saying, particularly when we were having chats about family life, but he usually didn't add anything to the conversation."

Dennis went out for basketball, but his lack of dependable transportation ended that. Said basketball coach Don Genasci, "We tried to get him involved, but it was very hard because he was such a shy boy. [But] I saw him and his dad having dinner at a restaurant one day, and they were talking and seemed to have a good father-son relationship. The man seemed to be really interested in the boy."

Soon after Dennis had enrolled at Point Arena High School, Ken went to downtown Point Arena and rented apartment 6, a cramped second-floor flat in a shabby old building grandly called The Garcia Center, a structure whose first floor boasted the town barber shop and a snack bar-newsstand. Ken planned to use the apartment as an office for his bookkeeping service but he never did get it going, and since they didn't use their television set at the cabin Parnell took it to the flat and tied it into the building's community antenna, thus providing Dennis with a hideaway to which he occasionally retreated when playing hooky, whiling the days away watching "soap operas, game shows, and old movies."

Their neighbors, the Pipers, thought Ken and Dennis odd. They were never invited into the caretaker's cabin, and when they dropped by to give Dennis a ride to school the teen would always be waiting outside for them, rain or shine. William "Billie" Piper assessed Ken Parnell as one of the strangest, most secretive people he had ever met, and said that when Ken did talk to him he wouldn't look him in the eye. "Then, as soon as I turned away, he'd look right at me. It would make me feel kind of funny in a way."

Perhaps this was because of the *real* reason Parnell had moved to the Stornettas' ranch: according to former Mendocino County D.A. Joe Allen and his Chief Deputy D.A. George McClure, Ken had actually been hired by Duke Stornetta to guard the brothers' hidden commercial plots of marijuana, which they grew in secluded areas of the Mountain View Ranch. McClure went on to say that during the 1970s and early 1980s some members of the Stornetta family were known to be cultivating cannabis and that the area's resident deputy sheriff had an income "many times greater than could be accounted for by his salary, although his usual public explanation was that he had been a very shrewd real estate investor."

The officers continued their story by saying that in Mendocino County in those days old-timers and newcomers alike who grew pot were arrested, *except* for the old-timers who grew it in the area under the jurisdiction of that particular deputy. Also, the lawmen told of a close relative of the Stornetta brothers, their cousin Henry ("Stogie") Stornetta trying to hire someone to kill his wife. Stogie's plot was uncovered, and this led to an investigation in which the same deputy sheriff opened Stogie's safe under a court order, dutifully reporting to the judge that he found "no drugs and nothing unusual . . . just fifty to two hundred thousand dollars in fifties and hundreds."

Stogie was tried and convicted and served time in prison, but one of these two former peace officers facetiously mused about the source of Stogie's cash and about the purpose to which Parnell had put the good wages he'd more than likely received for services rendered to the Stornettas.

Duke Stornetta liked Parnell's strange, quiet son and often took Dennis along with him when he went deer hunting or was out in the fields putting out salt for his sheep. But, he said, "The boy would never talk. He'd answer my questions, but I could never make him talk first . . . he'd just answer my questions. Even Parnell, you know, he almost never spoke. If you would see them out in the yard at the cabin and say hello, off they would go . . . [Parnell would] just turn and walk in the cabin with the boy. Parnell was a very peculiar type of fellow, but I never realized what he did to the boy."

Behind the cabin's closed door Parnell was still committing fellatio and sodomy on Dennis, but the frequency was continuing to decline as his sexual attraction to younger boys increased. Dennis said that while they lived at the ranch Parnell tried several times to coerce him into helping to kidnap a boy from Santa Rosa. But Dennis adamantly refused to help, although it wasn't long before Parnell found one of Dennis's friends who was willing to help him kidnap a new son-*cum*-sex partner.

Sean Poorman and Dennis had known each other since the seventh grade, but the two had never been really good friends. But Dennis got to know Sean better while he was hitchhiking to school in Mendocino City, since he and Sean rode the Mendocino school bus from Elk, the village where Sean lived. A dark-haired teenager, ruggedly handsome Sean Poorman lived with his mother, Chris, his two brothers Shea and Jim, ten and thirteen, and Henry K. "Hank" Mettier, Jr., their mother's live-in boyfriend, in a rented red-wood-shingled house next to the power station on the Philo-Greenwood Road at the edge of Elk.

Shea and Jim were much brighter and more socially adept than their brother Sean, a slow learner who was easily frustrated in the classroom and in most social situations. According to Sean's sworn statement, Mettier was a small-time drug dealer, having previously been arrested and convicted for selling pot in Marin County. Now, though, his operation was much more discrete . . . and lucrative.

During the fall of 1979 Damon Carroll and Sean came to know each other better and better, and one day Damon took Sean home to meet his mother, but Kathryn Vinciguerra immediately developed a dislike for Sean and his relationship with her son. "Sean was older," she said. "He was very manipulative of Damon, and Damon kind of put Sean on a pedestal. Damon was just fetching, and would do anything for Sean. Sean was definitely the leader." Kathryn did not involve herself in picking her children's friends. However, her son's friendship with Sean was different. "I did have a dream, and it was quite vivid, about Sean having a devilish personification, and I felt very strongly that it was not a good relationship for Damon. I felt that I had to communicate it to Damon, and I did so, and a little later on Damon came to me and told me that he did understand and respect my intuition about Sean."

Kim Peace also got "bad vibes" from Sean: "Sean's brother, Jim, was a very nice guy. They were best friends. But Sean was a troublemaker and into drugs . . . always cutting school, always getting in trouble with the law. And Jim was quite the opposite. He never was in trouble."

Sean first became acquainted with Parnell in November of 1979. Said Damon, a witness to their first meeting: "They went down to the beach and talked privately. It was really strange, because Ken was bringing Dennis to spend the weekend with me and Sean. As soon as they showed up Ken said, 'Sean, I've got something to talk to you about.' And they went down to the beach and talked for a while. And it was strange, thinking what would Ken have to do with Sean, 'cause Ken really didn't know him that well."

Dennis recalls that this occurred when Ken realized that he could make money selling marijuana that he probably took surreptitiously from the Stornettas' crop he had been hired to guard. In another twist Sean said that that fall he had learned about Dennis having been kidnapped years before by Parnell and that when he told Mettier, Hank had seemed extraordinarily interested in it.

The relationship between Sean Poorman and Ken Parnell grew in mid November when, invited by Dennis but at Ken's insistence, Sean came to the cabin to spend the weekend. Said Sean, "Ken picked me up in front of the Elk Post Office. I didn't even want to go, but I had to be polite. I didn't feel like going all the way back up in the sticks. And Parnell picked me up and started talking about how he wanted me to sell some marijuana for him. Then he got into this business of how he wanted a kid. I said, 'Why don't you adopt one?' And he gave me some reason how he couldn't do that . . . it was too much of a hassle, he had to pay out some money. He said he would just like to find some kid who doesn't have a home, whose mother and father don't like him anymore, and he's thinking about running away from home.

"And I got the impression that this guy was weird . . . he's telling me how he wants a kid, just pick him up off the street and bring him up here. He wanted a little kid, about five or six years old. He wasn't putting me on, either. He was really serious cause he whipped out a fifty-dollar bill from his wallet and kind of waved it in my face and said, 'You help me find a kid and this is yours.' And I says, 'Well, I'll do my best.' I thought it was cuckoo; I mean, I thought maybe I should hit him up for a hundred," Sean laughed.

When Parnell and Sean got to Manchester, Parnell stopped at the general store and bought a fifth of Jack Daniels and then drove straight to Point Arena High School, picked up Dennis, and took both boys to the Pirates' Cove drive-in for hamburgers, fries, and Cokes. Although while they ate there was no conversation about selling marijuana or kidnapping little boys, Parnell quickly brought up both subjects again once they were on the road to the cabin. According to Sean, Dennis had told Ken that he, Sean, would be a likely person to hire to "strong-arm some kid and bring him to the cabin." On the way to the ranch Parnell explained to Sean just how he wanted the kidnapping accomplished . . . even to the point of handing Sean a bottle of the Nytol sleeping pills with which he was to dose the intended victim. Sean slipped the pills into his pocket and later used them himself.

About sunset the trio arrived at the cabin and Ken gave the boys the fifth of Jack Daniels and told them to enjoy it while he sacked out for a nap before driving to his graveyard shift at The Palace Hotel. Although Dennis occasionally drank beer and hard liquor on his own, beginning that night Parnell not only allowed his son to drink whiskey in his presence but often purchased it for him.

When Ken returned the next morning he woke the groggy teenagers from their alcohol-induced slumber and drove them to Elk, dropping Sean off at the post office before taking Dennis south to Point Arena High. All the way into Elk, Ken reminded Sean of his offer: "Fifty dollars for a kid, and another twenty if you bring this kid up in a couple days." And Dennis saw Ken hand Sean a bunch of dime baggies of pot to sell when he got out at Elk, admonishing him not to spend the proceeds.

For Dennis, Christmas 1979 was quiet and very melancholy. For the first time in several years he found himself repeatedly thinking about his own parents, brother, and sisters in Merced, and sorely wishing that he was back there with them.

When the New Year began Parnell ended his sex acts with his son—"on about January third or fourth" Dennis recalls—but increased his efforts to kidnap a new, younger sex partner and possibly, it had begun to appear, rid himself of Dennis.

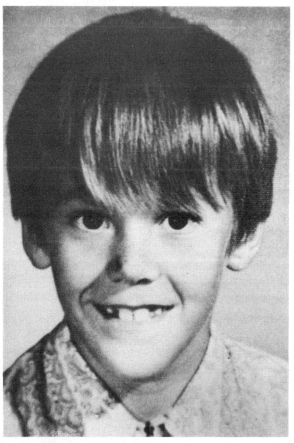

Steven's second-grade school photograph from Charles Wright Elementary School in Merced, California (1972). (*Courtesy of the* Merced Sun-Star)

Steven (in the middle, behind Santa Claus) attends a friend's birthday party. This was the last picture taken of him before he was kidnapped (December 3, 1972).

Steven scrawled his name on his family's garage wall December 1972 . . . the day before he was kidnapped by Kenneth Parnell.

Del and Kay Stayner pose for the author outside the Fishermen's Grotto Restaurant on San Francisco's Fisherman's Wharf on March 4, 1980, just two days after Steven returned home.

Parnell is sullen in this mugshot taken by Ukiah Police shortly after his arrest on March 2, 1980.

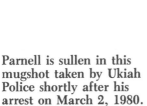

Edward Ervin Murphy smokes a hand-rolled cigarette in his cluttered third-floor room in the residential Hotel Covel in downtown Modesto, California.

The service station in Yosemite Parkway in Merced, California, where Parnell and Murphy kidnapped Steven on December 4, 1972 . . . just three blocks from Steven's home. The station wagon is parked in the same spot where Parnell drove up and convinced Steven to get into his car.

Parnell lived in the Curry Company's dorm F (employee housing) in Yosemite National Park. He hid the boy in his room there for several days.

Nineteen-year-old Steven poses in the doorway of room 18 at the Tropicana Motel in Santa Rosa, California, where he and Parnell spent their first Christmas together in 1972.

Steven revisits the old rental trailer where he lived with Parnell at the Mt. Taylor Trailer Park in Santa Rosa, California.

Registered as "Dennis Parnell" in sixth grade, Steven (last row, fifth from the right) poses for this class photo. Four of the other boys in his class were victims of Kenneth Parnell's attentions as well. (*Courtesy of Bill Patton.*)

Steven had lived as "Dennis Parnell" for five years when this seventh-grade school picture was taken. (*Courtesy of the Stayner Family.*)

Kenneth Parnell and his "son," Dennis, pose for a photo at the home of his landlady, Tyne Cordeiro, near Comptche, California, in 1978. (*Courtesy of Tyne Cordeiro.*)

This is the caretaker's stark cabin at the Mountain View Ranch where Steven lived with Parnell—without electricity or indoor plumbing—from July 1979 until March 1, 1980.

Steven stands in front of the Mountain View cabin where he lived with Parnell from July 1979 until March 1, 1980.

Some of the evidence successfully used by Mendocino County to prosecute Parnell in the kidnapping of Timmy White: Timmy's underwear and boots, the bottle of sleeping pills used to drug him, the hair coloring used to dye his hair, and the Peterbilt cap worn during the kidnapping by Sean Poorman.

Barbara Matthias's son Lloyd was sixteen when the author interviewed him outside Barbara and John Allen's remote trailer home in northern Mendocino County.

Dave Johnson was Ukiah's police chief when Timmy disappeared on Valentine's Day 1980.

Pat Hallford was the Merced County District Attorney who successfully prosecuted Parnell and Murphy for the 1972 kidnapping of Steven Stayner.

Timmy White and his mother Angela are shown here on the night they were reunited at the Ukiah Police Station. (*Courtesy of the White Family Collection.*)

Steven and Timmy as they appeared at the end of their press conference, the morning of their return. This photograph appeared on the front page of major newspapers around the world. (*John Storey*/San Francisco Chronicle.)

Steven poses with his youngest sister, Cory, at the Fishermen's Grotto Restaurant on Fisherman's Wharf in San Francisco, California, when he and the author first met, March 4, 1980, just two days after he returned home.

Timmy White beams at Steven after presenting him with a check for $15,000 as his reward for returning him to his parents. (*AP/Wide World Photos.*)

The summer after his safe return home, fifteen-year-old Steven cradles his beloved Manchester Terrier, Queenie, which was given to him by Parnell. To the left behind Steven is his name, which he had scrawled on the garage wall the day before he was kidnapped.

The Stayner family in front of their house at 1655 Bette Street in Merced, the same house they lived in when Steven was kidnapped (left to right, Cory, Jody, Steven, Cindy, Cary, Kay, and Del).

On June 22, 1981, Steven bravely testified at Parnell's trial for kidnapping Timmy White. (*AP/Wide World Photos.*)

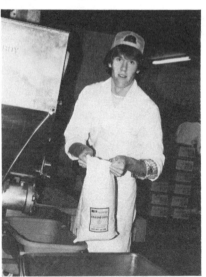

During the summer of 1984, Steven worked bagging hamburger at the Richwood Meat Company plant between Merced and Atwater, California. On September 17, 1989, he was killed in a motorcycle-automobile accident in front of the plant.

On June 13, 1985, Steven married Jody Edmonton in Atwater, California. (*AP/Wide World Photos.*)

Steven Stayner holds his son Steven Gregory II, left, and daughter Ashley. (*Mike Blaesser*/Merced Sun-Star)

Chapter Eight

The Valentine's Day Kidnapping

"Get the kid!"

By early February 1980 Sean Poorman had still not kidnapped a young boy for Parnell and brought him to the remote cabin . . . but he had smoked up fifty dollars' worth of Parnell's pot and Ken was not happy. Already that year Ken had forced a very reluctant Dennis to accompany him to Santa Rosa on a "shopping trip" for another "son." Said Dennis, "It was the same thing"—as the attempts in 1975—"identical, exactly. We were there a couple of hours."

On Wednesday, February 13, Parnell again picked up Sean in Elk and drove straight to his cabin by way of Boonville, leaving Dennis to take the Point Arena school bus and then ride the rest of the way home with the Pipers. According to Dennis, when he arrived at the cabin that afternoon, "Parnell told Sean right in front of me, 'Dennis is just no help at all. He never wants to help me.' And it made me mad. He said that

I was worthless, and at the time I didn't know what he was talking about, but that made me so mad that I didn't speak to Parnell for the rest of the day. I was insulted." Later that evening Parnell said that they were going to Ukiah the next morning to pick up a box spring at a garage sale and he needed Sean's help to load the box spring.

But Dennis knew better. Parnell had taken him and Sean into Ukiah several times early that month to follow one particular five-year-old boy. That boy's name was Timmy White.

After fixing and eating sandwiches for supper, Dennis and Sean started pulling on yet another fifth of Jack Daniels, topping this off with a "nightcap" marijuana joint outside before coming back inside about 8 P.M. and falling into a stuporous alcohol-and-drug-induced slumber.

Parnell had told Sean to wake him up at nine, but both boys were dead to the world by then and Parnell slept on until eleven, when he awoke with a start. Cursing, he angrily shook Sean awake, pulled on his shoes, and grabbed his partner-in-crime-to-be by the sleeve, sprinting out the door to his old Maverick. The car coughed alive and the pair roared off into the night.

They arrived at the hotel at midnight and Parnell apologized profusely to the evening desk clerk for his tardiness. Unconcerned, Sean watched a movie on the lobby TV. Later Sean curled up behind the front desk at Parnell's feet and fell asleep. At six-thirty the next morning, Valentine's Day, Parnell woke up Sean and sent him out for donuts and coffee. Then, when he got off at eight, he took Sean to McDonald's and over pancakes and sausage went over his kidnapping plans, twice having to spell out for the teenager exactly what role he was to play. About eight-thirty they left and went to scope out the "particular boy" among the children entering Yokayo Elementary.

Failing to spot him, Parnell told Sean they would try again later, and they began a tour of garage sales advertised in the *Ukiah Daily Journal*. Sean said that Parnell bought a black briefcase for him at one and, inexplicably, little girl's clothes at another. Then they went to the Salvation Army thrift shop, where Parnell bought a box spring but did not take it with him. The Thrifty Drug store was their next stop, where Parnell bought a small bottle of Nytol sleeping pills and handed them to Sean. By then it was a little past eleven. Parnell drove back to Yokayo Elementary and the pair began again to troll South Dora Street for their intended victim, Sean remarking that at first they saw youngsters who had gotten out at eleven walking home, including a little boy whose Slinky toy he helped to retrieve from a sewer drain. But it was not until the Yokayo kindergartners got out at eleven-thirty that the two kidnappers began their task in earnest.

Driving south past the school they saw their intended victim, delicate, platinum-blond, five-year-old Timmy White walking with classmate Christy Ryan. Parnell drove to Luce Street, made a quick left turn, headed east a short distance, and then made a rapid U-turn in his Maverick, coming to a stop by the curb.

Watching his prey carefully, Parnell anxiously reminded Sean of his role: get out, fake checking the right rear tire, ask for Timmy's help, grab Timmy, quickly get into the backseat with the boy, and close the door behind him as Parnell sped off. Sean did almost as instructed: when Timmy walked by alone, he asked him to hold the tire's valve stem to keep it from leaking air. Timmy emphatically said "No!" and continued on his way.

Not wanting to go after the boy, Sean went back to the car. But Parnell screamed and cursed at his accomplice to "Get the kid!" and so Sean ran after Timmy. Timmy ran too, but he was no match for the teenager. When Sean caught up to him the five-year-old had tightly wrapped his arms around a chain-link fence along the sidewalk, but Sean quickly slipped his arms under the youngster's and violently wrenched the little boy from the fence, ran back to the car carrying him, and threw the screaming, kicking child through the car's open right-hand door and onto the backseat.

Slamming the door behind him, Sean swiftly covered Timmy with an old green blanket as Parnell drove off, stopped briefly at the corner, turned right, drove directly past Timmy's school, and made another quick right to South State Street, down which he accessed the freeway and a short distance later the road to Boonville.

Timmy asked Parnell and Sean what was happening and where they were taking him. Parnell told him his mother was sick and in the same instant Sean said that they were taking him to a dentist. Timmy was confused by their conflicting answers but didn't ask anymore questions because he was afraid.

By the time they reached the freeway, Sean had given Timmy a sleeping pill and fruit punch to wash it down. Then he made the frightened little boy lie back down while he himself hunkered below the car's windows.

Less than thirty minutes later, southwest of Boonville on the Mountain View Ranch Road, Parnell roared up behind Duke Stornetta, who was taking his time, headed in the same direction. Said Duke, "Parnell passed me this side of Boonville—you know where the high school is?—and he was just a-flying. And so I stepped on it and I said to myself, 'I wonder what he is in a hurry for?' And as far as I could tell, it was just him alone. And when I got to the cabin, he was already gone into the house. You know, I didn't see him . . . he just outran me."

When Parnell reached the cabin he carried Timmy inside while Sean followed with the black briefcase Parnell had bought for him. At the kitchen table Sean quickly loaded his briefcase with two bottles of Jack Daniels that Parnell had given him in partial payment for his role in the kidnapping. Then he departed the cabin, leaving behind the black Peterbilt "gimmie" cap Parnell had made him wear during their crime, the teenager's only disguise.

Thirty minutes later, at the crest of the hill just past the Pipers' place, Sean flagged down Billie Piper for a ride to the Coast Highway. Remarked Billie, "He talked about the movie he was watching on TV with Parnell the night before. I mean, I don't think the kidnapping fazed him a bit, I really don't. He was a kid who to me looked like he was out of it all the time."

Without a word to Timmy, Parnell removed the terrified boy's clothes, put them in a sack, hid it in the closet, and dressed his new "son" in blue pajama bottoms and a brown shirt bought at one of the garage sales . . . apparently deciding not to disguise Timmy as a girl, his original plan for the little girl's clothes he'd bought. Then he laid Timmy down on his bed for a nap and stretched himself out beside his new son. As three o'clock approached, Parnell got up, carried Timmy out to the Maverick, and drove down to the coast to get Dennis.

"Parnell picked me up down at the bus stop, and that's when Timmy was in the back of the car," Dennis recalled. "He was asleep. I looked and just said to myself, 'Sure, ah ha . . . box springs, ah, yeah . . . right.' I didn't say nothin' to Parnell, and he didn't say nothin' to me, either. We just drove up to the cabin, I got out and walked up to the cabin, and Parnell went around and took Timmy out and brought him back inside and laid him on my bed."

With Timmy stretched out on his bed, and Dennis having only a spring-sprung couch on which to relax, seeds of jealousy were quickly sown in Parnell's oldest "son." Dennis selected a book from the stack Parnell had bought for him and, seething, flopped down to read it. At supper, Dennis recalled: "I was kinda' disgusted with the fact that Timmy was griping about what was being served. We was having a type of cube steak and mashed potatoes and white gravy. And Timmy didn't like the white gravy—'I don't like white gravy, I like brown gravy!'—and Parnell didn't like that either. So I ate my dinner real fast and then I went out to the barn. That was my place out there, at the barn. I'd just sit out there, or climb around in the trees, or I'd go down to the creek, or go around to the other side of the mountain and eat some apples. I'd go along the trails in back of the cabin because by then I hadn't even gone on all the trails. I liked going through the woods."

By the time Parnell and his two "sons" had returned to their cabin, all hell had broken loose back in Ukiah. A professional in every sense of the word, steely-blue-eyed Ukiah Police Chief David Johnson said of the series of events, "We got the call about twelve-thirty that day from Mrs. White saying that her son had not arrived at the babysitter's house. So we sent an officer down to take an initial report. Then we had two or three officers in the area looking for the kid, but not really too seriously until about three o'clock, when it was evident that maybe something had really happened to him."

At this point additional officers were pressed into the search; and as time passed, off-duty officers, then reserve officers, and by dark even police cadets were busily combing Ukiah's neighborhoods. Timmy's steps were retraced to the point where he and Christy Ryan had parted at the intersection of South Dora and Luce. "From that point on," Chief Johnson sighed, "it was an absolute mystery as to what happened to him because nobody saw anything. No one heard anything, even though there were people living there. One woman was ironing clothes by her front window right where it happened, but she didn't see a thing, didn't hear a thing. And it's actually incredible that no one saw what happened."

Timmy lived with his mother, Angela, an attractive, vivacious, blond native of England, and her slender, stoic second husband, Jim White. Timmy had one sister, Nicole, aged six. Timmy's mother and Jim had at first lived together several years and, when they married the previous year, Jim had adopted both children. Their home was seven miles south of Ukiah on Blue Oak Drive in middle-class Russian River Estates. Also the previous year, Angela began work at the Mendocino County Board of Realtors and Timmy began kindergarten at Yokayo, the public elementary school almost across the street from St. Mary's, the Roman Catholic school where Nicole was a first-grader. The previous fall the Whites had found a small private day care center run by Diane Crawford in her home on South Street, just a few blocks from their children's schools and a short walk for Timmy after his half-day kindergarten class.

On her way to work that Valentine's Day morning, Angela dropped her son off at school. At 11:50 A.M. Diane Crawford called to speak with Angela at work, but since she was on a long-distance call, Angela had a fellow worker tell Diane that she would call her back shortly. A few minutes later Jim walked in with sandwiches for their lunch. Still on the long-distance call, Angela scribbled a note to Jim telling him to call Diane.

"Jim went out to the outer office and dialed Diane's phone number," Angela recalled, "and he was talking to her, and I could hear him, and I finished my phone conversation and hung up. And he walked to the door and said, 'Timmy's not home from school yet. I'm going to go track him down.' And I said, 'Okay.' "

At that point Angela was not worried about her son, reasoning that since it was Valentine's Day, he had probably stayed late at school for a class party and

Diane would be calling her shortly to let her know that he had just arrived.

Angela suddenly became concerned, however, when she looked at her watch and realized that Timmy got out at 11:30, not 12:00, as she had first thought, and it was now after 12:00. Said she, "Then I scribbled a note to pin on the door for my assistant because we never close the office for lunch, and I locked up and left. I drove by Diane's house on the way to the school, and she was standing at her window and she shook her head no, and so I didn't even bother stopping, I just went on up to the school."

When Angela arrived at Timmy's school she went straight to the principal's office, where she found the principal telling Jim that Timmy's class had gotten out on time. At this Angela begged Jim to call the police, but the principal asked her to wait while he went outside and checked a nearby field where children sometimes played. "But when he went out," Angela said, "I told Jim, 'No, let's call the police,' because Timmy wasn't an adventuresome little boy and he wouldn't have gone off with a friend or anything.

"So we called the police from right there. They really didn't know what to do . . . they took the information, but that was really about it. And so we started driving around town as soon as we got back to the car. And we turned on the car radio and we heard Tim's description over the radio right away. It was real fast because Diane had called the local radio station right away . . . as soon as Timmy hadn't arrived.

"We kept driving around and looking and going back to Diane's house, and then Nickie got out of school and we made sure she got to Diane's, and we

were just driving around and around, and it was driz-
zling and it was an awful day. [Ironically, this was almost identical to the weather the day of Dennis's
kidnapping.] We were just driving and asking and
looking and trying to see if anybody had seen Timmy.''

Jim and Angela drove for hours that afternoon, asking everybody they saw if they had seen Timmy, occasionally returning to Diane's, checking their home,
and then resuming their driving and searching.

At 4:00 a policeman flagged them down and asked
them to go to the police station to file a report on
Timmy's disappearance. When they arrived at the station, Chief Johnson met them but he had nothing new
to tell them and, after making a detailed, dishearten-
ing report on their missing son, a dejected Jim and
Angela returned home.

At that time Angela's British parents were on holiday in the States, and after a visit with her sister in Los
Angeles were making a sightseeing auto trip up the
California coast. They were to arrive in Ukiah in a day
or two, but now it was imperative that they be reached
immediately. Through her sister, Angela located them
at a motel in Morro Bay and, on hearing the news,
they drove 350 miles through the night to be with their
daughter and son-in-law.

Angela described her emotions and routine while
Timmy was missing, "I remember my parents coming,
and then I really don't remember that night after that.
But you know, when Tim was gone, I slept well the
entire time. [Usually] I'll get up three or four times
in the middle of the night to use the bathroom . . .
it's just habit with me. But when Tim was gone, I used
to sleep all through the night. I wanted to go to bed

early, and I would sleep well. Then when I would wake up I would feel rested. You know, I never dreamt anything, but when Timmy came back, I went through a period when I'd wake up crying."

Added Jim, "I slept well, too. You know, I was mentally exhausted at night, and Angela thought at one time it was a defense mechanism—get to sleep and you can't think about it or worry about it—and you sleep."

Angela had an extension of her home telephone installed at her office and went back to work the next week, as did Jim . . . but, she said, "I really didn't want to because I was so afraid that, even if you resume your regular life, it is like you're resuming it without Timmy and everybody would forget. And I didn't want to get back to normal because I didn't feel normal. But I couldn't mourn him because I didn't want to think anything had happened to him. It was awful."

Usually, Diane Crawford stood on her front porch and watched for Timmy when he was due home from school, but she couldn't see more than the last fifty feet of Luce Street that Timmy walked down before turning onto her street, and Timmy's kidnapping had occurred hundreds of feet up the street. As she recollected, "I had other little kids at that time, and we would just wait until he came home so we could have lunch together. And when he didn't show up on time, I went up to my corner three times . . . but I didn't see anything that day. No panic, though, because I thought, well, it's Valentine's Day. And, too, he was a slow walker. But then about ten minutes 'til twelve—which would have made him about ten minutes later than he had ever been before—I phoned Angie at her office."

On Saturday, February 16, two days after Timmy disappeared, tracking dogs were brought up from Sacramento to scour the ten-square-block neighborhood between Yokayo Elementary and the Crawford home, but they couldn't pick up a scent because it had rained the previous three days. Then the trackers took the dogs into Diane's home to sniff out the closets and under the beds, but they couldn't detect Timmy's scent; and even a circuit with the dogs south of Ukiah along the Russian River near Timmy's home was equally fruitless.

"I continued to babysit, but the kids were upset," Diane said. "It was a real helpless feeling when Jim and Angie would come by to get Nickie, or phone me, and they hadn't found Timmy. But . . . well, what else can you do?" Diane sighed.

Besides the tracking dogs, Smith Air Service provided a helicopter for Ukiah policemen searching the remote hills west of town, but the persistent rain repeatedly washed grease from the rotor's bearings and cut the flights short. Radio and television stations from Ukiah to San Francisco alerted their listeners and viewers to Timmy's disappearance with information and photographs of the blond five-year-old. Also, some newspapers were very helpful, whereas others wouldn't help at all. Said Angela incredulously, "They wouldn't run a picture, and we had to pay money to have it done!"

Within a couple of days Jim and Angela's schedule at home had settled into a routine of addressing envelopes to mail out Missing flyers of their towheaded son with the faithful help of relatives and neighbors. Said Jim, "Every day we'd go out and drive somewhere, watch the river . . ." he trailed off. "We stayed around our house and around the city. Then we'd stop and go back home and start up writing letters and sending out posters again."

Beginning with the first night, Parnell had Timmy sleep with him. Timmy did not like it, even though, as he recalls, he always wore underpants or pajamas and Parnell never even attempted to fondle or molest him. But Timmy felt very strange sleeping next to this man he did not know, the odd man who had kidnapped him.

Before the kidnapping Parnell had tried to employ a babysitter "for a small child" in Ukiah. However, everyone with whom he spoke turned him down because of the distance to the cabin. Therefore, each day Timmy was left alone in the cabin from the time Dennis left for school until Parnell returned from his graveyard shift at The Palace Hotel. Usually, though he did not like doing it, Dennis followed Parnell's instructions and gave his "little brother" a Nytol sleeping tablet just before he left for school. But Timmy recalls rarely sleeping after Dennis departed: "Mostly I just sat there. I saw the phone, and I thought about trying to get away, but I didn't because I was afraid that Parnell would do something to me." (But Timmy could not have used the phone for Parnell kept a dial lock on it.) However, Timmy does not recall any sexual abuse, fondling, or photographs—nude or otherwise.

Dennis was afraid Parnell would sexually assault Timmy while he was at school, and so he began returning from Point Arena High School at noon each day. Confirmed Duke Stornetta, "One day, while Parnell had the little boy there, I passed Dennis as I was driving from Ukiah to our place on the coast. It was about twelve noon, and he was walking up the hill by the coast, so I turned around and went back and gave him a ride to the cabin. I says, 'Dennis, how come you aren't in school?' And he says, 'I didn't feel like going to school . . . I'm going home.' "

Billie Piper remarked, "Dennis was pretty regular going to school until he got mixed up with that other boy. Then, I'd take him to school and he'd come right back." One day, after he had noticed Dennis returning home about noon, Piper said he drove by and, "There was a small boy playing on that little hill by the cabin. And Dennis was out on the side of the road about half a mile away on his bike. Parnell's car wasn't at the cabin, but I figured maybe they had a friend visiting out there, and maybe the friend had a little boy."

As with Dennis years before, Parnell decided that one of the easiest ways to alter Timmy's appearance was to dye the boy's distinctive hair . . . from platinum blond to dark brown. So, eleven days after the kidnapping Parnell stopped in Ukiah at Thrifty Drug on his way home from work and bought a bottle of dark brown Clairol Nice 'n' Easy hair coloring. When he arrived home, Timmy was asleep. He woke him up. Timmy says, "He told me that he was going to dye my hair so people wouldn't recognize me and take me back." After he was finished, Parnell walked Timmy out back to the shower stall and had the youngster bathe and shampoo his hair.

Parnell kept Timmy hidden at the cabin the whole

time. But after changing Timmy's hair color, Parnell felt confident enough about the disguise to take the boy with him to pick up Dennis at Point Arena High. When Dennis got in the car, Parnell smirked to his oldest son, "How do you like his hair?"

Hurtful memories flooded his mind as a not-pleased Dennis responded through gritted teeth, "It's all right, I guess."

"Well, I don't think it's dark enough." Parnell superciliously smiled. "I got some more dye at the house and we're gonna dye it again."

"That's nice," Dennis parried with angry sarcasm.

Then Parnell surprised both boys by asking, "You want to go to Pirates' Cove and have a hamburger?"

"Sure!" was their joint response, and off they went.

A Point Arena friend of Dennis's, Marsha Beall, remembered the incident. "My cousins own the Pirates' Cove and one of them, Darla Reynolds, said that when they came in she looked at the little boy and she thought, 'Wow! He really resembles that little boy in the newspaper [referring to Timmy's picture in *The Ukiah Daily Journal*].' But you know how you think of something and then you take a second look and go, 'Oh, but I don't want to get involved.' "

Also, a couple of days after the dinner at Pirates' Cove, on February 27, Kim Peace saw Dennis and Timmy sitting in Parnell's car in the parking lot at the Manchester General Store. Then, that same evening, when she saw Timmy's picture in the newspaper, Kim recalled, "I kept thinking to myself, 'Where had I seen that little kid before?' And then it finally dawned on me that that was the little kid I had seen with Dennis in the parking lot in Manchester!"

Like Dennis before him, Timmy spent some of his time playing with small plastic toys Ken had bought at a flea market. But when Dennis was home the two often went across the road to the barn to feed Dennis's rabbits and chickens, climb the trees, and play hide-and-seek inside the barn and around the shearing shed and holding pens. As the two boys got to know each other better, Dennis told Timmy about his own life. Recalled Timmy, "He said he was my age and he got kidnapped by Parnell." And that, said Timmy, really scared him, for he couldn't even imagine himself as old as Dennis and still living with Parnell.

Dennis felt that sooner or later Parnell would sexually assault Timmy, and so the teenager began carrying his Bowie knife strapped to his side or hidden inside his boot. Ironically, Parnell was also concerned about the little boy's welfare and warned Timmy "Not to go with anyone and not to talk to strangers."

By the fourth day of his ordeal Timmy remembers that he considered Dennis to be "like a big brother" and he trusted the teenager enough to ask him to take him home. Dennis agreed to do so, but persistent rains and a lack of vehicles along the Boonville to Manchester road out front, plus Parnell's daytime presence at the cabin, caused a number of delays in Dennis's planned effort.

In Ukiah the investigation continued. But police had no clues and were at a virtual dead end trying to solve Timmy's disappearance. Detective Sergeant Dennis Marcheschi, now in charge of the investigation, said, "I think I probably lived with his family during that time, going over all his habits, where he went, what kind of food he enjoyed, his sleep patterns . . . I don't think there was anything about Timmy that I didn't know.

"Then, toward the end of the second week, Dick Finn from the D.A.'s office flew with me to Los Angeles to interview Timmy's natural father down there, and we spent the next four or five days contacting and interviewing every family member in the L.A. area. The Ventura County sheriff's office even gave us an office and all of the help in the world. They set up communications with all the family members, too. But still we had absolutely zero."

Filled in Chief Johnson, "In the meantime we had the sheriff's Aero Squadron activated, and they flew thirty-five or forty hours searching for Timmy. The creeks were running pretty good at that time and so they were searched, but still nothing. He had absolutely vanished right off the face of the earth. No ransom note had showed up, and we had searched everywhere and found nothing. So it became pretty apparent at that point that it was a kidnapping and not just a disappearance."

Even with Timmy concealed at his cabin, Parnell continued his habit of having a beer at the Samoa Club every morning after work. Jim Bertain, the bar's owner, said, "He used to sit in here every morning and we would be talking about the White kid. We'd be wondering what happened to him, and Parnell suggested that maybe he got washed away in a creek."

Also while Timmy was at the cabin, another inter-

esting yet confusing twist occurred when Dennis telephoned Damon and invited him to come to the cabin
for the weekend, Damon's impression being that Dennis wanted to do *anything* to get Timmy out of his
hair . . . or, perhaps, get someone else to take Timmy
home. "I remember this clear. This was on a Thursday
[February 28] that I talked to Dennis, and he wanted
me to come spend the weekend. I knew that Timmy
White was there because Sean had told me. I didn't
want to have anything to do with it, cause, like, if for
some reason Ken got the idea I knew, I'd be in big
trouble."

Even though Damon declined the invitation, he
phoned Dennis back the next night and told him
about the $15,000 reward that was being offered for
Timmy's safe return. He said that he then encouraged
Dennis to take Timmy into Ukiah himself and claim
the money, then reflected, "I should have gone out
there 'cause he probably wanted me to help him return the kid. Then I could have got the $15,000 re-
ward."

But even without Damon's encouragement Dennis
had already made plans to return Timmy to Ukiah,
his prime motivation having nothing to do with the
reward. He has never directly admitted it, but Dennis's
later actions and remarks point directly to a sibling
rivalry centering on the attention Parnell was lavish-
ing on Timmy. Dennis had been thwarted one evening
by Parnell's failure to go to work, and other evenings
by the persistent rain when he and Timmy got soaked
to the skin.

However, Dennis had no way of knowing Parnell
planned to kill him and then, with help from a teenage

acquaintance of Dennis, bury his body in a grave he and his accomplice had already dug along the upper, uninhabited reaches of the Garcia River. That done, Parnell would pull up stakes and move with Timmy to the cabin in Arkansas. But during the last two weeks of February 1980, the same winter rains made it impossible to access the remote upper reaches of the Garcia River, and delayed his plan.

As Saturday, March 1 dawned, Sergeant Marcheschi left southern California, driving north to follow up on yet another tip about Timmy's disappearance, this time a psychic in San Jose suggested by the F.B.I. As the sun came up Marcheschi departed Los Angeles in a repaired Ukiah Fire Department car he had picked up in L.A. and, as he drove, mentally reviewed the case, arriving in San Jose late that afternoon for his meeting with the psychic.

Recounted Marcheschi about the session, "She had Parnell's physical stature, hair, age, the fact that he had been an abused child and had served time for the same offense. Too, she described the cabin and that there were animals around it, but by that time both of us were mentally exhausted, and so I went to bed."

Chapter Nine

Nightfall, March 1, 1980

"Is my dad still alive?"

The sun set a little past six that Saturday. Because of the typical, rainy, wintery coastal weather, it was the first sunset that Dennis and Timmy had seen since Timmy's kidnapping on Valentine's Day. With the rainclouds gone, the dark pavement in front of the cramped old cabin reflected the glistening twilight, and with his dad almost ready to leave for work, Dennis was thinking of his plan to finally get Timmy back home.

The boys' dad, Ken, usually slept from late afternoon until nine at night, but today he had gone to sleep just after lunch and was up before sunset. For seven months he had been the graveyard shift desk clerk at The Palace Hotel in Ukiah, but tonight he would start his new position as the hotel's security guard. A punctual man, Ken was going to make certain that he arrived early enough to review his duties with the evening manager.

As was his habit, as soon as Ken awoke, he had a cup

of instant coffee Dennis had fixed him with super-heated water from the kitchen tap. Now, several cups and chain-smoked Camels later, the boys' dad was ready to leave. Characteristically saying little to his sons, Kenneth Parnell went out the front door, climbed into his seven-year-old white-over-purple Ford Maverick, and drove off east and into the gathering dusk for his hour-long commute over the winding, twisting county road toward the Anderson Valley, Boonville, and Mendocino's county seat.

Outwardly, Dennis was tranquil as he peered through the cabin window and saw his dad depart. But for several minutes he continued to stare contemplatively at the now-deserted road, lost in thought . . . thought about his own family in Merced, about the hell he had been through over the past seven years, about his determination that the same fate would not befall Timmy, about his fears of what lay ahead for him that night, and about his anger at his dad for the attention he had begun to give his new little brother.

Turning his attention to Timmy, Dennis watched as the grubby little boy sat cross-legged in the middle of Parnell's bed, "reading" his comic books. In some ways the teenager had begun to like the slight, now-brunet five-year-old and to care about his safety. Dennis was reasonably sure that Parnell had yet to make a sexual move on Timmy, but just the thought of it made the teenager shudder visibly.

Abruptly Dennis turned away from the approaching dark outside and went to the kitchen counter and made bologna sandwiches for their supper. He laid out the meal on the small kitchen table, along with bananas and milk, and called Timmy to come and eat.

Silently the two consumed what they knew without speaking would be their last meal at the remote one-room cabin they called home.

As he got up from the table, Dennis told Timmy to put on his gray-green jacket against the damp, chill breezes from the coast, and the teenager donned his dirty gray hooded sweatshirt. Dennis then went to the bureau which he shared with his father and pulled his Bowie knife from under the rumpled pile of clothes in his drawer, swiftly slipping its sheathed blade out of sight into his right boot. Then he knelt by his trembling Manchester Terrier, Queenie—his constant companion throughout his seven-year ordeal—and assured her that he would come back for her. Standing abruptly, Dennis took Timmy firmly by the hand and without looking back guided the boy out the front door and onto the tiny porch.

Closing the door behind him, Dennis scooped Timmy into his arms and briskly cut through the damp grass in front of the cabin before angling across the wet pavement toward the barn. A fleeting pang of fear hit the teenager as he passed the ranch house and for an instant thought about how angry Parnell would be if he should suddenly return home to find his sons out on the road, trying to escape. But Dennis had made up his mind to get Timmy back to his family and, well, he really didn't know what he would do then . . . but that decision would just have to wait. They had set out, and that was enough to worry about for now.

Remembering their previous attempts to hitchhike into Ukiah—with Timmy complaining about being cold, wet, and hungry—Dennis quickened his pace to put as much distance as possible between them and the cabin before Timmy's inevitable, "Ohhhh! I want to go inside!"

Glancing over his shoulder every few seconds, his heart pounding loudly as it crept up his throat, Dennis felt he had walked for miles. However, they were only a quarter of a mile from the cabin, up the hill and around the bend. Again he looked back fearfully and was startled to see approaching headlights reflecting off the distant wet pavement. He froze in fear for a moment before setting Timmy down in front of him and haltingly sticking out his thumb. It took an eternity and seemed an apparition, but the car finally drew near and braked to a halt. Dennis grabbed Timmy's hand and excitedly ran to the passenger door. When he jerked it open, a smiling brown face illuminated by the dash greeted him with, *"Buenos noches!"* Confused but not hesitating at this stroke of luck, the boys climbed in. But once inside, Timmy was frightened, remarking later, "I thought that this guy was going to kidnap me, too!"

But Timmy nestled into the safety of Dennis's lap as his big brother-protector shut the door and their Samaritan drove them off toward Boonville and safety, Dennis feeling a deep sense of relief that they were finally on their way.

The Mexican national knew little English, and therefore communication with him was difficult, but Dennis did understand that he was following a friend who was having car trouble and, almost unbelievably, he was following his friend all the way into Ukiah!

As they twisted through the deep, brooding red-wood forests east of the ranch, Dennis briefly ex-

plained to the driver that he and his little brother were
on their way from Point Arena to their home in Ukiah.
The mahogany face nodded and smiled, whether in
understanding or kindness Dennis did not know.

On through the pitch-black night they drove, following the confining road as it dropped down into a
canyon and threaded itself across the high, narrow
Rancheria Creek bridge before finally curling down
the eastern side of the first coastal mountain range
and entering the broad, clear-cut Anderson Valley.

The three figures in the front seat of the battered
old Volkswagen square-back stared silently at the road
ahead, Dennis alone glancing briefly to the left as they
passed the Boonville Airport where he had once
wanted to attend Anderson Valley High School's
popular pilot training program. Reaching California
128, they turned right and drove into the sleepy agricultural community of Boonville, where the Mexican
pulled up behind his friend's car across from The
Horn of Zeese—Cup of Coffee—Restaurant . . . that
odd little language, Dennis thought, that the Boonters
(natives) used. Some of his friends could actually
speak this odd language which their forefathers de-
vised over a hundred years before to converse secretly
when in the presence of outsiders.

As the boys sat mute in the car, waiting for their
savior to finish checking his friend's car, Dennis became lost in a mental exercise as he reflected on his
mission with Timmy, his fear of Parnell, what he was
going to do once he had liberated Timmy, and his
hidden Bowie knife—a *barlow,* the Boonters would call
it—this making him a little *collar jumpy* (nervous). But

the *tweed* sitting on his lap was innocently ignorant of his big brother's trepidation about what lay ahead.

Suddenly Dennis's ruminations were cut short, for after only a few minutes—It had seemed an entire evening to him—the Mexican was back in the car and they were soon continuing through Boonville toward the road's intersection with California 253 to Ukiah.

With their turn south they were again traversing a twisting, curving road, albeit a bit wider and better paved, as they climbed another coastal range and left behind the peaceful farms of the Anderson Valley. As Dennis settled back in the front seat and comfortingly wrapped his arms around Timmy's waist—as much to meet his own emotional needs as Timmy's—a wave of genuine care, concern, and determination to succeed swept over him as he recalled his feelings of love for his own younger siblings.

Retracing the route in June 1984, Dennis said, "We got over the last hill going into Ukiah and it really scared me, because I was trying to think about what I would do when we got there. I thought, 'It's me against the world. I'm alone now. There's no one to turn to and no one to help me make the decisions.' The main object and most important thing was to get Timmy home safe and sound. I just didn't think about doing anything else then. I knew that I'd be on the run then, but I didn't want to even think about it.

"The only person that I had to talk to was Timmy, and I didn't want to do that in front of this guy. I didn't know for sure how much English he could understand or nothin'. But then we started up South State Street and into Ukiah, and Timmy turns his head and whispers to me that we're near his babysitter's, and that's where he wants to go. So I told the guy to let us out by The Bottle Shoppe. Then Timmy and me walked over to where he said his babysitter lived, but nobody was home."

Timmy then told Dennis that he lived south of town, so they went back to South State Street and began trekking south. Once they reached the freeway, Timmy seemed totally lost, and Dennis became convinced that the five-year-old didn't know *where* he lived. They turned around and walked back north, stopping at a phone booth where the teenager looked up the address of the Ukiah Police Station. They continued north toward the police station and along the way double-checked Diane Crawford's home, but still no one was home.

At East Standley Street they turned east toward the police station, briefly passing along the southeast corner of The Palace Hotel as Dennis's heart jumped into his throat while he momentarily considered his options should Parnell see them. Dennis recalled, "Well, at that time I was thinking about using the knife on him if he came [at me]. I don't know if I would have or not, but that's what I was thinking at the time. I didn't think that he would have gone after Timmy. He would have tried and done something to me first. He wasn't afraid of me." Fortunately, the three did not meet.

Half a minute later Dennis and Timmy were safely across the street and hidden from The Palace Hotel by the surrounding two-story buildings and the narrowness of East Standley Street . . . and now they were only a block from their destination.

At the corner of the municipal parking lot, just west

of the police station, Dennis paused and hunkered down eye-to-eye with Timmy. Comfortingly he put his hands on the frightened five-year-old's shoulders and told him to go in the front door of the station and give his name to the first policeman he saw. Dennis assured him that the officer would see that he got home safely.

Inside the station, veteran Patrol Officer Bob Warner had just begun the graveyard shift. It was shortly after eleven, and he was talking to the dispatcher near the station's glass front door when he saw something strange. Recalled Warner, "I was getting ready to leave the station when I noticed a small boy come to the front door, push the door open, and then look back out toward the street, and turn around and run back out. He just started to come inside the door, and then he turned and went back out. Of course, being that time of night and seeing a small boy doing such things, I got a little curious as to what was going on; so I went out the front and I saw this young boy running across the parking lot. I noticed another, older boy walking westbound on Standley, just approaching Main Street. I was afraid that if I just took off running that the older boy would also run and we might not get either one.

"So I called for another unit using my portable radio. Fortunately, there was another unit coming down Main. It was Russell VanVoorhis, and he stopped them right in front of the Salvation Army Store. As soon as he said he had them, I got into my patrol car and went up to the location."

Continued Warner, "When I got there, VanVoorhis was holding the little boy in his arms, and he says to me, 'Would you believe it? *This is Timmy White!*' And I found it hard to believe, because Timmy had had his hair dyed dark brown.

"So VanVoorhis was basically talking to Timmy, and I started talking to this older boy. I asked him if he was with Timmy, and he says he was. I asked him his name and he told me it was Steven Stayner, and then VanVoorhis says, 'He says he's been missing from Merced for seven years.' Then I turned to Steven and asked him if this was true and he said, 'Yes. I was taken from Merced seven years ago.'

"Well," drawled Warner, "you know how you can get into a can of worms sometimes. Well, it was getting to that point . . . we were really getting into something there! It kind of got me . . . shocked me, you know to hear the kid say, 'I was taken seven years ago.' "

The officers put Timmy in VanVoorhis's car, Steven got in Warner's car, and they drove the short block back to the station and entered the back door. Said Timmy later, "I really felt that I was safe then."

Once inside, VanVoorhis took Timmy to an interrogation room while Warner placed Dennis/Steven in the booking room, locked the door, and telephoned Chief Johnson.

"I was at home in bed asleep when the phone rang," Johnson recalled. "It was such a mess that I couldn't understand all of what was happening, so I got up and got dressed and was at the station in about twenty minutes. I guess I couldn't understand what was going on when Warner called me because Steve's story was so absolutely incredible."

With confusion beginning to reign at the police station, one of the officers placed a call to the Whites' home. As Angela remembers it, "I don't remember his name, but I remember exactly what he said. He said, 'Hi. I'm calling from the Ukiah Police Department, and we have a little boy down here who says his name is Timmy White, and he looks like your son.' And I said, 'We'll be right down!'

"I hung up the phone and started getting dressed real fast, and I was telling Jim about it while I was getting dressed. And so Jim, being the real logical one, calls the police station and says, 'Did someone just call here and say that they had found Timmy White?' And they said, 'Yes, we did.' And then Jim starts getting all excited and dressed real fast. And we got Nickie up and wrapped her up in a blanket and took her to the car and got in and raced down to the police station.

"On the way down there I was thinking, and I said to Jim, 'He'd never be dead, would he? They wouldn't let me come down there unless they were real sure that that was him and he was okay, would they?' And Jim assured me that he would be okay, but it was a really long drive to town. I just kept all these things going over in my mind so that by the time we got there I was a wreck!"

Angela was so excited when they finally arrived that, she said, "I jumped out of the car and ran into the station. And the first officer I saw just pointed down the hall, and I didn't even wait to hear what he said. I just ran down to this room where another officer was standing at the end of the hall, and I looked in and here's this grubby-looking little kid with real dark hair. And I just said, 'That's not Timmy!' And then . . . I don't remember. I was on the floor . . . I guess I had fainted.

"There was the build-up to see my blond-headed son and then this! And the policeman at the door said I scared the hell out of him because, he said, 'If this isn't Timmy, *then who is it?*' And he helps me up and says, 'Come on . . . come and look closer. I think they dyed his hair.' So I went in the room, and I knelt down in front of him, and I was looking at Timmy like I didn't know him. And he just sat there silently twiddling his little thumbs. He was real nervous. He didn't blink or anything. He just stared straight ahead. And then I knew it was him, and I pulled him into my arms and he didn't do anything. He didn't cry, he didn't laugh, he didn't say, 'Mom,' he didn't say anything. He just let me hold him for, probably, fifteen to twenty minutes."

About that wonderfully joyous moment, Angela concluded, "I just kissed him and held him. Then Jim and Nickie came in, and I let Jim hold him, but I wanted him back. Then, when I was holding him again, he and Nickie started eyeing each other. But Timmy kept twiddling his thumbs. I'd never seen him do that before, and he's never done it since. But he did it that night."

Meanwhile, in the booking room where Steven had been locked up, Officer Warner, Chief Johnson, Detective John Williams, and Sergeant Vernon Black tried repeatedly to get information out of him about his dad's description and whereabouts. For seven years Kenneth Parnell had been the only parent the teenager had known, and now Steven was loath to say anything that would betray his "dad." With great conviction and fervor, Steven recalled, "I just felt gratitude toward him for taking care of me. You know, he took care of me for seven years, so what am I going to do? Return the favor by turning him in?"

As Chief Johnson put it, "He wasn't going to tell us who his dad was until we promised that if the man was sick, we would see that he got some help. Then, finally, he told us what his dad's name was and where he was working. But that took a lot of talking on our part."

Most of the questioning was done by Bob Warner, who remarked, "At the time, he was real hesitant because he considered Parnell as his dad and he was trying to protect him. I asked him basically where they came from, and he said that they came from over on the coast, but he wouldn't tell me exactly where. I got to kind of fishing around, trying to pinpoint where he went to school and so forth . . . found out he went to school in Point Arena. Then we got into Parnell and he wasn't telling us his name at first. He just said that his dad was at work. So we fished a little bit further, and finally he did tell us that his dad was working up at The Palace Hotel as a security guard. So at that time I informed Captain Maxon and he made arrangements to go and arrest Parnell."

Recalling his irritation, Steven said of the officers' quizzing, "I had finally given them all the information they wanted . . . that he was wearing a green plaid jacket, gray plaid slacks, that it was his first day as the security guard for The Palace. I had to tell them what his moustache looked like, whether he waxed it or not. And so finally they had enough information, so they went over there and picked him up. They practically wanted me to give them his life story before they'd even go over there!"

While Chief Johnson and Sergeant Bach stayed with Steven, Officer Warner, accompanied by Sergeants Budrow and Nelson, along with Detective Williams, made up an arrest party to go to The Palace Hotel. "We drove up to the hotel and walked into the lobby and I asked if they had a Parnell working there," Warner recalled. "The desk clerk said, 'Yes.' And I had just started to ask him where he was when Parnell just happened to walk around the corner and the desk clerk said, 'Here he is now.' And so we asked him to step out front. And when he had stepped out front, we told him that we were arresting him for kidnapping and we read him his rights. Then we drove him back to the station and locked him up in a booking room."

Once Parnell had been brought to the station, Steven said that a truculent police officer bullied him into identifying his father. "One of the cops takes me to the window of the room where they've got him and says to me, 'All right, I want you to look at him and I want you to tell me if it's him or not.' And I didn't want to face him. But I go, 'All right.' And I looked in the window and the cop says, 'Is that him?' And I said, 'Yeah, that's him.' And I started to turn around and go back to the room I was in. Then the cop grabbed my arm and opened the door to where Parnell was and pushed me in. And he says again, 'Are you *sure* that's him? Take a good look at him. *Is that him?*' And I screamed, '*Yes, yes . . . that's him! It's him! Now get my . . . get me out of here!*'

"Parnell just sat there looking at me. Then I pushed my way back out the room and I went back to the room I had been in before. From that point on I never did speak to Parnell again . . . *ever!*"

While the boys were at the station the police took photographs of them both. One Polaroid shows a sullen, unsmiling Steven; Timmy, though dirty and disheveled wears an impish grin in his. During the picture-taking, Timmy had his parents with him, but Steven was alone, frightened, and locked in a room, all of which served to heighten the adolescent's increasing fear that he was being considered a suspect in Timmy's kidnapping.

This impression of Steven was borne out by Bob Warner: "He never did show any emotion. He was just a stony-faced, serious type of a kid. He never showed his feelings one way or the other. He knew, I think, that what Parnell was doing was wrong, and that was why he brought Timmy back to Ukiah. He didn't want it to continue because he knew what he had gone through."

Besides Steven's concern about being implicated in Timmy's kidnapping—i.e., being mistaken for Sean Poorman—there were other things worrying him. He remembered having witnessed his real father, Del, suffer a slipped disk when he himself was just five, and all through the intervening years he had thought that his dad had suffered a heart attack. "At that age I didn't know how old my dad really was," recalled Steven. "I thought that he was around fifty years old. During that seven years I figured he'd be about sixty when I returned. And with thinking that he had a heart condition, my main worry was if he was still alive."

It was well after midnight by the time the Ukiah police telephoned their counterparts in Merced and confirmed Steven's story. "When I called," said

Warner, "their dispatcher didn't know anything about Steven or his kidnapping, but she put a sergeant on the line and he said, 'Yes, we're missing a boy by the name of Steven Stayner. He was taken from our streets seven years ago.' He told me that he'd get in touch with his chief and call me back. Then, a short time later, he called and said that they had two investigators on the way up here."

When Warner returned to the booking room to tell Steven he had called Merced Police and that a pair of officers were on their way to Ukiah to take him home, Steven's first question to Warner was, "Is my dad still alive?"

He was. The police sergeant in Merced was Mark Dossetti, and shortly after receiving that telephone call from Bob Warner, he phoned the Stayners to say that he had some news about their son and that he would be at their door shortly. Del and Kay's first thought was that something had happened to their oldest son, Cary, off on a camping trip to Yosemite National Park with his buddies. But when Dossetti arrived and told them that apparently their long-lost son Steve had been found alive and well in Ukiah, they found it almost impossible to believe. "I just sat down and cried," Del said. "I couldn't believe that he was finally coming home!"

It was around three that morning when eleven-year-old Cory was awakened by conversation coming from the living room. With her Boston terrier, Willie, barking and jumping all over her bed, she got up and went to the living room, arriving at her parents' side just as

Dossetti was telling of Steven's discovery. Sleepy, at first she didn't understand what was being said: "I heard Dad asking, 'Is it Cary?' And the policeman said, 'No, it's about your son, Steve.' And then I figured that he was coming back. I never did think that it was anything bad. I was just glad that he was finally coming home!"

Dossetti returned to the police station, but later, after he had received confirmation of Steven's identification from the Merced officers who had gone to Ukiah, he returned just before daybreak and confirmed the good news for the Stayners. This time Cindy and Jody joined Cory and their parents, and they all went into the kitchen and sat around the table while Kay fixed coffee and Dossetti sat down and visited briefly with the clan. Said Jody, "I was just stunned. I couldn't believe it! When Cindy came in and woke me up and told me, 'Well, they found Steve and he's *alive,*' I was just in shock. I would love to relive that moment . . . it was great! I loved it!"

After Dossetti left, Cory and her dad went from house to house around the neighborhood, telling their friends the good news. One of the first was next-door neighbor Alex Flores, who recalled Del as saying that he had burst into tears when Dossetti told him that Steven had been found alive: "He told me several times over the past seven years that he was miserable because of Steve's disappearance. But Sunday I told him, 'Delbert, you can begin to live again.' "

Remembered Del, "When the police officer came and told us it was Stevie, I musta hugged him a good deal. But since they never had no body to show me, I always believed Stevie was alive."

* * *

Just before four that morning, Ukiah Police Detective John Williams asked Steven to give him a statement in his own words. While Williams typed, Steven began: "My name is Steven Stainer [sic]. I am fourteen years of age. I don't know my true birthdate, but I use April 18, 1965. I know my first name is Steven, I'm pretty sure my last name is Stainer [sic], and if I have a middle name, I don't know it." Then Steven went on for two and one-half pages, telling of his strange odyssey with Kenneth Eugene Parnell, the man who had been his "father" for seven years, ending by signing the statement, "Steven Stainer" [sic].

Detective Williams affixed the time and date—"0415 hours, Sunday, March 2, 1980"—before he and Sergeant Bach took Steven to breakfast at the Denny's Restaurant in Ukiah.

Since shortly after midnight, the *Ukiah Daily Journal* had been trying to get information from the police. The considerable bustle of activity at the small city's normally quiet police station had tipped them off that something big was afoot. In turn, Chief Johnson realized that it would only be a matter of time before rumors would be running wild. So, at approximately 4:30 A.M., Sunday, March 2, 1980, while Steven was out eating breakfast, Johnson telephoned the story of Steven and Timmy's return to the Associated Press office in San Francisco, the world's first word of the boys' safe return. "As soon as I had given it to the wire service and hung up, the phone started ringing and just didn't stop," said Johnson, "and about two hours later the helicopters from the San Francisco TV stations started arriving, along with scores of reporters. That's when we decided to call a press conference."

When Steven returned from breakfast, the reporters weren't the only ones waiting to see him: so were the "two investigators" from Merced Police, Juvenile Officer Jerry Price and his Sergeant, Patrick Lunney, who had arrived after a red-eye trip up the middle of the state. They were the first Merced residents Steven had seen in more than seven years.

Secreting themselves from the press in Chief Johnson's office, they began a tape-recorded interview of Steven, asking about the details of his seven-year odyssey with Parnell. One of Lunney's first questions was, "Did he ever abuse you in any way?"

Without hesitation Steve replied, "Oh, no!"

Then Lunney asked, "Was he good to you?"

"Yes," Steve answered, "he kind of spoiled me, though."

Continued Lunney, "Did you ever think about your folks and brother and sisters back home?"

Responded Steve, "Oh, yes!"

Indeed, Steven's typed statement to the Ukiah Police contained the following: "Getting back to Ken Parnell. I call him Dad. He had never molested me, sexually, he had never been mean to me, and he never said why he stole me or why he stole Timmy. He has been like a father to me, and has always sent me to school." But it would be weeks before the truth about Parnell's sexual assaults on Steven would come out.

By the time the Merced officers had finished their interrogation of Steve, Mendocino County D.A. Investigator Richard "Dick" Finn had obtained his search warrant and, along with about twenty additional Men-

docino and Ukiah peace officers, was ready to head
for the cabin. In an attempt to elude reporters, photographers, and TV cameramen, the Ukiah police had
the station custodian drive the Merced police car to
the back, gas it up, and then, while the media people
rushed to the back of the station, quickly drive it back
around to the front, where Price, Lunney, and Steve
dived into it and roared off, followed by the Ukiah
and Mendocino County cars. But the ruse didn't work
for long, and by the time the law enforcement caravan
had cleared the city limits, a string of press cars
brought up the rear of the convoy.

"It took an hour-and-a-half to two hours to drive to
the cabin 'cause the road was crooked and there were
mudslides," Price recalled. "Too, they had extremely
bad weather up there . . . it was very, very, cloudy,
rainy, very cold, and very dark. And, I mean, when we
finally got there it was *no-man's land*. You'd never look
for somebody up there."

During the early morning hours the cabin had been
secured on orders from Finn (who had flown in from
Los Angeles very late the night before). Said Finn,
"Our office was going to handle the investigation of
those acts that took place in the county, and the Sheriff's Office didn't like that. They thought that *they*
should be handling the investigation. So when we
called them and asked them to secure the cabin for
us with one of their people on the coast, at first they
didn't want to do it. But they finally did."

Sergeant Daryl Dallegge, the Mendocino County
Sheriff's Department's deputy in charge of the southwestern part of Mendocino County, got a cryptic call
at 3 A.M. at his Point Arena home, advising him to go

to the Stornetta's Mountain View Ranch caretaker's cabin and secure it. Sleepily he climbed out of bed and did as told.

The cabin was deserted and apparently undisturbed when Dallegge arrived and parked his patrol car on the road's shoulder and dozed. At dawn he awoke and drove down to the Pipers', where his friend Billie put on the coffeepot and the two sat at the kitchen table drinking coffee and shooting the bull until Dallegge's two-way radio crackled to life, signaling the convoy's approach from Ukiah.

When Dallegge returned to the cabin, TV news helicopters following the small armada of law-enforcement vehicles were circling overhead. Soon the peace officers and ground news units arrived to join in the whirlybirds' commotion and, as Chief Johnson irritably recalled, "It was a hell of a mess. There were reporters everywhere. It was like a goddamned Vietnam War up there." Calming down just a tad, he concluded, "I know that they've [the news media] got a job to do, but sometimes they just don't use good common sense."

"The place was open," Price recalled about the remote cabin. "None of the doors was locked or anything. It was very, very cold inside there . . . like a dungeon, really . . . It was that bad! There were dirty clothes everywhere, there was food that had been left out, and there were cooking utensils that hadn't been washed. They had an outdoor toilet, and the whole place was a mess . . . dirty. And Steve was dirty, too! That's the one thing that I remember most. He had a terrible stench about him. That was their lifestyle, you know. It was very sad. In fact, on the way back to

Merced, Price and Lunney were forced to stop at the local Foster Freeze ice-cream stand in Cloverdale to air out the car."

Once he had assembled the press, Finn led them and the assorted law enforcement officers through the cabin as he delivered a constant stream of comments for the reporters' benefit; as Lunney and Price commented later, Finn conducted a whirlwind, none-too-professional search. After less than an hour, Steven scooped up Queenie and everyone jumped back into their cars and helicopters for the return dash to Ukiah and the scheduled noon press conference.

At the news conference—covered by reporters representing media organizations from as far away as London and Tokyo—Steven sat holding his tiny, trembling dog and apologized for her very apparent fright. Still dressed in the grimy gray sweatshirt and jeans he had worn when he'd left the remote cabin the night before, Steven spoke in a shy, quiet voice as he told the assembled reporters, "I got to like Timmy. I knew what Parnell was doing was wrong. I just gave him a whole life ahead of him with his parents."

During the news conference Timmy alternately sat on his parents' and Steven's laps. Timmy said that the teenager had become his friend during the sixteen-day ordeal and that Steven had read comic books to him to while away the long hours in the tiny cabin.

At the close of the news conference, photographers were allowed a few minutes to capture the two boys on film. Then Patrick Lunney, Jerry Price, and Steven got into the Merced Police cruiser for Steven's long-awaited trip home. As they headed south on U.S. 101, the long-lost boy settled into the rear seat, snuggled up to Queenie, and tried hard to remember what his father, mother, brother, and sisters looked like . . . and he prayed that they would still remember him, and love him, too.

Chapter Ten
The Boys Return Home

"I always believed Stevie was alive."

At 2 A.M. in Ukiah, Timmy was preparing to go home with his family, but first a few final police matters had to be dealt with. During the officers' questioning, Timmy had said that Parnell had told him that he, Parnell, knew Angela, and further, that it was okay for Timmy to stay with him. Therefore, Ukiah police officers had Angela look through the booking-room window at Parnell to see if she knew him; but of course she did not.

When confronted with this information, Timmy exclaimed to his mother, "He told me that you knew him, and you didn't! I didn't know big people lie!"

Before leaving the station, Angela went into the room where Steven was being held, kissed him on the cheek, and told him, "Thank you for bringing my son back home safe." Then it was off to the local hospital to have Timmy examined by a doctor for signs of physical or sexual abuse . . . and Jim and Angela were thankful to learn that there were none.

Even though it was nearly three in the morning when the White family arrived home, Angela asked Timmy what he wanted to do, and he responded that he wanted to eat some of her spaghetti and take a bath. Added Angela, "He wanted us to throw away the clothes that he was wearing because Parnell put them on him. He didn't want *anything* left around that would remind him of Parnell." Also, Angela recalled that when she tried to wash the dye from her son's hair, it wouldn't come out right away: "It took a few months because first it got red and then it turned a really strange color before it finally grew out blond again."

Finished with his bath, Timmy was so excited that he never did eat the spaghetti his mother made for him. But the family reunion continued with the four of them sitting around the kitchen table drinking hot chocolate and playing Old Maid until dawn, when the phone began ringing off the wall. One of the first to contact them was Diane Crawford, who had been out having dinner with her husband when Steven and Timmy had come calling the night before.

"The longest day in my life," is the way sixteen-year-old Cindy recalls her wait for her brother's return. "We learned that it was Steve at three in the morning, and then he didn't get home until seven or eight that night. And we made banners that morning with butcher's paper. And there was a big one in front of our house that said, 'Welcome Home Steve.' "

Twenty miles north of Merced, as they passed through Turlock, Lunney and Price established two-way radio contact with the Merced police dispatcher and Chief Kulbeth asked that they began relaying their location minute-by-minute. When they exited onto Yosemite Parkway, Lunney asked Steve if he recognized anything, and slowly it all began to come back to the nearly fifteen-year-old boy as he first identified a familiar drive-in grocery, then the route he had walked home from school, and finally the Red Ball Gas Station where he had been kidnapped as a seven-year-old in 1972.

Before he and Price left Ukiah, Lunney phoned Chief Kulbeth and filled him in on his and Price's interviews with Steve and their perceptions of him. "I told him, 'This kid is really almost self-sufficient, particularly because he was living up in the mountains.' And he carried his knife on him. In fact, he was wearing it when I first saw him, but then we took it into evidence."

When Kulbeth and Bailey arrived at the Stayner home, they took Del and Kay aside and counseled them, Kulbeth remembering: "In his parents' minds, he was this little child coming home, so I told them, 'Your son is a very grown-up young man, and he is somewhat independent. He's a fourteen-year-old near-adult, and you'll just have to recognize that.' " But even though Del and Kay acknowledged to Kulbeth that they understood, their relationship with Steven after his return clearly showed that they never, ever internalized what the chief had told them.

And Steve's impending homecoming caused then-twelve-year-old Jody to think back a few years, "I remembered when my Grandpa Tal [Del's father] died while Steve was gone. I prayed that God would take good care of him and, if Steve was up there, take good care of him, too. And I remembered those puff balls that are like flowers . . . that when you blow on them they go everywhere? Well, we used to blow them and make a wish that Steve would come back home. You know, you'd blow them and then clap your hands and make a wish? We'd always do that. But now Steve was really coming home!"

Added Cindy, "One of the most emotional things to me was seeing Steve's signature on the side of the garage. In that way Steve was always still around in our mind, you know . . . even after five, six years. And that memory is why my dad would never move. He always thought that if Steve came home he would find us."

It was dark when Jerry Price finally turned the police car onto Bette and saw the hundreds of people crowding the street from curb to curb, so thick that he had to halt several houses from the Stayner home. Lights from television cameras illuminated the area in front of 1655 Bette as Chief Kulbeth escorted Del and Kay to the reunion with their son. And at a little after seven in the evening of March 2, 1980, clutching his beloved dog, Queenie, Steve slowly emerged from the cruiser's backseat and stood motionless, staring in bewilderment at the crowd and his approaching family . . . 2,645 days after that cold, drizzly December day in 1972 when as a seven-year-old he had set out for home from Charles Wright Elementary School.

Remembered Kulbeth about Steve's parents' first sight of their son: "There was no problems at all with their recognizing Steve or his recognizing his family. They were overjoyed, but Steve seemed a little bit shy. When we got them back into the house, you could really see the emotion start to pour out. There were tears of joy everywhere, and if you have ever seen thoroughly happy people, then these people were just that happy! Everybody—the neighbors and friends—wanted to be in the house. And the press people wanted to be in there, too, and the family very graciously allowed some of these people to come in, especially close friends, and even a couple of local reporters from the *Merced Sun-Star.* Then, after awhile, they wanted to be alone, so we asked all of the people to leave. And we left, too, but we did maintain surveillance of the home for a couple of weeks after that."

Grinning ear-to-ear at the memory, Cindy recalled, "My parents took Steve to Cary's room so we could talk to him. And at first he remembered Mom and Dad's names and his name, but he didn't know our names. And we wanted to ask him about what happened when he was kidnapped, but we didn't want to upset him, and so we didn't. And there was one thing that I just never did want to ask him about, and that was how he felt about Parnell. I just didn't . . . just didn't want to know *anything* about it."

The initial excitement had hardly died down when an ecstatic Cary arrived home. He had first learned of his brother's return from a newscast on the radio in the family's pickup camper as he drove his buddies back to Merced from a weekend camping trip at Yosemite National Park. Exclaimed Cary, "I damn near drove off the highway when I heard that!"

That first night back at home, Steve chose to sleep on a pallet on the living room floor and Cary bedded down beside his long-lost brother. "I had a hard time trying to get to sleep that night," said Cary. "I stayed up a long time just looking at Steve while he slept and listening to him breathe. I just couldn't believe that my brother was finally back home again." Then, with tears in his eyes, Steve's big brother added, "You know, I went outside that night and I walked several blocks away and then looked up at the stars and started to wish on one again . . . but then I remembered that Steve was back home, and so I thanked the star instead."

Steve's return brought tremendous joy to Del, but the previous seven years had taken a serious toll on him. During his son's absence he had lost his deep faith in God and severely curtailed his practice of the Mormon faith. Explained Del, "I believe in God, but as a father I got mad at Him after four years. You're not supposed to, but He hadn't brought my son back!" Then Del angrily reflected on his son's years with Parnell. "It really affected our lives. We are not the same people we were before Stevie disappeared. After two or three years, Steve had accepted that kind of life"—with Parnell—"and he had a ball. He had a lot of friends. He had a lot of fun up there. This guy bought him funny books and all kinds of stuff, and Steve ate that up. When Steve was in the sixth grade, the damn guy even bought whiskey for him! So, Steve had a lot of stuff he would have never gotten if he was at home. But he would have had his family!" he cried.

After regaining his composure, Del added: "But most of the time that Stevie was gone, I had this hurting. I guess I was just about half crazy or something . . . I don't know. I'd take my anger out on Kay, my children, and I couldn't get along with anybody. I was tore up inside. I can't explain it except that I hurt all the time, and I know when Stevie came home, the hurting stopped."

A few blocks away that night, Ervin E. Murphy and his friend and fellow worker Pete Galessor registered at a motel. They were in Merced to enjoy their usual Sunday-Monday weekend, and early the next morning the pair walked down Yosemite Parkway to Carrows Restaurant for breakfast. On the way in, Pete bought a *San Francisco Chronicle,* and while they were eating he suddenly exclaimed, "Hey! Get this!"

"Then," said Murph, "he read this article to me about Steve and Parnell and the whole bit. I didn't say anything to him . . . not even on the whole way back to the park."

Based on their initial interview with Steve, Lunney and Price knew that there had been a second man involved in his abduction, but Steve had been reluctant to provide them with additional information. So, the next day, Monday, March 3, the two officers picked up Steve and drove him to the police station for an in-depth interrogation. It took several hours of questioning before the teenager told them that the mysterious second kidnapper's name was "Murphy," that he wore eyeglasses, worked "in Yosemite," and early on had stayed with Steve and Parnell "in a little red cabin on the road to Yosemite."

With this information, Lunney telephoned Lee Shackleton—in 1980 still Yosemite National Park's Chief Law Enforcement Ranger—and asked that he research National Park Service and Curry Company employment files for anyone working there in December of 1972 with the first, middle, or last name of "Murphy." This time Shackleton cooperated promptly and within hours Lunney and Price had photographs of two Murphys.

Late that afternoon Lunney and Price went by the Stayners' home and showed Steve the photographs they had received from Shackleton. With no hesitation Steve picked out Ervin Edward "Murph" Murphy, and the officers returned to the station to plan their arrest of the simple-minded kitchen worker.

That evening, as Steve, Cory, and his parents drove to San Francisco for an overnight stay before their Tuesday, March 4, appearance nationwide on *Good Morning America* from ABC-TV affiliate KGO-TV, Lunney and Price departed for the two-hour drive to Yosemite. There, with backup from park rangers, they waited in Yosemite Lodge's kitchen for Murphy to arrive for his graveyard shift. Right on time at 10 P.M. Murphy showed up and was promptly arrested for what was the very first time in his life.

But Murph was expecting them. "At five o'clock Tuesday morning I left my cabin and went over to the lodge and got a newspaper and read it myself. And the paper said that they were looking for an accomplice, so, more or less, I knew that they were looking for me. So I went on to work that night and I'm just starting to work when they came in and picked me up and I told them all about it. It was a relief to know where the kid was and that he was alive and not hurt or anything. He could have been dead! And I finally got it off my chest that I knew Parnell had kidnapped the kid, but at the same time I hadn't wanted to get myself involved."

The short, friendly, yet lonely little man paused and reflected a minute or two before adding somewhat sadly, "One time, years before that, I tried to call up the Merced police department, and the phone just rang and rang, and then when the lady answered I was still a little scared, and so I just hung up and went over and got drunk instead."

Before leaving Yosemite, Lunney and Price took Murph to his cabin one last time, where the dejected man sat on his glasses and broke them. With Murph's permission, they searched through his meager possessions. Among the things they found were science fiction novels and books on the occult. Lunney asked him if he read a lot, and Murph replied, "Yes, but a lot of it is way over my head. I had to quit the Book of the Month Club." Then they drove Murph to the Merced County Jail and booked him.

The next day, Wednesday, March 5, Murph was arraigned in Merced County Court for conspiracy in the kidnapping of Steven Stayner, with bail set at $50,000 . . . much more than Parnell's $20,000 bail in Ukiah. The Curry Company offered to provide Murph with private defense counsel—an offer he did not accept—but The Palace Hotel in Ukiah made no such offer to Parnell.

The arrest was a great shock to Murph's friends and fellow workers at Yosemite. They had always seen him as a little strange but perfectly harmless. Yosemite Lodge night auditor Nanette Ketterer—who, ironically, had Parnell's old job—recalled Murph telling a bizarre story to her in 1979 of how he befriended a runaway boy. He'd said that he'd lodged him in his employee cabin for several days, given him money for food, paid for phone calls to his parents, and, finally, bought the boy a bus ticket home. Then, Murph had told her, he was surprised to receive a "thank-you" letter from the parents with thirty dollars enclosed in appreciation for his help. But Murph had never told his cabinmate this story, and it was probably just his attempt to assuage his guilt for having helped Parnell kidnap Steven so many years before.

Also on March 5, Lunney and Price drove Steve out of Merced along Yosemite Parkway and California 140 to retrace the route that Parnell took with Steven and Murphy to Cathy's Valley. They found the little red cabin where Steven had spent portions of his first two weeks with Parnell and the two officers talked with the teenager again about his life experiences with Parnell.

Even though Steve continued to characterize his relationship with Parnell as a very normal one, Lunney and Price suspected Parnell had sexually abused Steve, for within hours of the kidnapper's arrest Ukiah Police had teletyped for and received Parnell's complete criminal history, including details of his 1951 arrest and conviction for kidnapping and sexually assaulting nine-year-old Bobby Green in Bakersfield. Ukiah Police had shared this information with the Merced officers, and so both jurisdictions knew from the start the potential crimes they were dealing with in Timmy's and Steven's kidnappings.

With Steve's safe return to Merced, Chief Kulbeth reflected on his department's lengthy search for him: "Certainly, in that seven-year period of time we made thousands of inquiries and arrests. There was always something you could do, even if it was just talking to people over and over and over. The case was kept alive.

"The Stayners are stable, down-to-earth people . . . I think they are great people. Over the seven years I don't think Delbert ever lost the hope that someday Steve was going to turn up alive. And for a long period of time Kay believed that, too, but then I think she slowly started losing a little faith."

He concluded pragmatically: "We didn't necessarily try to talk them into believing that Steve was dead, but in some way we wanted to condition them to the possibility that if he did turn up tomorrow in a grave someplace, for example, it would not be a total shock."

The chief concluded, "In my twenty-nine years on the department we devoted more time, more energy, and more manpower to Steven's case than probably any other case I can recall."

On Easter, April 6, Del, Kay, Steve, and his three sisters drove to Ukiah in their camper, their first trip to Mendocino County since Steve's return home. The trip's main purpose was for Steve to receive the $15,000 reward check from the Timmy White Fund for returning Timmy. A ceremony was held at two o'clock that afternoon in Ukiah's City Park, where Timmy was hoisted onto a chair to present the check to Steve. After brief remarks by Steve, the Stayners paid a short visit to Timmy's home before driving on to Comptche, where they met Steve's friends from his relatively happy three-year stay in the tiny backwoods community.

Recalled Kay, "The area was beautiful. The people up there were nice people . . . they're just not city people. The Mitchells were real eye-openers. They use a

Pacific Gas & Electric cable reel for a dining room table, and that's just not normal . . . just not ordinary."

Next the Stayners called on Damon Carroll and his family. Kay said that Damon is a "very intense kid. He is bright. He's a nice kid. What I mean by intense is he does sorta make sense sometimes, and other times you think, 'Boy! This kid's *deep!* He must know something I don't, because he doesn't always make a whole lot of sense.' He tends to be off in his own little world. And Damon told me that Steve had told him that he had been kidnapped while they were in Comptche. Steve hasn't recalled any of that, but if he was doped up on marijuana, high on that stuff, he wouldn't remember."

After spending Easter night in Comptche, the Stayners drove south through the small redwood forest communities of Navarro and Philo, turning southwest at Boonville and going to the Mountain View Ranch, a place Kay found "wild, desolate, and beautiful." They spent a couple of hours there looking over the place and visiting with the Pipers and Duke Stornetta.

Recalled Duke, "[When] the detectives brought Dennis to the cabin to get his stuff, I said, 'Now, you've got chickens and you got goats—penned up there in the barn—and you got rabbits. What are you going to do with them?' And he says, 'Eat 'em! I'm going home!' That's what he said, it is. And he left everything . . ." Then, when they returned at Easter, Duke said that Steve convinced his parents to let him take his favorite goat back to Merced in their camper.

* * *

After a month getting reacquainted with his family, Steve enrolled in the freshman class at the East Campus of Merced High School immediately following the Easter break. At the time, Principal Joseph Reeves was quoted in the *Sun-Star* as saying, "We are all going to turn ourselves inside out to help him, for one of the best things we can do is let the kid forget it. If he can handle this, he can handle anything. He can handle life."

But there were problems, Del recalled. "He was called a lot of bad names . . . gay, punk, all that kind of shit. He almost got into a fight. A lot of that stuff was at school, but there was some of it at a skating rink he went to."

And people were still asking the same question they had asked when Steve had first returned home: "Why didn't he ever run away from Parnell?"

Prior to his later evaluation of Steve for the Merced County District Attorney's Office, Psychiatrist Robert Wald of San Francisco was quoted in an article in the *San Francisco Chronicle* shortly after Steve's return home as saying, "Kids as young as the Stayner boy characteristically struggle with a lot of growth problems, behavior conflicts with parents, and feelings of guilt and shame. It takes no stretch of the imagination why a youngster might succumb to the blandishments and attention of a stranger, someone immature himself, who knows how to appeal to such a child."

In that same article, child psychiatrist Dr. Marjorie Hays said: "It's understandable that a child of seven could believe something like that. There's a textbook name for it, the *family romance syndrome*. It comes when a child suddenly develops an interest in the outside world and begins to devalue his parents and fantasizes that he was adopted and doesn't really belong to them. Normally, the attitude passes. With this boy, he might be just a normal kid who had some colossal bad luck."

At the end of the article, an unidentified psychologist was quoted as saying, "I'm sure the older boy felt tainted and damaged all along, but he couldn't leave because of the low self-esteem he may have developed. It was easier for him to mobilize himself on behalf of rescuing someone else."

Cindy remembered his sibling rivalry with Cary. "Cary was living at home when Steve came back and they argued and feuded all the time. They are both the kind of persons that think when they are right, they stick to it. They're not going to give up. And Steve, when he thinks he's right, I mean, he's right. You can't argue with him! Steve is very stubborn at times . . . *very stubborn.*"

Steve had problems making male friends; virtually his only one was his cousin, David Higgins . . . but he did have a lot of girlfriends. Ever concerned about others' perceptions of his sexual identity, Steve recalled, "I went through a lot of girlfriends starting as a freshman. Some were in the eighth grade and some were as old as nineteen."

After Steve's return home, many of his Mendocino County acquaintances went to Merced to visit him and his family. First it was Damon. He went down and spent several weeks with the Stayners that summer, driving Kay crazy with his moodiness and his habit of jumping over her furniture.

But the real shocker came the day Kay opened her front door and discovered on her porch Barbara Mat-

thias (the woman who'd molested Steven with
Parnell), her son Lloyd, and a television news crew.
Barbara had been promised several hundred dollars
by the TV station for her help in arranging an "exclusive" interview with Steve and his family, and she had
shown up out of the clear blue. Kay lost no time in
slamming the door in her face.

About the visit, Kay said, "I was just *boiling*. I can't
put my feelings into words . . . not printable, anyway.
I just feel that people like her should be put away for
good." And in the same way Mendocino County failed
to investigate or prosecute Parnell for his sexual assaults on Steven and his friends—Barbara's sons included—they exhibited the same lack of concern
about Barbara.

But the extensive sexual assaults her son had suffered were never, ever a subject discussed with Steven
by Kay, or Del, or Steve's sister Cindy, who recalled:
"I've never talked to Steve about that. During the trials
people would ask me questions, and I had to tell them
that I really didn't know. I never really talked to
him . . . *no one* talked about 'it.' My parents really
wouldn't talk about '*it.*' "

In the spring of 1980, Steve, with his family's approval, optioned his story to a Hollywood television
production company on behalf of ABC-TV. This
brought him $25,000, but because of the Stayners'
problems with the fictionalization of the script, the
story was never produced and by 1984 the option had
lapsed . . . and Steve had spent all his money.

Steve's fifteenth birthday on April 18th, 1980, was a

bright, happy occasion with an appropriately magnificent celebration. "It was a big blowout!" Steve grinned. "We went out to the lake and had a barbecue. I got all kinds of clothes, a new ten-speed bike, a calculator, and a fifty-dollar gift certificate for Stephanie's on the Mall. I had a lot of my friends there and practically the whole family came."

Chapter Eleven

The Investigations

"The value of taking Parnell off the streets forever is so obvious."

The Merced police department investigation of Steve's 1972 kidnapping was severely hampered by the more than seven years that had passed, the two hundred miles that separated them from Mendocino County, and particularly the less than professional efforts of some of their brother lawmen in Mendocino County, most especially the Mendocino County District Attorney's investigator Richard "Dick" Finn. According to former Mendocino County Chief Criminal D.A. George McClure, Finn was a public servant who always considered his personal agenda first and foremost. And McClure's boss, former Mendocino County District Attorney Joseph Allen, said, "I can say that Finn generally was a guy who had a reputation for playing his cards very close to his chest. I can recall the incident where George was in trial on Parnell and discovered to his amazement that Finn had evidence that George didn't know about. George talked to me about that later and said that he found that real surprising."

Early on it was Finn who took complete charge of the investigation of Parnell's kidnapping of Timmy White and on the whole provided little cooperation to his fellow lawmen from Merced. Finn was hired in September 1975 by then-D.A. Duncan James and by the time Joe Allen took office in January 1979 Finn had achieved civil service tenure. Said Allen tersely, "It certainly is true that Finn primarily interviewed Steve. It certainly is true that Finn primarily interviewed Timmy White. It certainly is true that Finn handled our relations—not exclusively—but the majority of the phone calls, contacts, back and forth with both the Stayner family and the White family."

It seemed especially odd to Merced Officers Lunney and Price that Finn didn't follow up on their discoveries that Parnell had committed hundreds of sexual assaults on Steve as well as a number of sexual assaults on Steve's young male friends during his four-year residence in Mendocino County. In fact, even though they detailed their findings to Finn on several occasions, the investigator seemed unconcerned about their information. Also, it was strange to Lunney and Price that instead of involving himself in this very major case, Allen was rarely in his office and delegated almost total responsibility for running the office to Finn while Allen himself spent a great deal of his time shooting pool at the Forest Club bar across the street from the Mendocino County courthouse.

Joseph Allen is a chunky, genial man who sports a bushy mustache and a brazen—friends called it colorful—manner both inside and outside the court-room. Joe, as he prefers to be called, is the sort of person even a stranger would find it difficult to address as "Mr. Allen." As the former Mendocino County Public Defender, he gained the attention of the local news media with his flashy, unconventional behavior.

As the P.D., Joe thought that his next career step should be running for District Attorney. He did, was elected, and took office in 1979. But Joe quickly found that he did not enjoy the prosecutor's role nearly as much as he did being the flamboyant counsel for the defense. Said Ukiah Police Chief David Johnson, "In the courtroom Joe is probably the most articulate man on his feet. He is sharp! But he does have different, unorthodox ways sometimes. He's a character!"

In Merced, Lunney and Price had been used to working with the county's efficient District Attorney, Pat Hallford, a true straight arrow who had been an F.B.I. agent for sixteen years before leaving the Bureau, getting elected D.A., and running an effective operation "by the book." Now they were having to conduct an investigation in another county by riding along on the coattails of what they thought was a disorganized district attorney's office.

Said Lunney: "Speaking about Mendocino County, those guys whipped through it [the first search of the remote cabin] and they didn't know what they were doing on the search warrant. They didn't know what they were looking for . . . they just went through it in a breeze. Here's Timmy White . . . he's been held for a short period of time. But we knew our case was going to be a lot more difficult because it wasn't an open-and-shut thing."

On Thursday, March 6, Lunney and Price drove back to Mendocino County to seek much-needed evidence for their case against Parnell. On their way north they began building their case by stopping in Santa Rosa and picking up copies of Dennis's school records. And they did the same in Willits, Fort Bragg, Mendocino City, and Point Arena. Although their trip lasted just three days, through long hours and dogged determination they were able to gather considerable evidence against Parnell.

During their first search at the desolate Mountain View Ranch cabin—the one organized and actually conducted by Finn—Lunney and Price had just one very confused, disorganized hour to try to locate and gather evidence. But on this second trip the Merced officers were surprised when they arrived and Finn presented them with a broad search warrant for the Mountain View Ranch to speed them on their way. This time it was just the two of them and they invested five diligent hours scouring the cabin, barn, and out buildings at the ranch. Unfortunately, though, the ranch had been just about picked clean of evidence by a number of reporters who spent the days after the initial, March 2nd search poking through the cabin, barn, and sheds. The ranch had remained unsecured since the Finn party's hasty departure the previous Sunday morning.

As a result of this, two reporters made very interesting discoveries. First, while searching the barn a reporter from The *San Francisco Chronicle* came across Parnell's nude photographs of Steve and Jeff Norton. He gave them to Duke Stornetta who in turn handed them over to Ukiah Police, and the photos eventually made their way back to Merced. But this series of exchanges destroyed the photographs' value as evidence against Parnell, since it no longer could be proved that he had taken them. Second, Miranda Dunn of KPIX-TV in San Francisco was going through the unlocked cabin when she noticed an open, huge jar of Vaseline on Parnell's nightstand. She thought it peculiar and later asked a blushing lawman what it might have been used for.

Lunney and Price went to Point Arena and searched Parnell's town apartment at The Garcia Center. There they found two sparsely furnished rooms. Next they went to Comptche, where Parnell had an old trailer set up as a storage shed. In it they found boxes of old junk and records, receipts for phone bills, and his parole papers.

While they were in Comptche, Lunney and Price interviewed people who had known Dennis and his father and in doing so stumbled onto a veritable nest of stories about Parnell's sexual assaults of Dennis's male friends. Said Lunney: "One boy's mother [George Mitchell's mother, Joann] was very upset about it. We told her that we would pass it along to the proper authorities. You see, by law we can initiate an investigation in the county of Merced, and we can go anywhere that investigation leads us. But if we come across another criminal act during the time we are conducting our investigation in another county, then we have to turn that information over to the proper authorities in that county. And that is what we did with the information we got about Parnell sexually assaulting these other boys. [Finn] should have gone after [Parnell] on those sexual assaults up there, but he didn't."

Joe Allen vociferously claimed that Finn had never told him anything about Parnell sexually assaulting boys other than Steve . . . and that Finn had minimized that by saying "damn little" about the kidnapper's sex assaults on the teenager.

Also, George McClure—who prosecuted Parnell—said that Finn never told him anything about Parnell sexually assaulting boys other than Steve. However, McClure did acknowledge that he had acted on Finn's recommendation not to prosecute Parnell "so as to protect Steve" for what Finn had told him were only "a few sex assaults" on the boy.

According to Mendocino County Sheriff's Department Sgt. Dallegge, in the early 1980s Mendocino County law enforcement had a strange attitude about prosecuting adults who were accused of sexually assaulting children: "Back then—the time I took over as [child sex abuse] investigator—you could catch a guy for sexual assault on a child aged fourteen and if you could get him for first offense and put him in county jail and get him convicted, you were lucky. I worked sex crimes and I couldn't get the District Attorney to prosecute. You know, *they wouldn't even file [the case]!*"

In fact, on their third investigative trip to Mendocino County, Lunney and Price continued to uncover more boys who had been victims of sexual assaults by Parnell. And each one of these boys had dark hair and were between the ages of nine and fourteen years old at the time Parnell assaulted them. As he had done in George Mitchell's case, Lunney filled out detailed reports of each incident and personally handed them to Dick Finn. But as with the Mitchell case, neither Lunney nor Price was aware that Finn nor any other Mendocino County law enforcement officer ever investigated these alleged assaults. In addition not a one of the dozen or so peace officers the author interviewed in Mendocino County knew for certain what had happened to the information that Finn had received. Finn himself, when asked, was vague and noncommittal.

However, George McClure believes that Finn put this evidence in the "short, two-drawer, locked file cabinet that sat behind his [Finn's] desk. Nobody else had access to it. Not even Joe Allen. I remember one day I was upset and had to get some evidence for a case of mine that was in that file cabinet. And the head secretary and I went to his desk and tried to find a key and there were several keys in [Finn's desk], but not a key to that file cabinet."

About Finn's personal, secure file cabinet, Joe Allen recalls, "It was one of those keyed file cabinets that would protect your papers in case of fire. I remember one time that George had to get some evidence for trial out of that cabinet. Finn was out of town and was the only one who had a key to it. So we had to let the charges against the defendant be dropped. That was his file cabinet and what he did or didn't have in there he kept fairly close to his chest."

* * *

In early March of 1980, several days after Parnell's arrest, fellow Palace Hotel employee Irene Cook went to see him in the Mendocino County Jail. Cook had a four-year-old son, Charlie, in whom Parnell had taken a very keen interest. Said Cook, "It was good for Charlie having Ken around. Young boys need a daddy. Ken did some good for Charlie, when he was there. My daughter didn't like him, though. She said there was something strange about him."

Concluded Cook, "His interest in my boy grew. Charlie started calling him 'Daddy Ken.' One time he asked Ken, 'Are you my daddy?' And Ken said, 'I'd like to be.' "

Two days after Lunney and Price's return to Merced at the end of their second trip to Mendocino County, on Monday, March 10, they went to talk to Steve again, but the teenager still denied there having been anything untoward about Parnell's relationship with him. But Lunney and Price knew better, and by early April their persistence finally paid off when they confronted Steve with the nude pictures of he and Jeff Norton and Steve admitted to them that Parnell had indeed sexually assaulted him . . . not once but hundreds of times over the more than seven years he had lived with the man. Said Steve, "For the first month after my return, Parnell was thought of as somebody who was looking for a family without having to be married. Then the nude pictures showed up. That's when Pat Lunney called me into the police station and started asking me about sexual abuse. At first I denied that there was any. Then Lunney asked me again, but I told him 'No' again. Then he said, 'Well, I've got a guy who says different and he will go and say it on the witness stand.' That's when I confessed and told him all that happened. From there I went to the D.A. [Hallford] and I had to tell it to him."

Since in California the statute of limitations for sexual assault on a child was and still is three years—and Parnell had left Merced County with Steve seven years earlier—charges against Parnell for his assaults on Steve would have to cover the period from 1977 to 1980 and have to be filed in Mendocino County. Therefore, Lunney and Price took both Steve's sworn statements about these assaults and Steve himself to Finn at his office in Ukiah and requested that Finn investigate Parnell for all eighty-seven sexual assaults on Steve which the Merced officers had by then documented. Also at this meeting the Merced officers personally handed Finn additional copies of their reports of several sexual assaults on Mendocino County boys in the trailer at Comptche.

"Yeah, we had the pictures of the one kid"—actually the nude photographs of Jeff Norton and Steve—"and we had a bunch of other people saying things," Finn said. "We knew that if we went into Comptche, we could come out with a whole shitpot full of sex assaults. We knew that! But we had a real situation there: small town, small department, small budget. We did the best we could. Everybody knew what was going on. And if anybody was a victim, they would have told their parents and talked at that time and come forward rather than us having to go in and dig them out.

"George McClure found out about Parnell's sexual assaults on Steve and he said, 'Find out the facts.' So, the first thing I did is ask Steve if this is true. Steve started talking about it . . . the last time he was molested. How Parnell fucked him, orally copulated with him. And Delbert was there, but about this time he [Del] got up and left. Then I decided, it's not worth putting Steve through. And at that time Steve was telling me that he had no problems in getting back into the normal hustle and bustle . . . Steve said he didn't have problems with that, but his friends did. Steve said, 'Hey, I can deal with it!' "

Therefore, on his own authority, Finn did not pursue a thorough investigation of Parnell's sexual assaults on Steven and the other boys.

However, Joe Allen accepts much of the responsibility for the decision not to prosecute Parnell for sexually assaulting Steve: "One of the things that the [Merced] police on the case had a difficult time accepting was our decision not to prosecute Parnell for any of the sex offenses committed against Steve, their reason being that here we have a series of crimes that could be sentenced consecutively to our kidnapping and could add many, many more years of imprisonment to Parnell's term; were prosecutable in Mendocino County without a statute-of-limitations problem; and within that three-year period there were eighty-seven counts of sexual assault [involving Steve alone] that we could have brought. Prosecuting him would have been a perfectly reasonable decision, except that after considerable meditation on the subject, I decided that, balancing the harm I thought it would do to Steve, it was not right . . . In retrospect, maybe Steve was stronger than I thought he was; and maybe from the standpoint of public safety, it should have been done. But it is an issue that I have never been really quiet about in my mind, because the value of taking Parnell off the streets forever is so obvious."

Merced law enforcement officers continued to have a very difficult time locating and organizing the evidence they knew they would need to make their seven-year-old kidnapping case stick. Although Parnell had actually done little to cover his tracks since December 4, 1972, the major problem was the three-year statute of limitations on kidnapping in California. But early on, Merced County District Attorney Pat Hallford personally, astutely, and successfully argued in court that the kidnapping of Steven Stayner had been of an ongoing nature for as long as Parnell had kept Steve with him. Therefore, when tested in a preliminary hearing, Merced County's kidnapping charge against Parnell as well as the county's conspiracy-to-kidnap charges against both Parnell and Murphy stuck. Following preliminary hearings in both counties Parnell was indicted by the respective counties' grand juries for second degree kidnapping* and in Merced County both were indicted for conspiracy to kidnap as well.

In late April, Joe Allen personally handled Mendocino County's preliminary hearing, which was held just up the stairs from his office in the Mendocino County Courthouse in Ukiah. George McClure, Joe's newly hired Chief Deputy Criminal D.A.—a musta-

---

*In California, a charge of first degree kidnapping requires that the crime result in the death of the victim or that a ransom demand be made for the victim's safe return. Second-degree kidnapping is applicable wherein there is no ransom demand made and no bodily harm caused the victim (California law does not consider sexual assault of the victim "bodily harm").

chioed man who speaks in an intense and direct personal fashion—assisted Joe at the hearing. Opposing them was the young attorney who had succeeded Joe as Mendocino County Public Defender, Scott LeStrange, a lanky man with a folksy presence who favored cowboy boots and a spare, Gary Cooper manner of speech.

During the hearing a rare degree of agreement surfaced when LeStrange made a motion for a change of venue and Joe immediately concurred, the judge then ordering that Parnell's trial be held in the Hayward Hall of Justice in Alameda County, just south of Oakland on San Francisco Bay's eastern shore. The judge also issued a gag order forbidding attorneys and law enforcement officers to talk with the press about the case. However, on exiting the courtroom Joe went no farther than the foyer before holding his own court for the assembled press and extensively discussing Finn's investigative efforts as well as the case's merits.

Said Joe about the gag order and his subsequent trouble for breaking it: "At that point I was attempting to enlist the citizenry through the press in the search that turned out to be for Sean Poorman. Therefore, that was quite successful, but it resulted in me getting cited for contempt by Parnell's public defender for violating the judge's antipublicity order; although looking at it carefully later, I'm not sure I did violate the order. We tried very hard to get the publicity we wanted for the search for Poorman, and yet avoid talking about the heart of the case, which is what the order was about?"

In the end, Joe was vindicated when the judge heard and dismissed the contempt citation against him.

Said McClure about Joe's close call: "We settled that in chambers, and the judge said, 'Joe, don't talk to *anybody, anymore.'* And then we go to lunch at Al's and Joe meets a reporter from *Newsweek* or *TIME,* and Joe, with his voice louder than anybody else's in the place, proceeds to talk to this guy about the case all lunch time. And after about forty-five minutes I'm done eating, and I said to Joe, 'I've got to get back to work. Talk to whoever you want, Joe, but remember what the judge said.' And I walked out and Scott LeStrange is about four booths over, having lunch. I just thought it was kinda amusing. I never heard anything else about it. Maybe Scott wasn't listening very well."

Since Parnell had taken Steve out of California three times—twice to Reno and once on the cross-country trip to Arkansas—Merced County had the option of deferring prosecution of their kidnapping charge to the federal courts. However, in a meeting with D.A. Hallford, Sgt. Lunney and Chief Kulbeth agreed with the D.A.'s position that he prosecute the case for Merced County under California law. Also, at that time all three of them felt certain that Parnell would be prosecuted by Mendocino County for his sexual assaults on Steve.

In the kidnapping of Timmy White Mendocino County had no such option: The only decision facing Finn was whether Parnell would be charged with the sexual assaults on Steve and the many sexual assaults on Kenny and Lloyd Matthias, George Mitchell, and a number of other Mendocino County boys just then coming to light. But even when Lunney and Price phoned Finn to remind him that Steve was ready and willing to testify about Parnell's sexual assaults on him, Finn acknowledged this concern but didn't act on it.

After working with McClure on the preliminary hearing, Joe Allen turned the actual prosecution of the kidnapping case against Parnell over to his assistant: "George just sat down with me one day and said, 'Would you have any great objections if I tried Parnell?' And I said, 'I don't suppose so. Why?' And he said, 'Well, I thought it would do me some good in the election.' And George was running for D.A. and I wasn't and we both figured George could use a win in an important case . . . it would help him politically. But from that point on, I sort of took a back seat to George."

McClure elaborates: "During the four years that Joe served as D.A. he tried less than half-a-dozen cases. As D.A., he liked to be known and to get his name in the news. But Joe is not a prosecutor. He has never been a prosecutor . . . it ran against his grain.

"The relationship between Joe and me was very strange. I ran the D.A.'s office for all practical purposes. Meanwhile, Joe would go to the Forest Club and all the pool tournaments and play pool. At that point in time I had been the chief deputy for five months and we had three brand-new deputy D.A.'s that had not been in the office long at all . . . a whole new crew. So who in the hell do I rely on? I rely on Dick Finn, because he's been there longer than anyone else. And I don't know what shit Dick Finn used to lie in, but at this point he was obviously doing a hell of a lot more to make Dick Finn important than anything else."

And so, McClure tacitly followed Finn's lead in the

investigation of Kenneth Eugene Parnell . . . sexual
assaults and all. Specifically, George said that Finn
came back to him about the sexual assaults and "recommended that we not go any further on it because
we probably aren't going to be able to do anything
much anyway."

When McClure first learned from the author that
Merced Police had provided Finn with evidence of
Parnell's 87 separate sexual assaults on Steve plus evidence of sexual assaults on nearly a dozen other boys,
he angrily said that Finn never did share anything of
the kind with him. "If in fact these assaults happened,
and if there was sufficient evidence there that I could
put on a good case, then I would blame whoever it
was that was supposed to give them to me . . . and the
person . . . was Dick Finn."

The change of venue to Alameda County for Mendocino County's kidnapping trial cost half of the
D.A.'s annual budget. These expenses included considerable court costs, transportation, lodging, and
meals. Also, Mendocino County was responsible for
substantial defense bills, since LeStrange did everything he could to defend his client. First he hired private investigator Joseph Burger to search out defense
witnesses. Also, before the trial, LeStrange spent considerable funds attempting to locate a psychiatrist who
would examine Parnell and then at trial give helpful,
expert testimony for the defense. It came to nothing.

However, when Parnell was transferred to the
Alameda County Jail in Oakland, LeStrange engaged
psychiatrist David Axelrad from the University of California at Davis to travel to Oakland to examine his
client. Afterward, Dr. Axelrad wrote to LeStrange,

"During the course of the examination, it became clear to me that Mr. Parnell is experiencing significant paranoid ideation and significant hostility toward the criminal justice system. . . . In view of the above, I respectfully request that you arrange for an evaluation of Mr. Parnell with the Mental Health Institute of Sacramento." This was done, but again without positive results for the defense.

Next, LeStrange got the Court to transfer Parnell to the California State Prison Medical Facility at Vacaville, thirty miles north of Oakland where, at considerable expense to Mendocino County, Parnell underwent several "truth serum" sessions during which he was injected with sodium pentothal and then questioned by LeStrange. These sessions were videotaped and reviewed by LeStrange who told the author that he considered their content so damaging to Parnell that he chose not to use the tapes nor any of the information derived from them in Parnell's defense. "There is information in those tapes that, if known, would put Mr. Parnell behind bars for the rest of his natural life." These tapes have remained under LeStrange's direct, personal control ever since.

Chapter Twelve

The First Trial

"Parnell is capable of killing a kid to protect himself."

Finally, more than a year after Steve and Timmy had hitchhiked into Ukiah, on Monday, June 8, 1981, the trial of Kenneth Eugene Parnell, charged in the kidnapping of Timmy White, began "in the Superior Court of the State of California, Alameda County, before the Honorable M. O. Sabraw, Judge." But matters ground to an immediate halt when there was considerable disagreement among the news media, the defense, and the prosecution about the media's right to be present in the courtroom. At the same time Judge Sabraw heard arguments from LeStrange and McClure about the methods to be used in questioning potential jurors—the *voir dire* process.

The next day Judge Sabraw granted the media's request for extended coverage, ruling that one television camera and operator and one still photographer with two cameras and four lenses could be present in the courtroom at any given time, that one broadcast audio system could be in place in the courtroom, and that individual reporters could use their small pocket recorders. However, these rules were for the trial itself, and to prevent intimidating potential jurors, no media coverage would be allowed during the *voir dire*.

Moving along quickly, Judge Sabraw granted LeStrange's motion to conduct an individual *voir dire* of each potential juror, denied LeStrange's second motion for an increase in peremptory challenges, and then had Bailiff Bob Artis usher in the panel of forty prospective jurors, seating twelve in the jury box and the remainder in the audience of his courtroom.

At this point Judge Sabraw spoke to the assembled jurors and delivered a polished and professional yet never patronizing explanation of their responsibilities and of the workings and procedures of a criminal court of law. A man of average build, with jet black hair highlighted by a few streaks of gray, and wearing black horn-rimmed glasses, Sabraw has the courtroom demeanor of a somewhat kindly yet learned uncle whose very presence demands attention. After a brief recess, the judge conducted the preliminary general questioning of the first twelve prospective jurors by inquiring about their ages, occupations, families, etc. One juror was retained for in-depth, individual *voir dire* while the remaining eleven, along with the balance of the panel of forty, were led out of the courtroom.

On through prospective jurors two and three the slow questioning process ground. Before juror number four took the stand, Judge Sabraw undertook to speed things up by suggesting to LeStrange that some of his repetitious questions be handled in a general session, but LeStrange was unwilling to relinquish any portion of his hard-won motion to question each prospective juror individually.

The process continued to plod along day after boring day until it finally ended the morning of Wednesday, June 17. The jury was sworn in and court was promptly recessed for lunch.

The *voir dire* filled nearly eight hundred pages of trial transcript, but there had been one startling bobble the morning before its completion. With the individual *voir dire* under way, and without asking anyone, Finn violated court protocol and casually strolled into the courtroom holding Timmy and his sister Nicole by the hand and, as if it were a perfectly normal thing to do, nonchalantly led the pair around the courtroom, chatting with the two children as he pointed out the various participants—intentionally ignoring a shocked Parnell—until Bailiff Artis realized what was happening and escorted them outside. The hapless McClure lamely tried to excuse his investigator's conduct, but Judge Sabraw quickly agreed to LeStrange's request to dismiss the prospective juror then on the stand.

The trial did not get under way after lunch that day because the defense brought up several more motions for consideration—all denied by Sabraw—including one wherein LeStrange sought a blanket prohibition of any mention by the State of "the alleged Merced kidnapping of Steven Stayner in 1972."

The next morning McClure offered the State's opening statement, consisting of a very logical, sequential explanation of Mendocino County's kidnapping case against Parnell. When McClure had concluded, Sabraw offered LeStrange an opportunity to make his opening statement, but he reserved the right to do that until after he had presented his case. He never exercised this option.

At long last the trial began in earnest when McClure presented his first witness, Angela White. She testified that Timmy was her son, recounted her personal knowledge of the events of Valentine's Day 1980, identified the clothes her son wore that day, told about her search for him, and finally over LeStrange's vociferous objections—identified Timmy when Dick Finn brought him into the courtroom. Angela left the stand and the State next presented several witnesses who knew Timmy.

Several days later, in anticipation of testimony by Sean Poorman, a special hearing was held at the request of Edward M. Krug, attorney for Henry K. Mettier, Jr. He was in court to represent Mettier's stepson. By then Sean had been convicted in Mendocino County Juvenile Court on a charge of false imprisonment and packed off for two years "in placement" at a northern California residential juvenile facility. Mr. Krug now introduced a motion requesting that the Court not allow the news photographer or television cameraman to photograph or videotape Sean while he was on the stand, arguing that as a juvenile he should be protected.

Attorneys from the *San Francisco Chronicle,* the *San Francisco Examiner,* the *Oakland Tribune,* and the *Sacramento Bee* argued strongly against any such prohibition, and McClure and LeStrange were in rare agreement with them. After hearing the arguments,

Judge Sabraw said that he would reserve his ruling until just prior to Sean's testimony and the trial continued with Timmy's schoolmate, seven-year-old Nat Kitcher.

Still more witnesses preceded the mid-morning recess, and when court resumed, Judge Sabraw ruled against Mr. Krug's motion and Sean was called to the stand. Quickly Mr. Krug approached the bench and requested that the State consider granting his client immunity from further prosecution in return for his testimony. McClure, LeStrange, Krug, Sean, and the court reporter followed Judge Sabraw to his chambers for a private discussion of the matter. McClure stated: "I have no objection to giving him immunity for any of those marijuana problems that he had. But unless I know what else we are talking about, if Mr. Poorman and Mr. Parnell buried twenty-five people in the woods, you know, I am not going to give anybody immunity for that." And that was the way it was handled . . . immunity was granted Sean Poorman for his minor offenses only.*

With the hearing ended, everyone returned to the courtroom. Sean was sworn in and began his direct testimony for the State, his account of the kidnapping, however, not as accurate as others' recollections of the events. But considering the legal jeopardy he was in, it was as close as one could expect him to make it.

When McClure steered Sean into his conversations

---

*In December 1984, Jim, Sean's brother, told the author that Mettier was still involved in "illegal dealings," and that "Hank" used Sean "to do his dirty work." Concerning his brother's relationship with Parnell, Jim spat: "He doesn't like Parnell. One time he said Parnell made him help to bury a couple of kids Parnell'd wasted."

with Parnell the day of the kidnapping, the teenager's responses became rather stilted. "We were going to abduct a little boy around—early that morning, and if we couldn't get one that morning, then we would in the afternoon. We talked about how we were going to partake in it, like you sit in the backseat, and I will sit in the front seat and we will go through some—go through some cruising around some schools, and then, basically, I would get out and grab a little kid."

Finishing his direct examination of Sean, McClure again brought Timmy into the courtroom, this time to identify Sean as the person who'd grabbed him and thrown him into Parnell's car. Again LeStrange objected, fearful of the sympathy the cute youngster's multiple appearances could engender with the jury. But Judge Sabraw again overruled his objection. Timmy entered and identified Sean.

With a transcript of the preliminary hearing in hand, LeStrange cross-examined the hunch-shouldered, sullen teenager using Sean's previous testimony to destroy the adolescent's contention that Parnell had *made* him kidnap Timmy by threatening him with a knife. All Parnell was doing, Sean finally admitted, "was cussing at me." With his meager success at spreading his client's guilt to include Sean, LeStrange forged ahead by pointing out additional discrepancies between Sean's preliminary hearing testimony and present testimony, but none was significant enough to further damage Sean's already limited credibility.

"I don't think there was any doubt at all that Sean knew more than what he was telling," McClure said

later, "and I say that because at one point I had heard
he was saying, 'Some other things happened, but I am
not so mad at Parnell at this point that I want to go
into it.' And I had some long conversations with Dick
Finn about how much do we want to delve into this
kid's life . . . it had been screwed up enough as it was.
I think that things happened to Sean by Parnell and
that Sean had observed what Parnell had done to
other kids."

Joe Allen agreed. "Poorman, I think, was in a position of attempting to protect himself as much as possible. He was a suspicious, paranoid kid, and perhaps
rightly so, considering the environment that he lived
in . . . hanging out with kidnappers and child molesters . . . I don't think he had any vested interest in
telling the truth. He wanted to tell enough of the truth
to get himself off the hook, but maybe not enough of
the truth to make himself look like the full, willing
participant that I'm convinced he was. Poorman had
no conscience about assisting Parnell with various
matters. What they were we can speculate."

Sean testified most of the afternoon, and when he
finally stepped down, his former best friend Steven
Stayner took his place on the stand . . . but not before
LeStrange again objected to testimony which he knew
could damage his client. Countered George McClure,
"As an offer of proof, I might mention to the Court
[that] we expect Steven Stayner at some point to say
that the reason he thought that Mr. Parnell had ab-
ducted Timmy White was based on the fact that he
had previously had the same thing happen to him."
After hearing both sides, Judge Sabraw agreed to allow

Steve's testimony about his own kidnapping and the teen took the stand and was sworn in.

His testimony began with his giving his "other" name, and then picking up his life's tale as of February 1980. Then, after a few more questions, McClure had Timmy brought in so that Steve could identify him. This accomplished, Timmy left the courtroom.

A few minutes later, LeStrange objected yet again when McClure asked Steve if Parnell had ever asked for his help in kidnapping a boy, but Judge Sabraw allowed the question and Steve answered affirmatively. The sixteen-year-old made a very good witness for the State and capably held his own during LeStrange's cross and re-cross-examination before stepping down on the third day of trial testimony.

Next Ukiah police officers Bob Warner, Larry Maxon, and John Williams testified in succession, each telling about his part in the events of the night of March 1, 1980. Court adjourned that day after Finn's testimony about serving the search warrant at the cabin.

The following day Steve and Finn were recalled briefly to the stand before the State called its final witness, Sgt. Lunney. At no point did McClure ask Steve any questions about Parnell's sex assaults on him or on other boys.

When Lunney stepped down, LeStrange put Parnell on the stand, and after slowly spelling his name for the court clerk, the balding kidnapper faced his attorney as LeStrange elicited from him a very long, convoluted story about the events of November 1979 through March 1, 1980. And when LeStrange asked Parnell if anyone lived with him at the Mountain View

Ranch in late 1979, he replied, "Yes, Steven Stayner. I called him Dennis."

Getting back to his story, Parnell said that he'd met "Hank" Mettier, Jr., in Elk in the fall of 1979 and that Mettier had told him that he knew he had kidnapped Dennis and asked for details about it. Parnell then vaguely related that Mettier threatened "the ones I care about . . . my mother and Dennis" should he not help Mettier kidnap a boy.

Parnell's recollection was that his next meeting with Mettier occurred in Ukiah at The Palace Hotel, when "he wanted to know how I came into possession of Dennis. And he reminded me that if I didn't cooperate, why, he would do either one of two things, and I don't remember what . . ."

After listening to this long tale, those in the courtroom finally heard this strange man tell his version of the events of February 13, 1980, the day before Timmy's kidnapping. He said that Hank phoned him: "He wanted me to go pick up Sean and bring him to Ukiah." Parnell went on to say that he did as he was told, picking up Sean in Elk before retrieving Dennis at the Point Arena school bus stop, the only portion of his testimony which matched Steve's.

But Parnell's account of the day of the kidnapping was the very antithesis of Sean's. Parnell's version had the teenager disappearing from The Palace Hotel before Parnell got off work that morning and himself going over to the Samoa Club for a beer and to shoot the bull for a spell. Next, he said, he went to the Salvation Army Thrift Store and bought a box spring, tied it to the roof of his Maverick, and—still without Sean—drove out of Ukiah, stopping at eleven for lunch at El Rebozzo Mexican Restaurant. Lunch finished, Parnell asserted he got back into his car and drove home alone

Parnell matter-of-factly intoned that he arrived at his cabin about one-thirty, fixed himself a cup of coffee, smoked a couple of cigarettes, and was then startled when Sean burst into the cabin and said, " 'We kidnapped a kid.' "

Then LeStrange asked his client when he first saw Timmy. Parnell replied, "It was about the twentieth. Hank brought him up to the cabin with a couple of sacks. I still didn't want him to leave him there, and he said he would get him in the next day or two." In response to his attorney's question about why Mettier brought Timmy to the cabin, Parnell launched into a spirited yet confusing story about his paycheck being late, his driving to Ukiah to pick it up, his running into Mettier at The Palace Hotel on February 16, and Hank's telling him that he had Timmy and wanted Parnell to take care of "the boy until he could work something out." Finally, LeStrange had Parnell deal with the problem of Steve's testimony that he first saw Timmy in the Maverick on February 14. Weakly Parnell explained, "Dennis might have been confused. He is right. He did see the boy in the car, but he just doesn't know the day."

Then it was McClure's turn to cross-examine Parnell, and after a few stale questions and answers, Parnell bumbled into a most confusing scenario about Mettier's reasons for kidnapping Timmy, summing it up with: "I think he mentioned something that he had worked out some kind of deal for making some money or trading the kid for dope."

McClure's cross-examination of Parnell continued into a second day when he opened by trying to make some sense out of Parnell's 1979-1980 cash flow, the only clear information being Parnell's statement that he made $600 a month at The Palace Hotel.

All through the trial McClure had noticed Parnell taking extreme interest in the legal minutiae of the proceedings: "During the trial, Parnell would turn to Scott and I could hear him talking, and he would say, 'Does *that* protect my appeal right? Do you think I could appeal on *that* issue?' He was almost paranoid about whether or not [he had] an appeal right on everything [LeStrange] did. And that probably indicates to some degree that the guy is looking into law books beforehand. He's got an idea about what kind of things are appealable and what kind of things you have to watch out for."

And in fact, during the time Steven was living with Parnell, the kidnapper owned an old law book in which he penciled in defenses in the margins for four different crimes: kidnapping, rape, robbery, and murder. Parnell had been arrested, tried, and convicted for the first three, but never the fourth, and he angrily refuses to respond when questioned about this.*

After Parnell finished his testimony, LeStrange presented a series of defense witnesses to try and support Parnell's story about his whereabouts on Valentine's Day 1980, but Jim Bertain, who owned the Samoa Club, couldn't recall whether Parnell was at the bar

*When the author interviewed Parnell about this in December of 1984 the convict was quite upset to learn that the author had recovered the law book from the Mountain View Ranch.

the day of Timmy's kidnapping; the lady who managed El Rebozzo couldn't recall Parnell having lunch there that day; and the couple who operated the Salvation Army Thrift Store where Parnell claimed to have bought the box spring didn't remember him either.

Steve's close friend from Comptche, Damon Carroll, then took the stand for the defense and gave a confusing recollection of the events of February and March 1980, rife with conflicts when compared to his sworn statements during the preliminary hearing.

McClure then offered a half-dozen State's witnesses in rebuttal, the shocker being Hank Mettier himself, who upon entering the courtroom looked about nervously. He was like a fish out of water. It was obvious that being there was *not* his preference.

> McClure: Do you know Chris Poorman?
> Mettier: Yeah.
> McClure: And could you tell us what your relationship is to her?
> Mettier: She and I have a son together.
> McClure: Beyond that, have you lived together for some period of time?
> Mettier: On and off, yes, for the last eight years.

As Mettier squirmed on the witness stand, McClure conducted a verbal block-and-parry with the conservatively dressed, convicted drug dealer as he went on to establish that Sean Poorman lived with him, called him "Dad," and referred to him as his "stepfather." Later, McClure asked the short, neatly bearded Mettier about his whereabouts from November 1979 through February 1980.

> McClure: During that period of time, did you ever come up to Mendocino County?
>
> Mettier: Yeah. I was living—in November I was probably living in Philo.
>
> McClure: And would you tell us during the latter part of November, possibly around Thanksgiving, did you ever meet the defendant sitting here at the end of the table, Mr. Parnell?
>
> Mettier: Never.
>
> McClure: Did you ever meet him by the post office in Elk?
>
> Mettier: I have never seen Mr. Parnell outside of this courtroom. The first time I ever saw him in my life was on Thursday afternoon in this courtroom.
>
> McClure: You saw Timmy White in my office today, is that correct?
>
> Mettier: Yes.
>
> McClure: Before seeing him today in my office, had you ever seen him before?
>
> Mettier: Only in this courtroom.
>
> McClure: Could you tell us when was the first time you ever saw Steven Stayner?
>
> Mettier: In this courtroom also. I think it was on Monday.

After attempting to discover an earlier possible first meeting with Parnell, McClure continued.

McClure: Did you ever go to the Palace Hotel
on February 16, 1980, about eight or
nine in the morning?

Mettier: No.

McClure: Do you remember where you were
that day?

Mettier: No, I can't remember.

McClure: How about February twentieth? Do
you remember where you were on
February twentieth?

Mettier: I can't remember that either.

And still later, there was this:

McClure: On February 14, 1980, Valentine's
Day of 1980, could you tell us between,
let's say, eleven and two o'clock in the
afternoon, do you recall where you
were during that period of time?

Suddenly, and most disingenuously, Mettier was able
to distinctly recall *all* his activities that particular day.

Mettier: Sure. I had a doctor's appointment in
Mill Valley at the Holistic Health
Institute at 9:30 in the morning. The
doctor was very late. I remember
waiting for at least forty-five minutes
for the doctor to come in. Then I
spent at least forty-five minutes with
the doctor, and then after lunch, he
prescribed some medicine for me, and
I ordered that over the telephone

around a quarter to two, I guess, from
Mill Valley.

McClure: Have you done anything to check to
see if your time frame is accurate on
that?

Mettier: Yes. I looked over my phone records
and that's what they indicated to me.

McClure: Did you do anything beyond that?

Mettier: Do what?

McClure: Well, did you check with the doctor's
office?

Mettier: Oh, yeah. I called the doctor's office,
and they told me exactly what time
my appointment was.

McClure: They had some sort of a record?

Mettier: They had those records, right.

McClure: And that refreshed your memory
about it?

Mettier: Oh, sure, yeah.*

Mettier's "convenient memory," illustrated by
McClure's direct examination, was made more evident during LeStrange's cross-examination of the former drug dealer:

*The defense's investigator, Joseph Burger, phoned the clinic
using the number provided him by Mettier. A person answered
and confirmed Mettier's testimony, and Burger then dropped
the matter. However, there has never been a "Holistic Health
Institute," in Mill Valley. Also, Burger's records reflect the doctor's name as "Coslinkco," but no such surname can be found
in Mill Valley telephone directories from 1977 to 1984, and
there is no such name among the 1985 professional directories
for all types of licensed California physicians, including holistic
physicians.

LeStrange:	Mr. Mettier, you were living where at that time [late 1979 or early 1980]?
Mettier:	I really can't remember, but I was probably in Elk. But I can't remember exactly what was going on at that time. I mean, I don't know, you know, where I was, specifically, at any point in November or December or anything like that. It's difficult for me to recall that.
LeStrange:	Were you employed in November of 1979?
Mettier:	I can't remember that either. I have changed jobs a few times, and I can't—I can't remember. I don't know.
LeStrange:	Have you ever been arrested on narcotics?
Mettier:	As a juvenile I was arrested for a very small quantity of marijuana, but that was a juvenile matter. And that was a long time ago, too.
LeStrange:	What year?
Mettier:	Well, it was probably eleven years ago.
LeStrange:	How old would you have been?
Mettier:	I think I was about sixteen.
LeStrange:	And where was that? In Marin County?
Mettier:	Yeah, it was.
LeStrange:	And are you sure you were a juvenile?
Mettier:	Yeah, I'm sure.

* * *

On the last day of trial testimony, June 29, LeStrange effectively impeached Mettier's testimony by introducing the official record of the witness's 1973 Marin County felony arrest, conviction, and probation for possession of a commercial quantity of marijuana—as a nineteen-year-old adult.

Next McClure called Timmy to the stand, and as LeStrange watched the little boy's testimony, he was very concerned about its precise, organized manner, feeling that he had been coached by Finn when he'd attempted to hypnotize the child during his investigation. (Actually, McClure had coached him.) Then, when his turn came to cross-examine Timmy, LeStrange walked on eggs so as not to anger the jury, an approach which resulted in an uneventful and unproductive cross-examination.

Before the trial, in an effort to counter Finn's amateurish hypnosis of Timmy, LeStrange had had Dr. David Axelrad—the same psychiatrist he had hired to attempt to evaluate Parnell at the Alameda County Jail—assemble a forensic case panel of his peers to make a professional determination as to whether, after being hypnotized, Timmy could be expected to testify honestly about the events surrounding his kidnapping. Among the panel's findings was ". . . that the hypnotic process carried out by Richard Finn was not valid."

Therefore, LeStrange wanted to introduce Dr. Axelrad's statement in court by having him testify to it, but Judge Sabraw would not allow it. This point became the sole trial error which was later appealed by

Parnell's court-appointed appeals attorney, Daniel Horowitz of Oakland . . . albeit unsuccessfully.

Finally, after the defense called several witnesses in subrebuttal to the State's case, it was time for McClure and LeStrange to make their closing arguments. LeStrange took forty-eight minutes before the lunch recess in a futile attempt to get Parnell acquitted; McClure began his closing argument immediately after lunch and took thirty-one minutes to sum up the State's exceptionally strong case.

On June 29 at 2:15 P.M. Judge Sabraw spent slightly more than thirty minutes patiently and carefully reciting detailed instructions to the jury, and at 2:52 they retired to deliberate Parnell's fate. At 4:50 they filed back into the jury box and stated that they had found Kenneth Eugene Parnell guilty of kidnapping in the second degree.

Judge Sabraw thanked the twelve profusely for their patience, time, and thorough consideration of the evidence, and then dismissed them.

Since Parnell had two prior felony convictions and had served prison time for both, California law precluded the possibility of probation. Therefore, two months later, Judge Sabraw sentenced Kenneth Eugene Parnell to the maximum prison time allowed for second-degree kidnapping: seven years.

Thus, Parnell's trial, conviction, and sentencing for kidnapping ended, and even though Mendocino D.A. Joe Allen was happy with the verdict, he did not feel justice had been completely served, saying: "I always thought there was a possibility that Parnell was involved in undetected crimes. I still think so. There is a similarity in my mind between child molesters and serial murderers. Child molesters who kidnap and retain their victims, like Parnell, are by far the rarest type.

"If we caught Parnell three times, I don't know if that means he did it thirteen times or three hundred times, but I'll bet there are a whole lot of incidents that we don't know about where Parnell did one thing or another. If Parnell took a kid and the kid fought back, or tried to run away, or for some reason Parnell thought that the kid wasn't going to work out, or perhaps there was a danger of this being detected, I think Parnell is fully capable of killing a kid to protect himself."

Chapter Thirteen

The Trial for Kidnapping Steven Stayner

"I'd like to point my finger at Mendocino County."

By September of 1981 Mendocino County's trial of Kenneth Eugene Parnell for the kidnapping of Timmy White was history, but many of the same participants in the drama just past would be reassembled for Merced County's scheduled December trial for his nine-year-old kidnapping of Steven Stayner. Also, this time there would be two defendants, since defense attorneys for Ervin Edward "Murph" Murphy were unsuccessful in their attempts to separate the simple-minded accomplice's trial from that of Parnell. The venue of the trial was changed to Hayward and Judge Sabraw would again preside.

Unlike Mendocino County's trial, where a Deputy D.A. represented the State, the Merced County trial would be prosecuted by the District Attorney himself, Pat Hallford, a dedicated, straight-arrow law enforcement officer who for sixteen years had been a highly respected F.B.I. agent before he resigned and ran successfully for office in Merced. He was a man as conservative and restrained in handling his job as Joe Allen was unconventional and verbose.

Within weeks of the trial the Merced County D.A.'s investigator, Lyle Davis, a trenchant, heavyset man with a jocular approach to life, took Steven on an intense four-day evidence-gathering trip to Mendocino County. About the trip Lyle recalled, "Our task was to photograph and document where he was, when he was there. I think the most memorable thing was the apparent ease with which we completed our task . . . Steve was always very, very well received, very well liked by a lot of the adults in that area. But in terms of visible trauma [to Steve], there was none. But I did realize that he has two feelings for Parnell. I think that there is a very paternalistic one. I think he would have also, if given the chance, probably removed Parnell's head."

Besides the trip with Steve, Lyle's responsibilities included uncovering as much as possible about Murphy's background and involvement in Steve's kidnapping, particularly how much Murphy knew about Parnell's sexual fixation on young boys. Said Lyle, "I don't think Murphy was ever totally honest with us, and I guess we shouldn't have expected him to be, but I knew that he knew a hell of a lot more than he told us."

Remarked Merced Police Chief Harold Kulbeth, "Murphy allowed himself to be used. While he's not intellectual by any means, certainly, I think, the man knows right from wrong; and he participated in a very, very serious crime. He covered it up and did not come forth with the information that was needed to help find Steve or clear the case up for all those years."

On December 1, 1981, Merced County's case against Kenneth Eugene Parnell and Ervin Edward Murphy went to trial in Judge Sabraw's courtroom in the Hayward Hall of Justice with a lineup of witnesses only slightly different from before. This time there was three defense attorneys instead of one: the Merced Public Defender, John Ellery, was representing Parnell and, because of that, Merced County had hired other local attorneys Wayne Eisenhart and Neil Morse to represent Murphy as privately contracted Special Public Defenders.

Parnell and Ellery never did see eye to eye. However, Ellery later explained that he had been disturbed about representing Parnell because he himself had been sexually abused as a boy; but, he hastened to add, he had done his "professional best" to defend Parnell.

As for Morse and Eisenhart's defense of Murphy, Eisenhart said that they used "substantially what was in the police reports [because] I don't think Murphy ever varied from what was in the police reports."

Recalled Morse, "Murph is not someone who is gonna spend a lot of time fabricating stories. He is a fairly harmless person who is always looking for someone to like him, either through telling them stories or buying them drinks or something else. He made a mistake: he helped Parnell. He shouldn't have, and he acknowledges that he shouldn't have. I can remember talking with him and he'd be physically shaking. He knew it was wrong and he worried about it for years and years after."

In preparing their defense of Murphy, Eisenhart

and Morse hired retired F.B.I agents Mel Shannon and Tom Walsh (Chief Kulbeth's friend) to do some investigative work for them. Morse quoted his client as saying, " 'I know I've done wrong, and whatever they're gonna punish me with is okay. I should be punished.' It was a real fatalistic type of thing, but the amount of information we needed from him, he had some trouble trying to recall. He's not what you'd call the most insightful person you ever met.

"What we were trying to do with Murphy was aim for the statute of limitations argument. We were trying to show too that at a certain point in time—early on in the kidnapping—Steven Stayner was able to control his own destiny, his own fate; that he had free rein and was not a mental captive."

As with the first trial, Judge Sabraw spent part of the first day hearing assorted defense motions dealing with striking or including various categories of evidence, and he made an identical ruling to one in the earlier trial about extended media coverage: there could be one TV camera and operator, one news photographer, and one sound system, and reporters would be allowed to use their own small audio cassette tape recorders. Then, late that day and continuing for the next six days, the boring but vitally important process of jury *voir dire* ran its course.

On Thursday, December 10, with jury selection finally completed, Judge Sabraw had the jury sworn in and then had them leave the courtroom so as to allow still more State and defense motions to be argued outside their presence. Among the defense motions, the major one Ellery presented was one to limit evidence about the kidnapping of Timmy White, the other side of the coin from LeStrange's concern during the first trial. After hearing Ellery out, Judge Sabraw walked a fine line by ruling that he would not allow testimony specific to that abduction, but would allow testimony "that would be appropriate covering that same period of time."

Then Judge Sabraw called the jury back and dismissed them for a late lunch, leaving just the lawyers, defendants, and court officials present. None of the attorneys were prepared for what happened next, but those familiar with Judge Sabraw, like Bailiff Bob Artis and court clerk Shirley Wensler, were not at all surprised. When the last juror had departed, Judge Sabraw began to speak, his voice rising in a carefully controlled crescendo of anger: "As counsel realizes, the matter of Mr. Murphy's glasses was first called to the Court's attention some two months ago, October 9th, and I indicated to Mr. Murphy at that time that I would ensure that he would have his glasses replaced and available to him for the trial.

"Now, in each session that Mr. Murphy has appeared since that time, inquiry has been made about these glasses, and, as a matter of fact, it's been done on a daily basis since the trial commenced on December 1st, and I indicated at the outset that I would not proceed with this trial until Mr. Murphy's glasses had been replaced."

Now wound tightly, Judge Sabraw concluded, "However, I'm going to invite the Sheriff and the Director of the county Health Care Services to be here at 9:30 on Monday morning if Mr. Murphy does not have his glasses at that time. . . . I'm inviting you, Deputy King, to communicate that to the Sheriff's Office and the

Court will communicate it to the County Director of Health Care Services." With that Judge Sabraw adjourned Court until 10:00 Monday morning.

Murph had his glasses well before ten o'clock Monday morning. Said Bailiff Artis about Judge Sabraw's pique over the delay, "He sure got their attention over at the Sheriff's Office! You bet!"

At 10:15 the following Monday morning it was a calm Judge Sabraw who greeted those assembled in his courtroom with, "Good morning, ladies and gentlemen, counsel . . ." before routinely replacing an ill juror with an alternate and having court clerk Shirley Wensler read the information on the charges to the jury, a five-thousand-word document prepared by Merced D.A. Hallford which detailed the two charges against codefendants Parnell and Murphy: kidnapping Steven Stayner and conspiracy to commit the kidnapping, a considerably more difficult charge to prove.

Ms. Wensler finished reading the lengthy document, the State and defense reserved their opening statements until the close of the trial, and Hallford called his first witness, Steven's mother, Kay. Her initial testimony was routine as she told about her family and children, and particularly about Steven and his school attendance, before she began relating recollections of the family's activities on December 4, 1972. There were no objections from the three defense attorneys during Hallford's steady, competent direct examination.

Wayne Eisenhart then cross-examined Kay and got right down to using what he felt might be helpful information on the subject of Steve's unhappiness about the family's move from the almond ranch into Merced and the alleged immoderate physical punishment of Steve. Before the trial the trio of defense attorneys had discussed and agreed to use this angle in an attempt to explain their clients' statements to police that Steve had been happy to leave his home, and so Eisenhart asked about Steven's tardiness in coming home from school. As he expected, Kay responded by explaining what she and Del had done to counter Steven's misbehavior before Eisenhart drove home with:

Eisenhart:	The second or third time, was it reinforced in any way?
Kay:	Yes.
Eisenhart:	And how was it reinforced?
Kay:	He got a paddling from his papa.
Eisenhart:	And how long before his disappearance was this?
Kay:	It was the week previous.
Eisenhart:	Were you present?
Kay:	I can't remember. I probably was.
Eisenhart:	Do you know whether the paddling was administered with a hand or otherwise?
Kay:	It probably was with a belt, but it probably wasn't very hard, knowing his papa.
Eisenhart:	Okay. "Knowing his papa." What do you mean by that?
Kay:	He tended to be a little bit easy with the kids.
Eisenhart:	Didn't punish them very often?
Kay:	Very, very seldom.
Eisenhart:	So it would be unusual that he

	would spank Steven with a belt?
Kay:	Very unusual, though he thought it was important that the boy know he was supposed to come home first.
Eisenhart:	My understanding would then be, if there was disciplining of Steven, spanking, it was your task more than your husband's. Is that correct?
Kay:	Typical mother, I nagged at him and paddled him a lot, yes.

Eisenhart was caught off guard by Kay's direct response but felt that this just might be the crack he had been seeking. Carefully he began to dig away at her, but it was to no avail, for Kay stood resolute in the correctness of her discipline of her children. Then, in turn, Ellery cross-examined Kay, but he, too, got nowhere.

Next Hallford brought Del to the witness stand to introduce Steven's Missing Juvenile flyer into evidence before turning him over to the defense for cross-examination. This time Neil Morse began with the ranch-vs.-town issue before nimbly shifting to the corporal punishment theme.

Morse:	Now, prior to December 4th, a week to ten days prior, had you had occasion to spank Steven?
Del:	I spanked him one time on a Friday before he disappeared on the Monday.

Then, after a few more questions, he got Del to admit that Kay spanked their children more than he did.

This put the onus of supposed immoderate punishment back on Kay. Then, Morse changed the subject and asked the witness about his family being approached about selling movie rights to Steven's story. Hallford quickly objected to this question and the objection was sustained by Judge Sabraw. John Ellery rose to assist in the argument that this was relevant, but it didn't profit the defense. Then came this exchange:

Ellery: Was the flyer sent to schools in Santa Rosa?
Del: Yes, they were. They were sent to every school in the state of California. I have a directory on that.

Ellery realized that his question and moreover, Del's response, opened a legal can of worms for the defense. By referring to Steven's school attendance while he was living with Parnell, Ellery had introduced a subject that could be damaging to his client's case. Prior to this point in the trial, the prosecution had been unable to raise this issue because it was not directly connected to the charges of kidnapping and conspiracy to kidnap.

Hoping that his strategic error would go unnoticed, Ellery quickly ended his cross-examination of the witness.

Hallford then solidified the jury's memory of this unexpected gift from the defense with a brief redirect examination of Del about the Missing Juvenile flyers and their distribution to the very schools Steven had attended as Dennis Parnell. Then he called Steven's second-grade teacher, Mary Walsh, to the stand. His direct examination elicited testimony from her that Steven was a young boy who needed "special strokes."

Walsh: He had to be recognized as a person. Sometimes I did that with children in my classroom with a wink of the eye or a smile or a touch on the shoulder.

Hallford: He wanted your approval?

Walsh: Yes, right. I tried to do that. And that evening [December 4, 1972] he had waited for a special approval before I sent him out of the classroom, and I sent him on his way after I'd fastened his windbreaker around his chin and told him to get on. It wasn't raining right then, but it would be raining before he got home.

Hallford: And that's the last you saw of him?

Walsh: That's the last I saw of him, yes.

Hallford: Until he was a big boy?

Walsh: Until he was a big boy.

Next Eisenhart cross-examined Mary Walsh, a teacher with thirty-four years of experience, trying as he did to turn her testimony into the notion that Steven had been neglected at home.

Steve then took the stand and Hallford led the tall, lanky teenager through a basic question-and-answer session covering the move from the ranch and his early family life before turning to a series of detailed questions focusing on the defendants' behavior. Inevitably these questions got around to the then mostly unknown knowledge that Parnell had sexually assaulted Steven.

Said Hallford of his approach to having Steve testify about the subject, "We had an agreement at the trial that the media wouldn't film the portion about sex. I had the promises of the media—and Steve knew that—and I used to turn around and give a signal to the press, and they would shut the lights off, and he would feel more comfortable. You could visibly see Steve was more relieved. Then he was able to come out with it. I thought that was good of the press to be that cooperative."

Hallford: Now, at some time or other was there anything of a sexual nature that occurred?

Steven: Yes.

Hallford: And where did that start, as far as you recall?

Steven: Cathy's Valley.

Hallford: What happened?

Steven: He made me do oral sex.

Hallford: On him?

Steven: Yes.

Hallford: What else did he make you do? [Steven blushed and looked at the floor, and Hallford paused.] It's embarrassing to tell, isn't it, Steve?

Steven: Yes.

Hallford: You go ahead in whatever words you care to use. Did he do something to any part of your body?

Steven: Yes.

Hallford: Steve, I asked you a question, [to] what part of the body did this other thing occur? If you can't find the word, show us.

Steven: It's the rectum.

Hallford: What did he do to your rectum? Did he put a part of his body into you?

Steven: Yes.

Hallford: What?

Steven: His penis.

Hallford: All right. Did this occur at other times after that?

Steven: Yes.

Hallford: Could you estimate with what regularity, if any?

Steven: Maybe once every two weeks.

Hallford: Were there times when he would stop?

Steven: Yes.

Hallford: Did you want this to happen?

Steven: No.

Hallford: Did you feel ashamed?

Steven: Yes.

Hallford: When was the last time any sexual acts occurred?

Steven: January.

Hallford: Of 1980?

Steven: Yeah.

Late that afternoon Steve's testimony progressed to his first sight of Timmy, in Parnell's car on February 14, 1980:

Hallford: What did you suspect?
Steven: That he had kidnapped Timmy White.
Hallford: Why? Why did you suspect that?
Steven: Well, I had never seen Timmy before
           and all of a sudden he just shows up,
           and because he done the same thing
           with me.

In preparation for the trial Hallford had ordered two professional evaluations of Steve's mental state, one by a Merced psychologist and the other by a psychiatrist in San Francisco. These were quietly but firmly opposed by Kay and Del, who believed, as did Steve himself that his mental health was just fine and therefore there was no need for any evaluations; and certainly, they staunchly insisted, there was no need for counseling, although counseling had been and would continue to be suggested to them repeatedly for years to come.

Steve and his parents were both very unhappy that these evaluations were both introduced into evidence at the trial. However, both seem very accurate and professionally prepared. Merced psychologist Dr. Phillip M. Hamm wrote:

Steve's parents present themselves as a very typical middle-American couple. They give the feeling that they are a close couple, conversing easily, spontaneously offering support to each other, and touching and holding hands at times during the interview.

Mrs. Stayner notes that she enjoys her children and relates well to them, but, on the other hand, is more a disciplinarian than her husband. They note that Steven was taught to do as he was told by adults and not question it. . . .

The Stayners also have many concerns about Steven's adjustment since returning to their family. They note that Steven has been reluctant to talk much about his experience, and they have been reluctant to force him to discuss it. They have a feeling that he is very much like Mr. Parnell in that he seems not to have much interest in a more structured life or in taking on the responsibilities of an adult person. Finally, Mr. Stayner expressed some concern with the fact that Steven has few male friends. "All his friends are girls." He apparently has only one male friend. His father feels that he is in a pattern of attaching himself to one female, and then moving on to another in a kind of repetitive fashion, not being able to maintain any relationship, and going through one girlfriend after another without much evidence of attachment or commitment.

They [Steven's parents] are confused about how to handle Steven's irresponsibility and, either out of guilt or fear, are confused as to whether they should be more firm with their discipline or more patient.

Steven, on the other hand, presents himself as a rather happy-go-lucky, easygoing, agreeable young man with a ready smile. However, this sunny disposition is frequently punctured when he is pressed to deal with various areas of his experience with Mr. Parnell. This is especially true as his face reddens as the subject of the sexual encounters with Mr. Parnell are brought up.

The results from the psychological tests administered provide a picture of Steven as a young man with average intellectual ability who is depressed, experiencing a great deal of emotional conflict, and who has a tendency to either act out or live out his very intense internal and conflicted experience. On the Minnesota Multiphasic Personality Inventory, Steven obtained an extremely high score on the L Scale. This is a scale designed to identify persons who attempt to give overly perfectionistic views of themselves; that is, to present a positive picture.

Steven's response to Card #6 [of the Rorschach Test] indicates that he has a tremendous amount of conflict about sexual matters.

While Steven attempted to fend off his abductors by initially declining their invitation, he appears to have been completely taken in and overwhelmed by their persistence and persuasiveness. I would note that in this connection, that I believe any seven-year-old child would be much moved by this persuasion, but that Steven appears especially vulnerable in as much as he was a rather trusting child who had been raised to respect the influence of adults.

San Francisco psychiatrist Robert A. Wald prepared a much briefer evaluation of Steven, stating in part:

Steven [was] essentially trapped and bound within the unconscious mind of Dennis. When

Dennis saw the active distress of the younger child, Timmy White, his satisfaction with the myth [of being Dennis] began to deteriorate. When he saw that Timmy was treated with kindness and concern by the officer, the mythic person was subordinated to the real person, and the young man spoke his true name. It is my absolute belief that with the acknowledgment of his true identity, Steven Stayner freed himself from his state of being kidnapped. From a psychological point of view, he was still in a state of kidnap until he spoke his name, thus ending a psychic capture that lasted two thousand, six hundred forty-four days.

Before and after Doctors Hamm and Wald introduced their evaluations from the stand, the State presented a lengthy list of witnesses: school officials, teachers, and some of Parnell's and Murphy's acquaintances. Following a redirect examination of Steven, several police officers gave evidence about his school attendance, the arrests of Parnell and Murphy, and Steve's frequent moves with Parnell. Then, on December 22, the State rested and the defense began its presentation, including testimony by Murphy, Steve, Sean Poorman, and Ukiah Police Officer Bob Warner.

From the stand Murphy told of his troubled childhood, his coming to California, his going to work in the kitchen at Yosemite Lodge, and his meeting and subsequent befriending by Parnell. It was exactly as he has always told it: simply, honestly, and matter-of-factly. And he patiently repeated the same honest story—indeed, it was the only one he knew—when he was cross-examined by Hallford.

At this trial, Parnell did not take the stand. Testimony ended two days before Christmas of 1981 and because of the approaching holidays Judge Sabraw dismissed the jury until January 4, 1982, but asked the attorneys to meet with him in chambers on New Year's Eve to deal with various motions and agree on his instructions to the jury.

With the jury back in place on January 4, Hallford made his previously reserved opening statement on behalf of the people. When he finished, Morse spoke on Murphy's behalf before Ellery stood and spoke in defense of Parnell.

As is legal custom, the tall, dignified Hallford then rose again and gave the State's closing argument. It was short and to the point, ending with, "Any verdict that's not kidnapping and kidnapping for conspiracy I think would be a cruel joke on Steven, and it would be a sad and tragic day for justice in Merced County and Alameda County, and any other county in this state."

After the lunch recess the jury, attorneys, witnesses, news reporters, cameramen, and anyone else still around a month after the trial had begun were witness to Judge Sabraw's hour-long jury instructions. At 3:12 the jury retired to begin deliberations, a formidable task, since they had to decide not just Murphy's and Parnell's separate guilt or innocence on the kidnapping charges but also on the highly complicated conspiracy-to-kidnap charges.

Also, as expected with two defendants with such apparently differing levels of involvement and culpability, the jury was sufficiently confused that it spent the balance of that day, all of the next, and nearly all of a third pondering the fate of Ervin Edward Murphy. Indeed, the jury repeatedly sent requests to Judge Sabraw for clarification of the detailed charges against Parnell's accomplice and rereadings of Murphy's testimony and the law, all of which the judge promptly responded to during the panel's nearly fourteen hours of deliberations.

At 3:25 the afternoon of the third day, the jury, having finally reached a verdict on one of the charges for both men, entered the courtroom. Parnell was first to learn that he had again been found guilty of second degree kidnapping, followed immediately thereafter by the pronouncement of Murph's guilt for an identical charge. But Judge Sabraw had already known the jury had been unable to reach a decision on the conspiracy-to-kidnap charges, and that to do so they needed additional, definitive information from him. Before the twelve returned to the jury room the judge furnished them with the requested information, but it was insufficient, for they were back in the courtroom fifteen minutes later for further clarifications.

Twenty-seven minutes later they finally came in with guilty verdicts for both men. Sentencing for the pair was set for February 3, and both were remanded to custody of the Alameda County Sheriff.

Just before he pronounced sentence that winter morning there were arguments before Judge Sabraw by all four counsel as to what the jury meant to do, what they did do, and how one or the other should be interpreted by him. After weighing both the State's and the defense's arguments, Judge Sabraw had

Parnell stand with his attorney and then imposed sentence.

> It is the judgment of this court and it's hereby ordered, adjudged, and decreed that in punishment for said offense, that the defendant be imprisoned in the State Prison of the State of California for the term of eighty-four months. . . .*
>
> I note that by reason of the bizarre nature of the circumstances surrounding this crime . . . that a seven-year-old boy was taken from his home and lied to, told that his parents didn't want him anymore, presumably didn't love him anymore, told that he was separated legally from his parents by reason of obtaining a court order, thereafter permitting this boy for the next seven years to lead a loose and permissive and undisciplined life, depriving him of the training at a most critical period in his life, religious training, moral training. The resulting psychological impact that this obviously had on this young boy, now sixteen years of age, is something that he's struggling with now and will be struggling with . . . for the rest of his life. The impact that

---

*Under California law, sentencing for each separate conviction (i.e., the kidnapping of Steven Stayner and the conspiracy-to-kidnap Steven Stayner) had to be merged. California law also prohibited Judge Sabraw from sentencing Parnell to more than twenty-four months for kidnapping Steven since he had already received the maximum sixty month sentence for his conviction on the second degree charge of kidnapping Timmy White.

this had on his family is difficult to measure and difficult to perceive and to fully appreciate. All this conduct was callous, deceitful, insensitive, and as far as the Court is concerned, fully justifies the imposition of the maximum sentence that's available to the Court . . .

The judge then turned his attention to Parnell's accomplice.

With respect to the defendant Ervin Edward Murphy, the record would reflect that I have read and considered the probation report that has been filed in this matter and have concluded, based on the circumstances of the crime, the serious nature of the crime, that the defendant's application for probation should be denied . . .

. . . it is the judgment of this Court . . . that in punishment for said offense that the defendant be imprisoned in the State Prison of the State of California for the period of 60 months . . .

I am also mindful in this sentencing that the prime mover in this crime was the codefendant [Parnell]. It further is evident from the facts that the greater responsibility . . . is with the codefendant. I also have in mind that you appear before the Court without a prior criminal record. I also have in mind that it was to your credit that you acknowledged eventually your responsibility in the crime. . . . Whatever wrenching and struggling you had with that crime during the intervening years did not result in you coming forward to the authorities and permitting the child to be returned.

For the kidnapping of Steven, Murphy received the average term allowed by law, 60 months, with an additional sentence of 60 months—to be served concurrently—for his conspiracy conviction. Thus, because of California law, for kidnapping Steven, Murphy received a prison term longer than Parnell's.

On Wednesday, February 3, 1982, the Stayner kidnapping trial drew to a complete and final close. Of course, there was the unsuccessful appeal made by Oakland attorney Daniel Horowitz for Parnell. But when the trial finished, Parnell and Murphy were remanded to custody of the California Department of Corrections.

Hallford was pleased with getting Parnell convicted for kidnapping Steven, but he said he wished that the sentences for the kidnapping convictions had at least been of equal length. "Consecutive sentences. Stack 'em! That is what the prisoners call them, in other words, one after the other. The second one is much less than the first.

"Now, in kidnapping Timmy White, [Parnell] got seven years. But since Steven Stayner was the second offense [to be tried], he only got twenty months. And that looked so bad when everybody realized that he got twenty months for keeping Steven seven years. The public was outraged! So they did change that law. Now, kidnapping is like rape: you can get seven years for the second one as well."

But under California law kidnappings like Steven's and Timmy's are still considered second-degree kidnappings . . . and the maximum sentence is still just seven years in prison.

Wayne Eisenhart and Neil Morse felt dejected for Murphy. Said Wayne, "We were trying to portray Murphy as a victim of Parnell's manipulations, just the same as Stayner was a victim."

Neil added, "To the extent that they found Stayner was a victim, Murph was a previous victim."

Remembering the protection Murph had unwittingly afforded him during those first days of the kidnapping, even Steve felt sorry for "Uncle" Murphy. "I'd like to see him. The only time I ever saw him [again] was during the trial. That was sort of a sad thing to watch, especially since the judge sentenced him to five years. It was kind of heartbreaking. . . ."

With the trials over, Hallford had still not given up trying to convince Mendocino County to prosecute Parnell for the 87 sexual assaults on Steve. "After my trial was finished, I called Mendocino County and Dick Finn came down here to talk to the Stayners and Steve. He wouldn't have come down at all except at my insistence. They were going to let it go! But after he got here, he didn't do anything other than 'Well, Steve, would you like to do this?' And that really didn't impress me.

"I don't know that this is a case [where] they should have even allowed Steven to make the decision, because we're talking about a lot of other kids besides Steven. So there's a lot of finger pointing going on, and I'd like to point my finger at Mendocino County. The problem is, the sexual abuse did occur in their jurisdiction. And sexual abuse ought to be a crime anywhere! But they didn't press Parnell, because if they had, Parnell would be in prison for another fifty years!"

Chapter Fourteen
Closure

*"I fought too hard for those seven years to make it
to give up now."*

In February of 1982, with the trials over, the news media's focus on Steve and his family moderated, but the teenager still had major problems to tackle, not the least of which was passing his classes so that he could graduate from Merced High School the next year. At first he missed classes for the interrogations by Merced Police and the Merced D.A.'s Office, then he was absent for appearances on *Good Morning America*, *The Today Show*, and other national and local television shows, and finally he had to be excused to testify at both trials, all of which added considerably to his already marked academic weaknesses. Furthermore, Del and Kay had still not decided whether they would treat their son as a seven-year-old—thereby trying to pick up where they had left off in 1972—or as an adolescent male standing on the very edge of manhood.

Compounding things for Steve was his parents' continuing opposition to his receiving professional counseling. Many family friends felt it reasonable that a boy kidnapped and forced to live for seven years as a pedophile's sex partner could not help but have serious psychological problems. But the fact that the whole family was not prepared emotionally for Steve's return and reintegration into their midst caused daily problems which, though not immediately evident, held major consequences for the family years later. "I've never talked to Steve about that," Cindy Stayner said, referring to Parnell's sexual assaults. ". . . People would ask me questions, and I had to tell them that I really didn't know. I never really talked to him . . . *no one* talked about '*it.*' My parents really wouldn't talk about '*it.*' "

Since his return to Merced, Steve had maintained a reasonably good front . . . or so it appeared to those outside the family. But all was definitely not well, and most difficult for Steve was his inability to work through his feelings about those seven-plus years he spent with Ken Parnell as his "father". . . years he would have spent with his own family but which he had now lost forever.

Four years after coming home, while Steve traveled around Merced and Mendocino Counties being interviewed by the author, he spoke of a desire to meet with Parnell face to face, "to ask him why he ripped me off. People are always asking, 'What would you say to Parnell if you ever saw him?' . . . 'Do you have any feelings toward him?'

"I told them straight out: 'I spent seven years with him . . . he treated me well . . . he looked after me. I thank him for keeping me alive.' And I am grateful to him for that.

"Then I went on to tell them that I hate him with a purple passion for stealing seven years of my life. The reason I said that is because when I got home my mom and dad, brother and sisters, told me about all the things that they did while I was gone. It's just that I hate him for stealing the time, the time that I would have been there and I would have had the experiences."

Steve characterized his relationship with Kenneth Parnell as a genuine love/hate relationship . . . one which he has never been able to resolve in his own mind and one which he never felt comfortable talking about with his parents.

One summer night in 1984 Steve tried to bring this up with his parents at the kitchen table and ended by telling Del and Kay that he wanted to go to Soledad Prison to talk with Ken. Del and Kay didn't even respond; they just stared off into space. Then, when they did begin to talk again, they pointedly ignored their son's statement as if he had never made it.

Therefore, the author understood when Steve prefaced many of his revelations about his relationship with Parnell with: "I'm going to tell you something, but don't say anything about it to my parents. Let them read it in the book."

When he returned home it was quite apparent to Steve's parents that his morality and personality had changed considerably during his seven-year odyssey with Parnell. Family members said he was much quieter and more reserved and tended to keep his own counsel more than had the seven-year-old who disappeared in 1972. "Due to my experiences with Parnell, I like to be alone with my own thoughts. In fact, I do this a lot, like I did when I was with Parnell. I'm not as easy with other people."

As a seven-year-old, Stevie had been inseparable from Del; after his return home, they found themselves screaming angrily at each other almost daily. Steve's use of pot was the cause of many such quarrels, for that was one thing that Del refused to brook in his house. But Steve didn't want anybody, his own father included, telling him what to do. He wanted to smoke pot, drink beer and Jack Daniels, drive cars fast and recklessly, and stay out all night if and when it suited him. In short, Steve wanted to do what he wanted to do when he wanted to do it.

Later, when Steve turned eighteen and received the $25,000 TV-movie option money and the $15,000 reward for returning Timmy, there were rumors about Steve dallying with harder, more expensive drugs. Perhaps this accounted for the tremendous sums he occasionally withdrew from his bank account, as much as $1,000 in a single day, said Cindy, with nothing to show for it a day later. There were many who tried to get Steve to invest some of his money. But continued Cindy, "No, no, he had to take it all out and buy a car . . . blow it on his friends. It was gone in three months!" To Steve's credit, he did loan Del $2,000 for Cindy's wedding.

Cars—to be exact, three of them in less than a year—were a passion for Steve, but he wound up wrecking two of them. "When I was sixteen—just two weeks after I got my license—I wrecked one of my cars when I hit a parked car. I got charged with making an illegal left-hand turn. And I've gotten all kinds of speeding tickets . . . maybe about ten. I just can't remember all of them."

When word got around Merced that Steve had been sexually assaulted by Parnell, most people failed to understand that it had been forced on Steve. Steve remarked that some asked, "Is Steve gay?" while others maliciously went around telling his classmates, "Steve *is* gay," and "Steve *let* Parnell do that stuff to him!" This provoked brother Cary, sisters Cindy and Jody, and many of his classmates to run interference for him, Steve happily recalling one incident at Merced High School: "I heard one guy say I was queer, and he almost got his ass beat . . . not by me, but the whole class got up and was ready to take him on. Having that happen felt good enough to make me forget what the guy said!"

Heterosexually, Steve hit the ground running when he returned home. In 1984 he bragged that as a fifteen-year-old in 1980 he had had scores of girls clamoring to date him. Also, he shyly told about his first heterosexual intercourse, right after his fifteenth birthday. "She was the same age. It happened in the rocket at Applegate Park. They have a little rocket . . . well, it's not a little rocket . . . it's a rocket that you climb on. Straight up to the top there's a little cone. And you sit there and there's a little steering wheel. I used to climb that when I was little.

"So we went up there—me and Liz—and it was kind of funny. The sucker was not very stable, either. So . . . it was quite late, actually . . . and it was her first time, too. There was a little bit of awkwardness for her, and there was a little for me, too, in the way to approach *it*. And at the time I didn't think anything about what had happened to me with Parnell. I was just concerned about what was going on right there. And when we started doing it, that rocket started wobbling back and forth. That was funny!"

But it was a one-night stand for the pair, Steve saying that he had his first, serious relationship later with a girl named Laura. They had a very close, very active relationship, Steve remembered, but the on-again, off-again variety. "We were supposed to [get] married . . . but I broke up with her. [She claimed] she was pregnant three times, but I tossed her off like a wet rag, literally. I mean, I didn't care. It was really easy to do that. It's just something I can do." But deep inside it was an apprehensive Steve who went from girl to girl and did everything he could to allay the disturbing local rumors about his sexuality.

At eighteen, shortly after finishing his senior year in high school—without graduating, because he had failed several courses—Steve moved from home into a rented house trailer (which he shared with his cousin, David Higgins) in a mobile home park in Atwater, a town of 20,000, ten miles northwest of Merced. There Steve enjoyed his first true independence since his return to Merced. By then he had gone through the entire $40,000 he had received and had nothing but his dinged, dented gold Pontiac Trans-Am to show for it. So he went to work in a meat-packing plant, bagging hamburger for fast-food restaurants, and spent his spare time completing his high school General Equivalency Diploma.

In 1984 Steve still frequently smoked marijuana, but by then he had given up alcohol. As a high school senior he suffered a potentially fatal reaction to a drinking bout, serious enough to tear his stomach lining, cause severe internal bleeding, and require hospitalization for several days. This scared him so badly that he swore off beer, wine, and hard liquor, although his one-to-two-pack-a-day cigarette habit continued.

Cory—eleven when Steve returned and thirteen when he moved out—missed him terribly as she grew into adolescence. In June 1984 Cory told the author that she wished Steve would come to see her more often, though during her softball team's season that summer Steve attended several of her games and thus made this adoring youngest sister very happy. After one of those games Steve drove Cory home and then sat with her at the kitchen table and with genuine brotherly concern and interest rehashed the game's high points with her. After he left, Cory lamented, "We all have a lot of laughs when we're all together, but now it's getting where everybody is just going and growing and we never have the time together that we used to have."

Before she knew about the sex assaults her brother had suffered, Cory said, "I used to just feel like going up to Parnell and saying, 'Thank you for keeping my brother alive and healthy.' " But now that she knows about the assaults, she says, "Somebody that does that must be insane. I mean, they are sick! And they should be somewhere where they are not around somebody that they could do that to."

In June 1984, on a trip to Mendocino County with the author to retrace his life there, Steve ran into a rude, obnoxious man who knew who Steve was and had the audacity to approach him and ask that he tell him all about the sex acts Parnell had committed on him. Admirably, Steve firmly but politely declined to do so, and as we drove away, Steve commented: "He's the first one that's ever come right out and asked like that . . . nobody ever asks anything sexual." But Steve did admit that whenever the subject of homosexuality comes up, he feels himself quickly building up walls deep inside.

During his first two years back at home, Steve exhibited behavior that upset his grandfather, Bob Augustine, who remembered his grandson as a nice, courteous, active boy; but on Steve's return he saw a sarcastic, discourteous, disrespectful stranger. Said Bob in 1984, "He is simmering down a bit now. He seems to be normal . . . anyway, I've learned to accept it. He was a good kid before, and he is still a good kid. I'm just curious as to how much harm has been done."

Kay talked with the author about pedophiles who just sexually assault their victims (as opposed to the rare ones who kill them). "Because of Steve's abilities, it wasn't him [who was killed]. His whole make-up is probably why he survived . . . 'cause he is a survivor. And he has the ability to put up this wall, and I can see him doing that. I know he does it. And if that's what it takes to survive, it's the thing to do.

"I think that maybe we did a good job of raising Steve so that he was malleable, you know, he was the type of kid who, when he was presented with a set of circumstances, he just lived with them. You don't become unglued just because things aren't going the way you want them to go. Maybe that's how come he's a survivor.

"I've wondered about whether or not Steve was just the lucky one, and if there were others that just never made it."

"All I know is that it wasn't me that was killed, and I'm thankful," Steven said. "I'm sorry that stuff like that does happen, but to be realistic, it's been happening since the dawn of time. Some people may think that it's something new, but it's just . . . *I know better.*"

Finally, summing it all up, Steve said: "But I think that my survival has a lot to do with the way I was raised the first seven years of my life. And I can't let what happened to me with Parnell get to me. I fought too hard for those seven years to make it to give it up now."

In June of 1985 Steven married Jody Lynn Edmonson, the woman he'd met the summer before, in a private Mormon service in Atwater, California. Del, Kay, Cary, Cindy, Jody, Cory, and Steven's new wife's parents and grandparents were in attendance. In December that same year Jody gave birth to their first child, a daughter, Ashley. In May of 1987 Jody delivered their second child, a son they named Steven Gregory Stayner II. They call him Stevie.

For a while Steve worked as a self-employed landscaper while he dreamed of becoming a deputy sheriff. A happily married young couple, he and Jody lived briefly in his old home on Bette Street, where Steven's scrawled signature is still visible on the garage wall.

In 1986, over Easter weekend, the entire Stayner family camped out at Lake Shasta in northern California. "It was sorta' like old times," Steve remarked happily.

But later that same year personal problems related to Steven's kidnapping and tumultuous return home finally took their toll on Del and Kay's marriage, and they separated. Two years later, however, these loving parents who had shared so much suffering reconciled and moved together to Atwater. Del still does maintenance for a local cannery, and in 1987 he finally saw his Stevie get baptized into the Mormon faith.

Cindy and her husband, Rick, live in Modesto, where she works in a bank and he is a maintenance mechanic for another cannery where Del once worked. They, too, have a young son.

Cary, still single, works as a glazier in Merced.

Jody Stayner, Steven's sister, married a cabinetmaker, Grant, and in June 1986 she had their first child, a boy.

In early 1989, Lorimar-Telepictures produced the miniseries "I Know My First Name Is Steven." At the time Steven was working for the Pizza Hut in Merced, but he was given a leave of absence and served as an adviser for the filming and appeared in the production as one of the policemen who reunited Corky Nemec—the actor who portrayed the teenaged Steven—with his on-screen parents. NBC Television premiered the miniseries to critical acclaim in May of that same year. In August of 1990 it was retelecast by NBC, and by 1991 it had been shown in over three dozen foreign countries, including Australia, Brazil,

Britain, Germany, France, Italy, and Yugoslavia . . . a new record for a miniseries.

Although it meant his return to the public eye, the miniseries gave Steven the opportunity to make a number of talk-show appearances on behalf of his cause: missing and sexually abused children. Also, as Steven told the author, he felt a great sense of relief once the miniseries was televised ". . . 'cause people now know what really happened to me." With the miniseries hoopla over, Steven returned to the Merced Pizza Hut as its new assistant manager.

The afternoon of Saturday, September 16, 1989, Steve ended his shift at the Pizza Hut but hung around with a friend in the back to smoke a couple of marijuana cigarettes. Shortly before 5 P.M. Steve mounted his new Kawasaki motorcycle for the fifteen-minute ride to his home in Atwater. As he rode north along rain-slick Santa Fe Drive directly in front of Richwood Meats—the meat packing plant where he had worked in 1984—migrant worker Antonio Loera, driving a friend's car with which he was not familiar, pulled in front of Steve and stalled.

A car traveling alongside Steve was able to stop and avoid Loera's car, but Steve kept going, crashed into the driver's door, and was thrown forty-five feet from his motorcycle. He was rushed to Merced County Medical Center, where at 5:35 p.m. he was pronounced dead of massive head injuries. The helmet he normally wore had been stolen three days earlier.

Perhaps equally sad is the fact that Steven's last years continued to be filled with reckless driving. At the time he was killed he had no driver's license. It had been suspended for the third time in his young life due to his having yet again racked up a number of traffic tickets.

But Steven will be remembered as a very loving, affectionate father to his young, now-orphaned son, Stevie, and daughter, Ashley. A large heart-shaped wreath on his casket read simply "Daddy."

Five hundred people attended Steven's funeral service at the Church of Latter Day Saints' (Mormon) Merced Stake Center on September 20, 1989. The author was there, as were Harold Kulbeth, Jerry Price, Pat Hallford, and scores of radio, newspaper, and TV reporters. And two of the pallbearers were Dennis's old friends from Mendocino County, Damon Carroll, and tall, slender, fourteen-year-old Timmy White.

After the eulogy, Steven's sister Jody delivered an emotional good-bye to her brother, remarking that he had "brought our broken-hearted family back together again" before adding "even though he has passed into another life, we're so very grateful that he went as Steven Gregory Stayner, our brother."

Then she tearfully concluded, "We will always remember you and will never forget you; but remember, this is not good-bye, this is until we meet again."

Kenneth Eugene Parnell was paroled from Soledad Correctional Training Facility at dawn, Friday, April 5, 1985, an early release due to his light sentence and his excellent behavior while in prison. Because there had been numerous death threats, two parole officers surreptitiously drove him to a boardinghouse in a residential section of Berkeley.

Much to his consternation, Parnell's parole was extended to two years rather than the usual one. His parole officer checked on him "five or six times a week, including Saturdays and Sundays," he could not leave Alameda County; he had to attend regular counseling sessions; and he could not be in the company of children.

On April 5, 1987, Kenneth Eugene Parnell completed his strictly supervised parole and became a free man: he is free to drop out of sight, to travel wherever and whenever he pleases, to live however he wants, and to associate with anyone he chooses . . . even young boys.

Author's Epilogue

Pedophilia—the sexual attraction of a man or a woman to a child—has existed since the beginning of recorded history as a dark blotch in the fabric of adult-child relationships. In fact, of all the criminal acts perpetrated by adults on children, sexual assault of children is by far the least known, least discussed, and least understood. Sadly, though, in a few gut-wrenching cases, these assorted crimes against children have coalesced into sickening, gruesome outrages by Art Bishop (Utah), Ted Bundy (Utah, Colorado, Florida), Arthur C. Goode (Florida, Maryland, Virginia), John Wayne Gacy (Illinois), John Joubert (Nebraska), and others of their ilk whose nauseating crimes are covered year in and year out in our newspapers and magazines and on our televisions and radios.

At the F.B.I. Academy in Quantico, Virginia, Behavioral Unit Agent Kenneth Lanning observed that most pedophiles are gentle and nonviolent with children. The glaring exceptions are those cases which catch our attention, such as the 1980 abduction and brutal murder of John and Revé Walsh's six-year-old son, Adam, apparently committed by homosexual serial murderer Ottis Toole, who first admitted and then recanted his guilt for the atrocity.

After his son's death, Walsh left his lucrative hotel-management career in south Florida and goaded and badgered the U.S. Congress into founding and funding the National Center for Missing and Exploited Children in Washington, D.C. At Colorado State University, in an address to a conference of law-enforcement officers, social workers, and other professionals who work with missing and sexually exploited children, Walsh movingly told of the disappearance of his son from a Sears store where Adam had gone with his mother; the ensuing futile search for his son, which cost him many thousands of dollars; and his shocking realization that looking for a missing child in the U.S. is not top priority for law enforcement agencies. Walsh also bared his soul as he recounted his and his wife's gut-wrenching horror when a Florida detective called to tell them that Adam's head had been found floating in a canal 120 miles from his home. (The rest of the Walsh's six-year-old son's body never was found.)

Of that day Walsh said: "That was the day I found out in the worst way that there is a lot we don't know about missing children. It has often been called a national tragedy. I say it is a national disgrace. A country with the resources that we have, and what we haven't done for our children is a disgrace. The figures are staggering. Everyone says it is an epidemic. We say it is the tip of the iceberg. We are just starting to see it. It is nothing new. It has always been there. It is something we haven't wanted to deal with . . . something we have wanted to bury our heads in the sand about, and say it only happens to the other guy.

"I think we disadvantage our children by teaching them to respect authority figures. In many cases those authority figures are the people who hurt kids because, in cases of sexual assault, the estimates are that seventy percent of the people that molest children are people that they know and many times [they] are a figure of trust and authority."

He went on to recount a conversation about missing children which he'd had with the Broward County (Florida) Coroner. Walsh said: "He was a doctor and a lawyer and an expert with this type of thing. He said, 'Right now on the morgue tables we have a dozen unclaimed bodies. Four of them are adolescent girls, and, in fact, one of them is only nine years old. The rest of them are between eleven and fifteen. A couple of those girls I have had for six months. I don't want to bury them. I know somebody is looking for them.'

"He said there is no system to exchange information in cases like this. He said we guesstimate that coroners and pathologists have maybe between four and five thousand unidentified dead to bury every year in this country. In any given year, hundreds and hundreds of these are children."

Walsh's fervor rose as he continued: "Lots of people don't love children as much as I do. They use them. They abuse them. They molest them. They use them in child pornography. They use them in child prostitution. They murder them and leave them in fields and streams and in canals *all over* this country.

"I testified before Congress—I don't know how many times; I lost track. But a man begins to choke when he realizes the scope of the problem. The first few times I was asked to testify, I was asked the same question: What are the statistics? I went to Cornell University's law library and sat there day and night, researching microfilms, trying to garner the national statistics on missing children. I researched the F.B.I. uniform crime reports. *They* keep records of crimes against Americans, I thought. But, in categories for crimes against children, well, there just weren't any there. For instance, in homicides of children, they were lumped into homicides of adults."

After his address, I interviewed Walsh at length about his work and asked his advice to parents about protecting their children. From his extensive experience, he said, "I urge people to take videos of their children, because when the media comes that night [when a child is missing] and says, 'we will put it on TV,' the parents can choose to do that. And that can help to find their missing child. [But] a second aspect of that is, imagine the nightmare of spending the rest of your life searching for your child and never having known that his body is buried in another state. Not because he wasn't entered into the National Crime Information System—that should be done—but because you didn't have the identifiers. . . . Parents can put their children's fingerprints, dental charts, recent pictures, videos, everything in a safe deposit box. But if they have a misconception that this makes their child safe, it is a ludicrous misconception, because this is just a matter of prevention, awareness, and attention."

Concerning adults who work with children, Walsh's ire rose as he remarked: "It is a nightmare that we don't do background checks on these individuals. Big Brothers and Big Sisters say damn well they should check the backgrounds of their volunteers, even if they might lose some volunteers."

A major concern of Walsh's is the handling of abused children by social service departments, principally their return to abusive parents. "We have tens of thousands of children that were returned by a social service worker that was underpaid, underskilled, undertrained. A family court judge said, 'Let's keep the family intact.' I personally believe those children are a lot better off alive in the foster care system than dead of a broken neck or broken back within their own home. It is as simple as that.

"We have got to get over the old adage that we have to keep the family intact. There is no qualification to become a parent. You couldn't teach school without some kind of degree; you couldn't practice law; you couldn't repair a Mercedes without some type of schooling. I believe in parents' rights to a certain extent, but when you are given the greatest gift of all—the birth of a child—you can turn that child into a Henry Lee Lucas [the partner of his son's murderer, Ottis Toole] mobile murderer, or into a Nobel Peace Prize winner.

"Let's get over that assumption that everybody is a good parent . . . that old assumption by the court system and social services. We have tens of thousands of children in graves that were returned to their parents by social services, or not removed from their homes, because their parents weren't good parents. Who is responsible for those kids? Society! *We* are *all* responsible for all the children, whether they are our own naturally or not. Children are God's special little people. They need special protection. They certainly can't physically take care of themselves. . . ."

Concerning the criminal justice system's handling of those who murder children, Walsh observed: "If life imprisonment *was* life imprisonment in the United States, then we wouldn't have so many murderers that get out of prison and continue to murder children. The penalties for the murder of children or crimes against children should be stiffened. The death penalty is only applicable in the most heinous of situations. [But] when an individual is sentenced to death, he has gone through the finest criminal justice system in the known history of the world. He has had the benefit of that, and he should be held responsible for his crime."

Also in attendance at the Colorado State University conference was Jay Howell, the first Executive Director of the National Center for Missing and Exploited Children, and one of his greatest concerns is the use of the word "stranger" when cautioning children.

" 'Stranger,' " he said, "is a word we do *not* advise using with children. Children will tell you that if they see somebody on the way to school everyday—even people who introduce themselves to the child by name—then they are not strangers. They don't understand 'stranger' because it suggests somebody who is weird-looking. The other half of the problem with using that word is that sixty to ninety percent of the people who commit crimes against children are known in some way to the child. You have told the kid to look out for the wrong person! Children just aren't getting the right messages. We would like for them to get better messages that they can understand . . . messages like, No one should be picking you up, Nobody should be making secrets, Nobody should be taking pictures in the bathing suit areas . . . those kinds of things." And Howell stressed the inherent danger of parents allowing children to wear T-shirts with their names emblazoned on them.

Many people are surprised to learn that, according to Derek Hudson's biography of Lewis Carroll (*Lewis Carroll: An Illustrated Biography*, Derek Hudson, Clarkson N. Potter, Inc., New York, 1977), the author of the beloved children's classics *Alice's Adventures in Wonderland* was a pedophile who was sexually attracted to little girls. According to Hudson, portions of Carroll's diaries clearly show him wrestling with his conscience over his hidden sexual feelings for young girls, although no evidence remains that he ever actually had sex with any of them.

When he wrote his most famous book in 1862, Charles Lutwidge Dodgson—Lewis Carroll was a *nom de plume*—was a respected mathematics don at Oxford's Christ College, an Anglican Church deacon at Oxford's Christ Church Cathedral, and a pioneer photographer of children, taking many nudes and seminudes of little girls, for in Victorian England nude photographs of children were considered asexual and thus acceptable. Indeed, the Prince of Wales, later Edward VII, collected many such photographs.

Dodgson was a heterosexual pedophile fixated on prepubescent girls. In a letter to an individual who had offered him a lucrative position at a public school for boys, Dodgson said, "I am fond of children (except boys) . . . boys are not in my line: I think they are a mistake." And in a letter to Harry Furniss—the illustrator for Dodgson's book *Sylvie and Bruno*—Dodgson wrote, "Naked children are so perfectly pure and lovely. . . . I confess I do *not* admire naked boys. They always seem to need clothes—whereas one hardly sees why the lovely forms of girls should *ever* be covered up."

There are hundreds of thousands of Dodgsons in America today, such as David Tichnor of Chicago, a notorious heterosexual pedophile who is well known to Chicago Police, the F.B.I., and U.S. Customs agents. Tichnor founded and operates the Lewis Carroll Guild, which—recalling Dodgson's dark secret—publishes the periodical *Wonderland*. Unfortunately, though, the Guild is but one of several public organizations in the United States which openly advocate and promote their *raison d'être:* sexual liaisons between adults and children.

Another such organization is the Rene Guyon Society of Beverly Hills, California, whose spokesperson, Tim O'Hara, occasionally pops up on television and radio talk shows. One of the Society's missives—a single, sloppily printed sheet—bears the group's motto: "Sex by year eight or else its [sic] too late!" The paper also states, "Because of our efforts, the day will come, and come soon, when children will have sex [sic] freedom (provided contraceptives are used) of a bisexual nature with other children an [sic] with adults. They will be allowed to happily participate in kid porn activity. The soonest of all this [is] to come about depends on your sending funds and offering to provide your special talents."

However, the real winner in this nefarious category has got to be *NAMBLA*, the North American Man/Boy Love Association, which is headquartered in New York City, "with chapters in Boston, Los Angeles, New York, San Francisco, and Toronto." As stated in a brochure they distribute, "Our membership reflects a cross-section of the population. It includes members of both sexes, teachers, artists, clerks, writers, students, social workers, cooks, professors, taxi drivers, editors, priests and ministers, prisoners, and so on."

In late 1984 I began writing to NAMBLA's New York address, falsely representing myself as a wealthy homosexual pedophile so as to gain access to NAMBLA members and material. Finally, on April 12, 1985, my efforts were rewarded when, while I was in New York on business, NAMBLA's National Membership Secretary, Robert Rhodes, phoned me at my hotel from his office with the Social Security Administration in Newark, New Jersey, and invited me to be his guest at that evening's meeting of the NAMBLA Collective, the executive editorial committee for the *NAMBLA Bulletin,* "Voice of the North American Man/Boy Love Association." (Indeed, Rhodes had swallowed whole my story that I wanted to help NAMBLA financially.)

I met Rhodes at NAMBLA's postal box at the midtown post office on West 38th Street and the two of us then traveled by subway to the apartment of Editor Renato Corazza, located on the fifth floor of 222 East 10th Street. On arriving, I was introduced to and warmly greeted as a fellow homosexual pedophile by Corazza; Peter Melzer, NAMBLA's Treasurer; David

Thorstad, NAMBLA's Founder and President; and Peter Reed, who was introduced to me as "a teacher with the New York City schools."

Over the next five hours I was privy to this groups intimate conversations as I helped them stuff their current *NAMBLA Bulletin* into preaddressed nine-by-twelve-inch plain brown envelopes marked "First Class," with a return address reading simply, "P.O. Box 174, Midtown Station, New York, NY 10018." Finishing this, I was asked to singlehandedly sort the four hundred and twenty issues by the addresses on the labels. I was only too happy to oblige: almost seventy-five percent of the labels bore the recipient's name, and some of those even had a title and/or organizational name which identifies the recipient as one who comes into contact with children (i.e., ministers, rabbis, social workers, teachers, youth choir directors, etc.). Also, I saw that virtually every state in the union has members of this organization receiving this monthly communique advocating sexual liaisons between men and boys.

I sorted the individual copies while Melzer packed one hundred to ship to Rock Thatcher (P.O. Box 10675, Phoenix, Arizona 85064), Director of NAMBLA's Prison Ministry (indeed, it is called this), which each month attempts to surreptitiously mail the *Bulletin* to incarcerated homosexual pedophiles in prisons all over the United States. And as he worked, Melzer paused to proudly show me NAMBLA's financial records, files which clearly indicated that NAMBLA receives regular, large contributions from a variety of celebrity member supporters, including internationally prominent novelists and poets.

As an unknown "newcomer," my being given the task of stuffing and sorting the *NAMBLA Bulletin* was contrary to Rhodes's own lofty pronouncement in a previous issue in response to "M.R., Hawaii," who wrote expressing his concern: "A NAMBLA member incarcerated for four years has warned me to discontinue my membership in NAMBLA and other boy-lover organizations. He warned that just sending for and receiving NAMBLA publications is very dangerous and that agents consider NAMBLA a threat to the U.S. government. Please advise!"

To "M.R.," Rhodes pompously responded: "Be assured that these rumors are unequivocally false. No one has ever been arrested simply because of membership in NAMBLA. NAMBLA's mail is handled only by a small group of longtime members. Our records are kept in highly secure locations. We need not panic, but we should be prudent."

Early in that truly unforgettable evening, when I referred to one of those present as a "pedophile," Rhodes quickly corrected me: "Pedophile is an unfortunate choice of a word; we would prefer boy lover." Later, when the subject of a letter from a heterosexual pedophile David Tichnor came up—he had written to Melzer suggesting a closer alliance between his Lewis Carroll Guild and NAMBLA—Rhodes haughtily remarked, "Personally, I can't understand a man being into little girls."

Before I left the meeting those present tried to induce me to become a member of NAMBLA so that I could purchase back issues of the *Bulletin* and receive future issues. It was an offer I could not refuse. In those issues of this abhorrent publication I found many insights into NAMBLA and its members.

The May 1984 issue featured a poem on the back cover entitled *Adam*—"Dedicated to Adam Walsh, dead at six"—by boy lover Russell T. Kinkade. Also, inside that issue appeared a short piece by Nat M. Black, who recounted his experiences as a soccer coach for a team of ten-year-old boys and his finagling a couple of unsuspecting mothers into allowing him to have two of the lads stay with him overnight, a night during which he took sexual liberties with both.

The December 1984 *Bulletin* had a feature article "by a busy boy lover" entitled *Boys at Sport*. The article gave detailed advice to those pedophiles who wanted to follow in Mr. Black's footsteps and become soccer league coaches. Said the pedophile/writer: "As long as the league is running decently, it will self-perpetuate with new young boys coming in every year. . . . Occasionally, exposure to adult males is a consideration in a mother's signing her son up for a sport. While the majority have caring fathers, you shouldn't assume that because a boy is in one or more seasonal sports, he's too busy to have time for a caring adult friend."

In the May 1985 issue, Rhodes used his monthly "Quid Nunc" column to discuss his chastisement for his column's content: "Several members (including our kindly Editor) felt there was too much bad news. The point was that readers are depressed by reading only a list (and graphic details) of arrests and convictions [of fellow pedophiles], and thereby are inhibited from acting for their own liberation. . . . One Collective member raised the point . . . that I am using the language of our oppressors. This involves using the language of violence (i.e., molestation, assault, rape) about acts often notably consensual, non-violent [sic], and pleasurable." In fact, this vapid periodical is always filled with such prevarication.

A case in point is Richard Boyer's *NAMBLA Bulletin* column "Boys in the Media," featuring television program notes and motion picture reviews pointing out those which contain scenes with boys wearing underwear (or, Boyer hoped, nothing at all) and ripped-off, sometimes-revealing photographs of boy actors (on one occasion a photograph of a young, half-naked Ricky Schroeder). But the March 1985 issue had sad news indeed: "Former Steering Committee member and Bulletin Collective Member Richard Boyer has been arrested and charged with having sex with two underaged boys, eleven and fourteen, in the Bronx."

On the whole, though, the really frightening thing about NAMBLA's members—especially the likes of David Thorstad and Robert Rhodes—are their articulate, astute efforts to spread their skewed gospel of legalizing sex between men and boys. Whereas they are reasonably careful that the material they publish is protected by the First Amendment, they are not so careful in their private lives, thus the unfortunate Mr. Boyer and his arrest.

However, NAMBLA and their ilk are only part of the problem. The most devastating stories of sexual assaults of children include those of the victims of gruesome murders committed by serial killer-homosexual pedophile Arthur Gary Bishop on five boys in and around Salt Lake City, Utah, from late 1979 until mid 1983. Bishop—with a long yet neglected history of sexually abusing boys dating back to his days as a teen-aged Mormon Boy Scout leader—had the same sexual desires as do NAMBLA's members, but he killed his prepubescent and pubescent victims to prevent them from telling about his photographs of and assaults on their naked young bodies and even occasionally practiced necrophilia on their dead bodies.

Bishop's first victim was four-year-old Alonzo Daniels, who disappeared on October 16, 1979. On November 9, 1980, eleven-year-old Kim Petersen went to meet a man who wanted to buy his roller-skate wheels at a street corner. He never returned home. On October 20, 1981, four-year-old Danny Davis went to the grocery store with his grandfather. He vanished without a trace while playing in the toy aisle. June 22, 1983, was Troy Ward's sixth birthday; he went for a birthday ride on a motorcycle with an unknown man and never returned home for his ice cream and cake. And on July 14, 1983, the oldest, thirteen-year-old Graeme Cunningham, disappeared.

On that November Sunday in 1980, Kim Petersen walked to a street corner near his home to sell his skate wheels to a man he had met at a skating rink the night before. When Kim arrived at the corner, Bishop talked the boy into accompanying him, drove the lad into the desert southwest of Salt Lake City, and at gunpoint forced the eleven-year-old to strip naked and pose for a series of pornographic pictures. But as Kim started to get dressed, Bishop shot the youngster. Kim begged for his life, but another shot rang out and ended the blond eleven-year-old's life. Bishop dumped the limp body into a shallow grave.

About life without her son, Kim's mother said: "The real hard thing is—you know, we have two little girls now—it is such a feeling of loss, not to have Kim here with us as part of our family . . . and for the girls not to ever be able to meet him or be with him. We told our first girl, Edwina—she's four now—about Kim, and that she does have a brother, and she knows she had a brother Kim, and she talks about him quite often, in fact. Her friends come over to play with her and the first thing she says is, 'My Kim lives with Jesus.'

"And she will go shopping with me and she will see a boy that looks like Kim's picture, and she'll point him out to me and ask, 'Is that my Kimmie?' "

Thirteen-year-old Graeme Cunningham was small for his age, a boy with a mischievous smile and an affectionate nature, the youngest son of Scottish immigrants John and Shona Cunningham. Graeme was deeply loved and doted on by his eighteen-year-old sister Jacklene, and his older brother Ian, sixteen. For over a year before Graeme disappeared his best friend had been Jeff, a thirteen-year-old boy living with Art Bishop.

Although their contacts with Bishop had been casual, John and Shona felt that they had come to know the man—Jeff's father, they assumed—over the year prior to July 1983. So when Bishop asked permission for Graeme to accompany him and Jeff on a camping trip to the red rock canyons around Moab, Utah, they approved. It would be two weeks and their son would be dead before the Cunninghams would learn that

Jeff was not Bishop's son and that the man had been
sexually abusing his young live-in charge for two years.

After their return from Moab, on the night of July
14, 1983, Bishop telephoned Graeme and told him
that he could earn some money for their planned trip
to Disneyland if he would come to his apartment and
help him to deliver something. Art also told Graeme
not to tell anyone that he had called, nor where he
was going.

Graeme went to Bishop's apartment, where the man
convinced the boy that he was being blackmailed and
that he needed to get some nude photographs of
Graeme for the blackmailer. Very reluctantly, Graeme
undressed and posed naked for a dozen frontally nude
Polaroids before he started to get dressed and tell
Bishop never to tell his mother. At this, Bishop picked
up a hammer and struck Graeme in the back of his
head, gravely injuring the boy.

Assuring Graeme that he would be all right and that
they would still go to Disneyland, Bishop carried his
groggy victim to the bathroom, filled the tub with
water, and drowned Graeme before undressing and
fondling the lad's naked body. Later that night he
drove up remote Cottonwood Creek, dumped
Graeme's body, and then picked up Jeff at a local
amusement park.

Even with the search for Graeme under way, Art and
Jeff went to Disneyland on July 16 while the Cunningham's, their friends, and the Salt Lake City Police
searched frantically for Graeme.

When Art and Jeff returned to Salt Lake City, they
immediately drove to the Cunninghams' home, where
Bishop told Shona, " 'Well, the trip would have been

more fun if Graeme had been there, because I was looking forward to showing him all these new things he had never seen before. I'd have waited a week to make the trip if I had thought it could help find Graeme.' "

About Bishop's visit, Shona remarked, "It wasn't a real abnormal conversation, other than the fact that I was having it with the man who had come into our lives and murdered our son."

And Shona recounted a conversation Jeff told her he had had with Bishop on their way back, when Jeff had said to Bishop: "You lived in the same apartment house as Alonzo Daniels; you lived close by Danny Davis; you were supposed to meet Kim Petersen; you don't live too far away from where Troy Ward lived; and you were friends with Graeme? And Jeff was going through this turmoil of, *'My God! . . .'* "

Thanks to Shona's sharp instincts, Art Bishop was arrested at her home that afternoon, Shona concluding, "At that point I was bound and determined that Art Bishop would pay for the sexual abuse of my son because that happened when Graeme was alive, healthy, loyal, loving. Art Bishop sexually abused Graeme by taking the nude photographs of him. That in itself would have changed Graeme's life."

As Shona summed up her son's death, "It's just awful when you realize the only thing you can do for your thirteen-year-old son is make up a basket of flowers to take to the cemetery. When you are asked to part with your child, you give part of yourself away. I think to lose a child is the most unnatural thing in the world. Art Bishop has ruined our lives. He has taken life from us. We exist. We don't live anymore. He took our hearts. I don't think anybody can ever understand what it means to get dressed to go to church to bury your child. I get upset just putting the dinner out. I go to pick up five plates, and it's a reminder that I don't have my son. I know that one day I'll die, too, and I'm glad that I know that now."

And Shona has strong advice for other parents: "The thing I would say to parents is, I don't care what the situation is, whether it's a neighbor, an uncle, baseball coach, or whomever . . . take the time to *personally* interview that person. And if they are offended by it, *tough luck!* I have to live with that because I didn't do that. And take the time to say, 'You've called my son and I would like to meet you before you call him again.' And if the individual doesn't want to do that, then you say to your son, 'This was the offer I made to this individual, and he refused it, and I don't want you to have any contact with him.' And that goes for women, too. It's not just men that are harmful. But I would not hesitate to do that anymore. But, you see, I gave Art Bishop the right to his dignity as an individual not to be interviewed . . . not having to qualify to come into my son's life and our lives. And because of that we're in the position we are in today. Had people, parents been harsher, he might not have murdered these children.

"There are parents who are maybe too busy, divorced, or maybe economically depressed or whatever, and here's an adult that enjoys their child's conversation and company, is nice to the child, helps the child with their problems, and can maybe afford to give the child some of their time . . . taking the child to see something that maybe the parent can't afford. In this sort of situation the child doesn't see himself as the victim. They have a friend. But it could be another Art Bishop."

At Bishop's 1984 trial, six boys testified that he had forced them to strip naked, photographed them, and sexually assaulted them, but for some reason had not murdered them, although he had threatened them with the same pistol with which he had killed Kim Petersen.

The jury found Bishop guilty of all five counts of first-degree murder and he was given a death sentence for each. Finally, after almost four years on death row at the Utah State Penitentiary at Draper, on June 10, 1988, Bishop was executed by lethal injection.

But the horrible memories have hardly begun to fade.

During the 1970s a similarly deadly homosexual pedophile, one Arthur C. Goode, Jr., kidnapped and killed a dozen or more young boys up and down the East Coast. In 1976 he was apprehended while traveling with then-ten-year-old Billy Arthes, whom he had kidnapped and forced to travel with him as a sex slave. The son of a surgeon at Johns Hopkins Hospital in Baltimore, Maryland, young Arthes was the only one of Goode's victims to live to tell of his harrowing experiences with this murderer-sodomist of young boys.

"I had a paper route in the afternoons, and when I went to get my papers at this corner, Goode approached me and started asking me questions about bike routes," Billy told the author. "I pointed off in a direction, and then he asked me to show him. At first

I said no, but he persisted, and so I did. Then, when we were off in these woods, he grabbed me by the neck and said, 'You are going to do everything I tell you to do or I will kill you.' And he showed me a list of people he had supposedly killed. He told me stories about how he had drugged some of them and a lot of really sick things. And for the first few days I begged him to kill me, too.

"Outside a shopping mall in Falls Church [Virginia] he lured Kenneth Dawson [an eleven-year-old boy] into the woods. I was with them, but I just could not believe what was going on! Goode took everything that Kenneth had on off. Kenneth was crying and asking him, 'What are you doing? Are you going to leave me here?' Art assaulted him anally once and then put Kenneth's pants over his [Kenneth's] face and Kenneth's belt around Kenneth's neck and then he just strangled him. Art even had me hold the belt. He made me watch. I just stood there. I was a total blank. I just could not believe what was going on. The whole time, really . . . I couldn't run. I was just too stiff.

"Art would make me sleep with him, and that is when he would have sex with me. He did it every one of the nine days I was with him. It was both oral and anal sex, and when it was anal intercourse he would put his hands around my neck and threaten to kill me."

After more than a week traveling and sleeping with Goode, Billy was rescued by Baltimore police and Virginia state troopers who laid a trap for Goode in the basement of a home where he had secured work for himself and his young "son."

"The Baltimore police really went out of their way . . . Please mention how grateful I am that they were that excellent!" Billy said of his rescue. "I will *always* be indebted to them . . . There is no way I could ever repay them. And my father has been extremely great. He has been my support through everything through my whole life. Really, it was my upbringing from both of my parents that enabled me to endure this. I could never, ever have asked for more from them!"

Early the morning of April 5, 1984, Arthur C. Goode, Jr., was put to death in the electric chair at the Florida State Prison at Stark for the rape-murder of nine-year-old Jason Verdow. The night before his execution, during an eerie death-row press conference, a reporter asked Goode if he had made any special requests of the warden before his execution. A grinning Goode said, "Yes, I asked him to bring in a nine-year-old boy so I could have sex with a little boy for one last time before they kill me . . . but he wouldn't do it."

Of Goode's execution, Billy sighed, "Justice was carried out, I feel, but it wasn't carried out fully, because Goode is not suffering anymore, but his victims, the families of his victims, everybody whose lives he did hit . . . they are still suffering."

There are many who disagree with executing the Arthur Goodes and Arthur Bishops of this world. Some feel that there are alternatives to both incarceration and execution. One such person is Dr. Fred S. Berlin, Co-Director—along with Dr. John Money—of the Johns Hopkins Hospital's Sexual Disorders Clinic in Baltimore . . . a program which at one time unsuccessfully attempted to treat Goode.

In part, Dr. Berlin said in a lengthy interview I conducted with him in 1985: "Going back about seventeen years, there was some research at Johns Hopkins in the area of human sexuality and particularly in the area of the biological aspects of human sexuality. In terms of the clinic as it is now structured, that has really been going on for the last four to five years. The term used to refer to someone who is sexually attracted to children is 'pedophile.' If they are exclusively attracted to children, the term 'fixated pedophile' has sometimes been used. If they are attracted to adults as well as children, the term 'regressed pedophile' has sometimes been used. So, all that pedophilia really tells us is that this is a person experiencing sexual attraction to children in the way most of us don't, but it does not necessarily mean that we know something about that individual and his character or any other aspects of what he is all about as a person.

"At present we have as outpatients in the community approximately 150 men. At any given time we usually have about eight people who are hospitalized. And at any given time we might be seeing in treatment approximately forty individuals who are incarcerated. In types of people we are treating, we treat on an outpatient basis exhibitionism and pedophilia, but we have also seen people with voyeurism, sexual sadists, and sexual masochists. Too, we have seen a number of rapists, some of whom seem to be individuals where rape is a reflection of a sexual compulsion. Overall the success rate has been very high: in excess of eighty-five percent of the people seem to be doing well. We have a handful, literally, of females.

"Most of the people we see are people who want

intimacy and affection and love—all the things that most of us want—from children. And most of the men we are seeing have been involved with young boys in homosexual pedophilia.

"We and a couple of other centers have been working with males who become involved with young boys. I don't think you can 'cure' it, but we have had a high percentage of success. Just as the alcoholic can learn to control himself and resist temptation, I think these men in most of the instances that we have been involved in have been able to do that as well. [However] sexual sadists—who are clearly the most dangerous of pedophiles—draw the most attention because the consequences of their actions are clearly the most horrifying and alarming.

"Interestingly enough, some of the men who are sexually attracted to little boys might have a better chance of trying to develop an erotic interest in females than in adult men. Too, many, if not most, homosexual pedophiles are in no way sexually attracted to men. To them, pornography isn't the centerfold of *Playgirl*, but rather a little boy in his undergarments in the Sears catalog.

"What we do is to try and suppress the patient's sexual appetite with medicine, the idea being that if you hunger sexually for children, hopefully you would be less hungry in that fashion and it will make it easier to resist temptation if you control one's behavior appropriately. The medicine we use Depo-Provera—is a form of progesterone. What it does is it lowers the hormone testosterone in the body, and so by lowering the testosterone we lower the sexual libido. We know we are lowering the testosterone with the medicine we give because we give it by injection and it is deposited into the muscle and released out of the muscle into the bloodstream and then we give a blood test to confirm that.

"Now, I am not suggesting that this is a cure. I think it clearly seems to be helping some people to help themselves, but the treatment we have also has to include counseling. That is a very important part of our approach to the problem. The injection of Depo-Provera is only a part of a much bigger picture.

"Many of the men that we now label pedophile victimizers are simply the former victims of other pedophiles that have now grown up and were warped by their experience. It is very clear that some youngsters are warped in the development of their sexuality as a result of premature sexual involvement with adults.

"If we look at the variety of kids that become involved sexually with adults, thankfully, most of them don't become pedophiles. But if we look at a group of pedophiles, tragically, most of them were involved sexually with adults when they were children. One of the things we have seen over and over again is the little boys who become involved sexually with men: there were things about it that they didn't like, but they were also turned on sexually. They were erotically aroused at a time in their life when they weren't prepared to deal with it. Because they were turned on to sex early in their lives, they began to persuade their friends—other little boys—to become involved sexually with them.

"Then, by the time they were older, they had developed habits that they really had a difficult time breaking. They had learned to enjoy having sex with boys and the fact that they were now finding out that it was wrong didn't seem to change the fact that there was a tremendous desire to do it. Indeed, many homosexual pedophiles are simply the former victims grown up. It is very rare indeed that we see someone who is biologically intact [and] who had healthy early experiences who comes to us presenting predilections of homosexual pedophilia."

I completed my interview with John Walsh by asking him, "Why do you continue going around the country talking about missing and exploited children?" His answer surged forth like a flood.

"Why do I continue? It is not the best thing I could be doing for my family right now, but I will point out one thing: Adam didn't have a chance. The system let Adam down. Who the hell is going to go out and battle for the new Adams? I want to tip those scales for those little people. I will never be able to understand how this country has allowed these crimes to be perpetrated to the tremendous extent that they have.

"This is no longer a catharsis. It is no longer therapeutic for me. I need to be with my family. I probably need a week off . . . I probably need a *day* off! I probably could use a good night's sleep. But I know what is happening. I know as I land in a different city every day. I see the slides of the mutilated and raped children . . . the horrible things that are done to them. The public doesn't see it. Juries don't see it in many cases when they should. I see it and I know what is happening. I know how terrorized they are. I can feel it! I interview them and talk to them.

"I had eleven little girls give me a plaque in Colorado . . . sexual assault victims with tears in their eyes. Double victims of the system. They said, 'Thanks for speaking out for us and helping us. We want some justice in the system.'

"I know that nightmare . . . what a child goes through when they are sodomized, tortured, raped, murdered. . . . *You have just got to do something to stop it.*"

Right now, today, *we must begin to care about the safety of our own children, our relatives' children, our neighbors' children, and even strangers' children* by being ever-vigilant about the backgrounds, motives, and interests of all persons with whom they come into contact, never forgetting that over eighty percent of all sexual assaults on boys and girls are perpetrated by persons they know.

Further, we must make certain that *all children are protected by being educated about the dangers of sexual assault and kidnapping* and by making certain that they truly have someone whom they can trust and turn to whenever they feel so threatened. And we must call, lobby, speak to, and write to our elected officials to force them to pass laws which both adequately incarcerate and attempt to treat pedophiles while at the same time effectively keeping them away from children. We have been given the responsibility to care for and protect children and, therefore, we can do no less.

* * * * *

Since this book was first published in late 1991— outside of the terrible crimes that Cary Stayner has now confessed to—some interesting things have occurred and developed due to my researching and writing *I Know My First Name Is Steven.*

As a result of researching and writing this book and publicity for it in late 1991 and early 1992, I became an aggressive child advocate. In January of 1992, I went undercover in San Francisco and infiltrated the North American Man/Boy Love Association—NAMBLA—for NBC-TV affiliate KRON-TV, which, in turn, led to additional coverage on NBC News, CNN, and *Geraldo Rivera.* This led to the gay and lesbian community—initially in San Francisco but soon spreading nationwide—to slam the door on this nefarious organization of child sex predators and child pornographers. And this led to their membership plummeting from a high of over 4,000 members to fewer than 400 today. In fact, at the 1994 Gay Pride Day Parade in San Francisco, gay community leaders told me that televangelist Jerry Falwell could march in the parade with greater impunity than could an acknowledged member of NAMBLA. (You can read the full story in my Author's Epilogue in my second book, *Brother Tony's Boys* [Prometheus Books, 1996: Amherst, NY].)

As for Kenneth Eugene Parnell, Steven's kidnapper, after completing his parole in 1987 he went to work as a night watchman for a boys' home in Oakland, California. But his background and criminal record remained undiscovered until the Lorimar/NBC-TV miniseries of *I Know My First Name Is Steven* premiered in May 1989. He was fired and forced to move out of his apartment in the Oakland suburb of Berkeley. Once again Parnell folded his tent and disappeared.

Although he was required to do so because of his 1951 Bakersfield, California, kidnapping and sexual assault conviction of nine-year-old Bobby Green, Parnell did not notify law enforcement authorities of his change of address. In 1995, a private investigator located Parnell for the author. I went to his house and, surprisingly, Parnell welcomed me, proudly showing me a boy's bicycle and toys just inside his front door, saying, "I've got to keep up with the younger generation, Mike!"

I called and gave Parnell's address to the Berkeley Police and the Alameda County Sheriff's Office. Parnell was not prosecuted for failing to register his new address. Over the new few years, I kept in regular touch with Parnell in an attempt to keep track of him, occasionally taking him out to eat and interviewing him repeatedly. During one interview, Parnell challenged Steven's remark that he had sexually assaulted Steven "over 700 times," the child sex predator correcting his then dead victim with, "Steven never was very good at math. It was more like over 3,000 times."

During these interviews, Parnell repeatedly reacted with shock and stuttered and coughed whenever I asked him about the murdered children's bodies found buried in Mendocino County—crimes that have never been solved. And he reacted the same way during an August 1999 dinner and on-camera interview with reporter Steve Noble of TV's *Inside Edition* and staff writer Lance Williams of the *San Francisco Examiner,* remarking disingenuously: "I know who killed and buried those two kids, but I can't remember his name right now." And these two children and their murderer all have yet to be identified.

The sum of all of these experiences led the author to found the proactive, nonprofit, tax-exempt child advocacy organization Better A Millstone, Inc. (BAM). Calling itself "the Internet eyes and ears for law enforcement," BAM is composed of a group of Internet-savvy child advocates who lurk on-line and gather intelligence and information about Internet child sex predators and child pornographers and then provide same to law enforcement around the world. Thus far BAM has helped in the identification and arrest of over sixty such criminals.

You can learn more about BAM by visiting their Web site at http://www.shadow-net.com. And if you have children using the Internet, they can learn how to become safer on the Internet by visiting BAM's "For Kids Only" Web site at http://www.shadow-net.com/forkids.html.

And sadly, children continue to be kidnapped, sexually assaulted, and murdered. One young life lost to such damnable acts was that of ten-year-old Anthony Michael Martinez, of Beaumont, California, who was kidnapped on April 10, 1997. You can help find the man who kidnapped, raped, and murdered him by visiting BAM's Web page, http://www.shadow-net.com/nam.htm. Another young life lost was that of beautiful Christina Marie Williams, a thirteen-year-old girl who was kidnapped from my hometown of Monterey, California, on June 12, 1998. You can help find the men who kidnapped and murdered her by going to http://www.shadow-net.com/kidnapped.htm.

Always do whatever you can to help protect the children. Thank you!

Cary Stayner:
The Yosemite Serial Killer

Late on a quiet June afternoon in 1984, this author, Mike Echols, kidnap victim Steven Stayner, 19, and Steven's brother Cary, 23, sat talking around the kitchen table at Del and Kay Stayner's new home on Mirror Lake Drive in northeast Merced, California. The brothers' mother, Kay, divided her time between preparing dinner for the family and their guest, chatting with the three at the table, and setting the table for dinner.

When she had finished setting six places at the table, Kay returned to the stove to stir the beans. After surveying the table Steven suddenly remarked to his mother in his slow, distinctive way of talking, "You forgot one."

The spoon still in her hand, Kay turned and queried her second son, "Who?"

Without pause, Steven pointed to his brother Cary and said with a smile, "Cary!"

Kay looked quizzically at Cary and then said, "Oh . . . Cary."

* * *

Sadly, that is the way it was for the ruggedly hand-some oldest son of Del and Kay Stayner after his younger brother returned to his family on March 2, 1980. Steven had returned home after spending seven years, two months, and twenty-eight days as the "son" and unwilling sex partner for his "father," previously convicted kidnapper-child molester Kenneth Eugene Parnell.

Steven's return marked the decline of attention and family prominence for Cary. But during an interview in his jail cell in late July, 1999, Cary reportedly asked a TV journalist if someone might be interested in making a TV miniseries about his life story, as was done with Steven's life.

Steven's ordeal became the basis for the first edition of this book and the Lorimar/NBC-TV miniseries, which was also *I Know My First Name Is Steven*—a mini-series that continues to be shown two to three times a year.

While Steven was missing, Cary attended a Hoover Intermediate School program for gifted students. He was so good at drawing that while he was attending Merced High School he was the cartoonist for the school paper, *The Statesman*. His journalism teacher Sharon Wellins remembers an exam that Cary apparently failed to study for. At the bottom of the blank page, Cary had drawn a picture of a little man holding a picket sign that read, "Unfair test."

But much of the time, Cary hung back alone. His male friends started going out with girls, but no one recalls Stayner ever having a date in spite of his good looks. And some remember disturbing incidents involving Cary as a teenager. In an interview with the *San Francisco Chronicle*, Victoria Flores-Tatum recalls that he "was very frustrated at all the publicity Steven was getting." And she remembers a dark occurrence involving her. When she was 14, she attended a slee-pover with Cary's sister Cindy. Victoria said that Cary crept under her cot as she slept and reached up and touched her breasts. She was startled awake and told him to go away, but a few minutes later, Cary reappeared in the doorway stark naked and just stood there. Victoria told him to go away and he did.

After graduation from Merced High School in 1979, where his classmates voted Cary the "most creative" senior, he drifted through a series of relatively menial jobs, hauling furniture, exterminating insects for a pest-control firm, working for an aluminum company, and finally going to work for the Merced Glass and Mirror Company. There he worked with Mike Marchese, who recalls about Cary, "He'd say a woman was nice looking and he'd go so far as saying it would be nice to get together with her . . . but nothing ever came of it."

Marchese remembers a day a few years ago when he found Cary slamming his fist into a piece of plywood and bleeding from cuts on his hand. "He said he felt like he was having a nervous breakdown and said he was all nervous and didn't know why. He said he felt like getting in his truck, driving it into the office, and killing the boss and everyone else in there and torching the place.

"I told him he might have a chemical imbalance,

and he said, 'I have been told I have, but nothing's ever been done about it.' "

As he stated in an interview with the *Los Angeles Times,* company owner Gordon Ekas drove Cary to a Merced psychiatric center, where he was counseled. But soon thereafter, Stayner came into the Merced Glass and Mirror office, picked up his check, and never came back. Instead, in the summer of 1997, Cary Stayner took a job as a maintenance man at the Cedar Lodge in the tiny mountain community of El Portal on California Highway 140 near the entrance to Yosemite National Park—the same highway his brother Steven had been taken along when he was first kidnapped in 1972.

Cary was so highly trusted by Cedar Lodge owner Gerald Fischer that Fischer allowed his children to work alongside the new handyman as he repaired plumbing, arranged pool furniture, and took care of many other tasks at the large, busy motel.

But his apparent difficulty in getting along with the opposite sex continued. Cary's friend Jake Jones, who works at the Yosemite View Lodge a few miles from Cedar Lodge, said that Cary never talked about dating any specific woman. And once, when Jones was telling him about his own four-year relationship, Cary expressed surprise. Recalls Jones, "He said, 'Four years? Man, I never had a relationship that lasted more than three weeks.' "

But apparently Cary did associate with some females. Nancy Wilson of the Yosemite View Restaurant, where the wiry Stayner often ate, said Stayner identified himself as a "sun worshiper" to teenage girls he met. And one evening in early July, 1999, Wilson went to the Merced River at the Two-five Beach, where Stayner often smoked marijuana and sunbathed and swam in the nude. And she said, "He asked me if I wanted to get high. I said no."

But when he was arrested, Cedar Lodge Restaurant's manager Lisa Hansel said, "It really affected a lot of us that this monster could be walking around amongst us . . . so trusted! How could we have missed someone we felt was part of our family? Everyone living in this community knew and embraced this monster who was capable of such horrors!"

But instead of working at the Cedar Lodge during the busy summer tourist season, Cary Stayner spent his 38th birthday locked up by himself in a jail cell in Fresno, California, having been arrested on July 24, 1999, for the July 21, 1999, decapitation murder of 26-year-old Yosemite National Park naturalist Joie Armstrong . . . a murder to which—along with the February 15, 1999, kidnapping-murders of Eureka residents Carole Sund, her daughter Juliana, 15, and the Sunds' family friend Silvina Pelosso, 16, from Argentina—he confessed later that same day, shortly after he was arrested by the F.B.I. at the Laguna del Sol nudist colony outside Sacramento, California.

As Cary Stayner confessed to television news reporter Ted Rowlands of KNTV-TV and KBWB-TV: "I am guilty. I did murder Carole Sund, Julie Sund, Silvina Pelosso, and Joie Armstrong. I wish I could have controlled myself and not done what I did."

In the week following Cary's arrest, his father Del, a simple man who worked most of his life as a machinery mechanic at canneries around Merced and who is described as salt of the earth as you can get, could not talk about the crimes his son Cary confessed to without recalling the crime that still shadows their lives: The seven-year-and-three-month-long kidnapping of his second son, Steven Gregory Stayner.

Said Del, "Thank you for all your support since December 4, 1972, when you helped look for Steve. You helped celebrate his return in 1980; you helped mourn his death in 1989. Now we must ask you for our privacy during this terrible tragedy."

It was Del who had passed on his love of the backwoods and camping to his oldest son, Cary.

But if he was brokenhearted by the image of his son desecrating an area that had become almost religious for the family—the lakes and the foothills of the Sierras—he did not let on in his few muffled statements to TV cameras and reporters from behind his closed screen door in Merced.

"The Cary we know is not capable of these crimes," Del Stayner said. "We love you, Cary. You will always be loved by your family."

Beginning with the arrival of the white man in the middle of the 19th century, the Yosemite Valley has had a homicidal history. It was home to American Indians for thousands of years before the Mariposa Battalion—part U.S. Calvary and part vigilante group—entered the Valley in March of 1851 and all but wiped out the Ahwahneechee Indians under Chief Tenaya in a bloody battle perpetrated by the Battalion. A dozen years later, President Abraham Lincoln set the Yosemite Valley aside as a protected park. And not long thereafter, philosopher Ralph Waldo Emerson visited it and wrote, "This valley is the only place that comes up to the brag about it—and exceeds it." And it is this assessment and not the almost 150 years of violent killings with which most of today's visitors—up to 20,000 a day in the summer—would surely agree.

On President's Day, 1999, Carole Sund, her 15-year-old daughter Juliana, and 16-year-old family friend Silvina Pelosso from Argentina had hamburgers for dinner in the 1950s-style diner at the Cedar Lodge in El Portal, California, near the entrance to Yosemite National Park. And then, for what they did not know would be their last night alive, they retired to their motel room at the Cedar Lodge.

During the day the girls *oooed!* and *ahhed!* at Yosemite Falls, Half Dome, the snow-covered mountain meadows, and skated on a frozen pond in Yosemite, where they posed for the last photographs ever taken of them.

After the busy holiday weekend, almost all of the tourists had left the Lodge when at about 11:00 P.M. Cary Stayner knocked on the door to Room 509 in a remote corner of the nearly deserted motel.

In a detailed statement to one investigative journalist, which appeared in the *San Francisco Examiner*, the *San Jose Mercury-News* and other news media, the 37-year-old motel handyman admitted he had been watching the three females, and when Carole Sund asked who was there, Stayner responded, "Maintenance. There's a leak behind the wall in your bathroom that I need to repair." Carole opened the door and pleasantly greeted the maintenance man, who returned her kindly greeting by pulling out a pistol, pointing it at her, and assuring her that if she kept quiet no one would get hurt. Apparently thinking that the man would rob them and then leave, the frightened mother of four believed him, and along with her daughter Julie and their friend Silvina, she complied with Stayner's orders.

By his own admission, Cary Stayner bound and gagged the three and then separated them from one another. Then he took some rope and strangled Carole and then Silvina out of sight of Juliana. After he placed their bodies in the trunk of Carole's red rental car, he returned to the room where he forced her to perform oral sex on him for hours.

Then, he drove Juliana and the bodies of her mother and her friend for over an hour through the Sierra darkness before pulling into a paved overlook near Moccasin Point at New Don Pedro Reservoir, a lake where he and his family repeatedly camped and fished as he grew up.

Forcing the terrified 15-year-old out of the car, Stayner dragged her up a trail and over a rise so that they were out of range of the headlights of any cars. Then he stopped, sexually assaulted Juliana, and slit her throat so savagely that he almost severed her head. Afterward, he calmly left her body on the trail, walked back to the rental car, and drove into Tuolumne County, where he pulled onto an old dirt logging road.

His plan was to ditch the car in an isolated reservoir he knew about, with the bodies of Carole Sund and Silvina Pelosso still in the trunk. But in the dark, he high-grounded the car on a tree stump and couldn't get it to move.

Frightened by the arrival of first light, Stayner walked two miles back to a phone and called a cab to come and pick him up for a ride back to Yosemite. When driver Jenny Paul arrived she was surprised that the casually dressed, "decent-looking" man with a backpack, who was "beat tired" and "didn't look like he'd slept," was willing to pay $125 for the cab ride to Yosemite.

Paul said Cary told her that friends had abandoned him. Then he fell asleep in her cab on the drive. Toward the end of the trip, he awoke to talk about trucks and to point out a cabin where he said he once saw Bigfoot, the legendary mountain ape-like creature. "I told him I didn't believe in Bigfoot," Paul said, "but he said, 'Oh, you should! You'll see!' "

When they arrived at the entrance to Yosemite National Park, the passenger argued with the ranger about paying the $35 entrance fee, insisting that he worked in the park and was therefore exempt from paying it. But when Stayner refused to tell the ranger who exactly he worked for, the ranger insisted that he pay the fee, he did, and Paul drove him on into the park.

As instructed, she delivered Cary to the Yosemite Lodge, the motel where Kenneth Eugene Parnell had worked at the time he kidnapped Cary's brother Steven. Paul went inside to use the restroom before the trip back, and when she came out, she spied Cary in the lobby staring at the pictures on the wall, as if lost.

Reports indicate it took two days before law enforcement began searching for Carole and Juliana Sund, Silvina Pelosso, and their red rental car . . . believing all the while that they had been the victims of an auto accident. Soon the search moved into high gear when the Sund family offered a $250,000 reward for finding the trio alive.

The search was one of the most extensive in California history and eventually involved airplanes, helicopters, and even search dogs and teams on snowshoes. But no trace of Carole Sund's red Pontiac Grand Prix rental car could be found.

Back at his cramped apartment at the Cedar Lodge in El Portal, Cary Stayner watched the search begin and then drove his baby blue International Scout back to Tuolumne County, took Carole Sund's wallet, and then torched the rental car.

In an apparent effort to confuse investigators, Stayner then drove to Modesto and dropped Sund's wallet—chock-full of credit cards—on a Modesto street, where a high school student found it and handed it over to police.

This discovery alarmed investigators and led them to believe that there had been no automobile accident—rather, that the trio's disappearance was due to foul play.

The F.B.I. was called in and agents were soon swarming all over Cedar Lodge, where handyman Cary Stayner had worked for two years. When Stayner volunteered to help them, F.B.I. agents accepted his offer, and Stayner opened up each room for them to inspect and even gathered samples of acrylic blankets so that the fibers could be examined and identified at the F.B.I. Crime Laboratory in Washington, DC.

But despite the fact that F.B.I. agents interviewed him twice, they did not arrest this quiet, unassuming caretaker could possibly be a suspect.

In mid-March, a target shooter discovered Carole Sund's burned-out rental car and investigators found Carole's and Silvina's charred bodies inside the trunk.

Soon the F.B.I. turned its investigation toward a group of Modesto prison parolees known as "cranksters"—ex-cons with a history of methamphetamine use. In short order, a half dozen other suspects were pulled in, including a pair of half brothers who violently reacted in standoffs with police. F.B.I. agents thought their irrational behavior might have been prompted by their need to hide something. And they believed that they did have the men responsible for the murders in custody, but lacked sufficient evidence to charge them in those murders.

Soon thereafter, an anonymous letter arrived at the Modesto F.B.I. office; it led investigators to Juliana's body. Stayner now admits he wrote that letter to throw investigators off the trail, even etching random names on the page above the one on which he wrote the letter and referring to the murderer as "we."

These events only served to fuel the F.B.I.'s case against the Modesto "crankster" suspects, especially when the F.B.I. crime laboratory discovered that acrylic fibers found in the half brothers' cars matched those found in blankets at the crime scene that Stayner helped agents gather. And then one of the half brothers told agents that he had participated in the murder of Carole Sund and helped to dispose of Juliana's body and that the matching fibers had come from a blanket used to hide the teenager's body.

But the F.B.I. may well have put too much credence in the F.B.I. Laboratory's report since the fibers came from an orange acrylic blanket—not exactly a rare find—and now an F.B.I. official has acknowledged the match was of "almost zero significance. . . . Nobody attached a lot of weight to it."

Also, the F.B.I. could have performed a simple investigative check of the trip records of cab companies in the area, such as those of the Courtesy Cab Company in Sonora, for which Jenny Paul drove. The record shows that this was not done.

Further, even though the half brother who had confessed began backing away from his confession and his other statements grew increasingly suspect, the F.B.I. pressed ahead, trying to gather the evidence that they would need to make a case against those they had arrested around Modesto.

Then in June, 1999, Sacramento-based F.B.I. Agent in Charge James Maddock and task force chief in investigating the kidnapping-murders of the Sunds and Pelosso announced to news media, "I do feel that we have all of the main players in jail."

When Cary Stayner heard this announcement, he was still living and working at the Cedar Lodge and he must have figured that he had gotten away with the triple murder.

On Wednesday, July 21, 1999, Stayner drove into the small enclave of Foresta on the western edge of Yosemite National Park and saw 26-year-old environmental educator Joie Armstrong packing her car for a trip. He later said that when he realized that she was alone he couldn't resist attacking her. But this time, his chosen victim fought back so viciously that Stayner was forced to leave clues everywhere, including fingerprints and footprints in her house as well as distinctive tire tracks from his baby blue International Scout, a vehicle with different tires and treads on each of its four wheels.

On Saturday, July 24, investigators confronted Stayner at the Sacramento County nudist colony in Laguna del Sol and arrested him. Almost like Ervin Edward Murphy—the accomplice who had helped Kenneth Eugene Parnell kidnap his brother in 1972— Cary Stayner went quietly as if he had been expecting them. And within hours, Cary Stayner confessed to having stalked and murdered all four females, claiming that he had been dreaming of committing such mayhem since he was just seven years old.

Accordingly, investigators not only have Stayner's confessions, but they know that he knows too much about the crimes and that there is too much evidence to back up his statements for him not to be the killer: He knew what was taken from the Sunds' and Pelosso's room, the conditions of the bodies, and the fact that knives were used in the killings—all details that had not been released to the public.

And in an interesting twist it wasn't until Paul saw Cary Stayner's face on TV the night of July 25 that she recognized him and chillingly learned that he had confessed to the four murders. "I didn't know who he was until I saw his picture on TV. I said, 'Oh, my God! That's him!' "

Controversy surrounds the F.B.I.'s handling of this case. Some law enforcement authorities say that the

F.B.I. should have looked closer at Cary Stayner when they interviewed him and then used him to gather evidence at the Cedar Lodge in February, 1999, shortly after Carole Sund, her daughter Juliana, and their friend Silvina Pelosso disappeared.

The flaws in the Bureau's investigation seem best illustrated by statements made by Agent in Charge, Maddock. In June, 1999, he said, "I do feel that we have all the main players in jail, but we are in no rush to charge them." On July 25, the day after Cary Stayner was arrested for the murder of Joie Armstrong and indeed confessed to that murder as well as those of the Sunds and Pelosso, he stated: "I had previously expressed a belief that the key players in that case were already in custody on unrelated matters. That was my sincere belief based on the results of intensive investigative efforts and the best information available at the time. I have asked myself whether we could have done anything differently that might have prevented the murder of Joie Armstrong, [but] I'm confident we've done everything that we could have done."

Senator Charles Grassley (R-Iowa) has sharply criticized the F.B.I.'s handling of the case, saying, "Homicides have never been the F.B.I.'s strong suit. Perhaps the F.B.I. should stick to what it does best: investigate complex white collar crimes."

Besides initially dismissing Cary Stayner as a suspect, Grassley said, the Bureau rushed to judgment in claiming the killers of the Sunds and Pelosso were in custody, "raising the specter once again of the 'Richard Jewell syndrome.'" (Jewell was the security guard whom the F.B.I. falsely accused of the 1996 Olympics bombing in Atlanta. The F.B.I. later recanted.)

"This is not the first time that this F.B.I. agent has been involved in controversy," continued Grassley. "Mr. James Maddock was also involved in the F.B.I. crime lab fiasco, and had the primary responsibility of containing the allegations of whistle-blower Fred Whitehurst (a former lab employee).

Grassley summed it all up by saying, "I think you can safely say that they're looking into this right now in Washington. Incidents like these by the F.B.I. tend to undermine public confidence in federal law enforcement."

But on July 28, 1999, the only statement from Maddock's office in Sacramento was a recorded telephone message from Agent Nick Rossi, who said: "To respond to criticism, we would have to discuss details of our pending case. If we are forced to choose between defending ourselves against critics and preserving the integrity of our case, we will always choose preserving the integrity of our case."

According to Peter Keane, Dean of Golden Gate University Law School in San Francisco, "The danger is, you may be mistaken, and by ruling out other possibilities, you are allowing other trails to go cold. An investigation should always remain open until a jury comes back with a verdict."

With what it now knows about Cary Stayner, the F.B.I. has assigned a team of investigators to search California for unsolved crimes, particularly ones in which the victims were beheaded (as Cary Stayner has confessed having done to Juliana Sund and Joie Armstrong). Although Stayner says that his killings only began in February, 1999, experts who study serial killers say such a sudden, late debut is unlikely. Therefore authorities are looking at Cary Stayner's whereabouts over the past two decades in an attempt to solve half a dozen unsolved murders, including that of his uncle, Jesse "Jerry" Stayner, who was murdered in the home he shared with Cary on December 26, 1990.

In reference to Cary's claim that he only began his "career" as a serial killer at the age of 37 on February 15, 1999, a San Jose State University sociologist who studies the minds of multiple murders said, "It's very rare for a seven-year-old kid to fantasize about killing women. The average age is 35. Almost all serial murderers have low-paying jobs that don't seem to be going anywhere. Thirty-five seems to be about the age that they crack and can't handle the strain of knowing what their lives are going to be like. Plus, they're afraid that maybe they're losing their sexual attractiveness."

As to Stayner's claim that his fantasies began at age seven, Dr. Scott W. Allen, a senior staff psychologist with the Miami/Dade County Police Department, agrees that Stayner's claim of violent fantasies in early childhood is suspect and thinks that it is an attempt to establish a classic legal defense for himself with his confession. "This fellow is extraordinarily manipulative," said Allen. "This is the nexus for an insanity plea, that he had irresistible impulses. He may just be making it all up."

Adds Dr. Reid Meloy, a San Diego forensic psychologist and author of *The Psychopathic Mind,* "My hunch is there's a high probability these were sexual homicides. Women were targeted who were unknown to [Stayner]. Violent fantasy plays a predominant role in these killings. These fantasies can precede the actual killings by a long latency period. Typically these fantasies start in adolescence. They are subterranean fantasies, not discussed with anyone. The perpetrator will masturbate to them, but doesn't act on them for years."

Robert Ressler—who developed the F.B.I.'s Behavioral Sciences Unit, which profiles criminals, as portrayed in the 1991 motion picture *The Silence of the Lambs*—said serial killers' fantasies do typically start early in life. "It becomes sexual violence when it's played out in fantasies, and they are fantasies about taking a matter of authority and control over an individual. If he is 37, I'd start when he was 25 or 26 and look for homicides and sexual assaults in areas where he lived," Ressler said. "You have to go back [and] look for evidence of moves toward that behavior."

And what about Cary Stayner's years as a good worker, albeit in low-paying jobs? Michael Rustigan, San Francisco State University Professor of Criminology, cited the case of Ted Bundy, who confessed to committing 31 murders and was executed in Florida in 1991. "He was a charming, good-looking guy. [And] I could rattle off the cases of many serial killers who worked by day and crept by night."

But all of the experts did agree that, if Stayner had not been caught, he almost certainly would have killed again and again.

Traveling in a dark blue government van, on Thursday, July 29, 1999, federal marshals drove confessed Yosemite serial killer Cary Stayner from the state capitol of Sacramento south down California 99 right through the very middle of California. They traveled through his hometown of Merced and on south to Fresno, a city of over 400,000 in the same agricultural San Joaquin Valley of California, an area where his brother's kidnapper had been raised and where Cary had grown up the eldest child of a loving, hardworking blue collar family, and where his brother Steven had returned home on March 2, 1980.

On arrival at the Fresno County Jail, in downtown Fresno, news photographers jostled each other and even climbed atop a nearby roof to try to get pictures of the 37-year-old motel handyman as he arrived at the facility's rear entrance.

Once inside, Cary was placed by himself in an 85-square-foot cell with only a steel toilet, a sink, a desk, and a bunk. And a suicide watch was established for him after a medical evaluation.

This isolated cell will remain his home for the foreseeable future, except for one hour every other day for a shower, twice a week for a 30-minute visit, and a total of three hours each week for exercise.

"This inmate is a celebrity," said Fresno County Sheriff Richard Pierce. "That alone and the type of crime [he committed] can cause other inmates to want to harm him."